Managerial Paper P7

Financial Accounting and Tax Principles

For exams in 2005

Practice & Revision Kit

In this January 2005 new edition

- Targeted at CIMA's new syllabus

- New format for ease of use

- Question formats reflect exam question styles

- Guidance on study planning and techniques

- CIMA's Pilot Paper included as a mock exam

BPP's **i-Pass** product also supports this paper.

PROFESSIONAL EDUCATION

First edition January 2005

ISBN 0 7517 2145 X

British Library Cataloguing-in-Publication Data
A catalogue record for this book
is available from the British Library

Published by

BPP Professional Education
Aldine House, Aldine Place
London W12 8AW

www.bpp.com

Printed in Great Britain by
WM Print
45-47 Frederick Street
Walsall
WS2 9NE

We are grateful to the Chartered Institute of
Management Accountants for permission to reproduce
past examination questions. The answers to past
examination questions have been prepared by BPP
Professional Education.

Contents

	Page
Question search tools	
Question and answer checklist/index	iv
Topic index	vi
Revision	
Effective revision	viii
Detailed revision plan	xi
The exam	
The exam paper	xiv
Exam technique	xv
Tackling multiple choice questions	xviii
Tackling objective test questions	xix
What the examiner means	xxi
Additional guidance	
Exam update	xxii
Formulae to learn	xxii
Useful websites	xxii
Question practice	
Questions	3
Answers	65
Exam practice	
Mock exam 1	
• Questions	123
• Plan of attack	139
• Answers	142
Mock exam 2 (Pilot paper)	
• Questions	153
• Plan of attack	169
• Answers	172
Mathematical tables and exam formulae	183
Review form & free prize draw	
Order form	

Question and Answer checklist/index

		Marks	Time allocation Mins	Page number Question	Page number Answer

Part A: Principles of Business Taxation

		Marks	Mins	Question	Answer
1	Objective test questions: General principles of taxation	20	36	3	65
2	Objective test questions: International tax	20	36	4	65
3	Objective test questions: Indirect taxes	20	36	5	66
4	Objective test questions: Company taxation	20	36	7	67
5	Objective test questions: Deferred tax	20	36	9	69
6	Section B questions: Taxation I	25	45	11	70
7	Section B questions: Taxation II	25	45	12	72
8	Section B questions: Taxation III	25	45	12	74
9	Section B questions: Taxation IV	25	45	13	75

Part B: Principles of Regulation of Financial Reporting

		Marks	Mins	Question	Answer
10	Objective test questions: The regulatory framework	20	36	14	77
11	Objective test questions: External audit	20	36	16	78
12	Section B questions: Regulation	20	36	18	78
13	Section B questions: External Audit	15	27	18	80

Part C: Single Company Financial Accounts

		Marks	Mins	Question	Answer
14	Objective test questions: Presentation	20	36	19	81
15	Section B questions: Presentation	15	27	21	82
16	Leonardo	20	36	22	84
17	Objective test questions: Cash flow statements	20	36	23	85
18	Cee Eff	20	36	26	86
19	T cash flow	20	36	27	88
20	Objective test questions: Non-current assets, inventories and construction contracts	20	36	29	89
21	Section B questions: Non-current assets, inventories and construction contracts	15	27	32	90
22	Geneva	20	36	33	91
23	Objective test questions: Distributable profits and capital transactions	20	36	34	92
24	Objective test questions: Accounting standards I	20	36	37	93
25	Objective test questions: Accounting standards II	20	36	40	93
26	Section B questions: Accounting standards	15	27	42	95
27	Evans	20	36	43	96
28	Newcars	20	36	43	98
29	L Manufacturing	20	36	44	99
30	PW	20	36	45	101

		Time allocation	Page number	
	Marks	Mins	Question	Answer

Part D: Managing Short-term Finance

31 Objective test questions: Short-term finance I	20	36	47	103
32 Objective test questions: Short-term finance II	20	36	48	104
33 Objective test questions: Short-term finance III	20	36	50	105
34 Section B questions: Short-term finance	25	45	52	106
35 DF	20	36	53	109
36 Objective test questions: Working capital management I	20	36	54	112
37 Objective test questions: Working capital management II	20	36	56	113
38 Objective test questions: Working capital management III	20	36	58	114
39 Section B questions: Working capital management	20	36	60	115
40 STK	20	36	61	118

Mock exam 1

Questions 41 to 49

Mock exam 2 (Pilot paper)

Questions 50 to 58

Topic index

Listed below are the key Paper P7 syllabus topics and the numbers of the questions in this kit covering those topics.

Syllabus topic	Question numbers
Advanced tax	1, 6
Auditing	11, 13
Audit report	11, 13
Balance sheet	14, 15, 29, 30
Baumol model	60
Cash flow forecast	39
Cash flow statement	17, 18, 19
Company taxation	4, 6
Compound interest	31, 32, 33
Construction contracts	20, 22
Contingencies	24, 26
Deferred tax	5, 8, 9
Development costs	20
Discounts	37
Distributable profits	23
Economic Order Quantity (EOQ)	37, 38, 40
Employee tax	1, 7
Events after the balance sheet date	24
Expectations gap	13
External audit	11, 13
Factoring	31
IAS 1	14, 15, 16
IAS 2	20, 21
IAS 7	17, 18
IAS 8	14, 16
IAS 10	24, 25, 26
IAS 11	20
IAS 12	5, 8, 9
IAS 16	20, 21
IAS 17	24, 25, 26
IAS 24	25, 28
IAS 36	20
IAS 37	20, 24, 25, 26
IAS 38	20, 21
IFRS 5	16
Income statement	15, 16, 29, 30
Indirect taxation	3, 6
Inflation	32, 33
Intangible assets	20, 21
International tax	2, 9
Inventories	20
Leasing	24, 25, 26, 27

Syllabus topic	Question numbers
Miller Orr model	34, 38
Non-current assets	20, 21
Operating cycle	39
Overdraft	31, 34
Regulatory framework	10, 12
Research and development	20
Rights issues	23
Share capital transactions	23
Short-term deposits	31, 32, 34
Sources of finance	34, 35
Statement of changes in equity	30
Withholding tax	7
Working capital	36, 37, 38
Yield curve	32, 33

Effective revision

What you must remember

Effective use of time as you approach the exam is very important. You must remember:

> **Believe in yourself**
>
> **Use time sensibly**

Believe in yourself

Are you cultivating the right attitude of mind? There is absolutely no reason why you should not pass this **exam** if you adopt the correct approach.

- **Be confident** – you've passed exams before, you can pass them again
- **Be calm** – plenty of adrenaline but no panicking
- **Be focused** – commit yourself to passing the exam

Use time sensibly

1 **How much study time do you have?** Remember that you must **eat**, **sleep**, and of course, **relax**.

2 **How will you split that available time between each subject?** A **revision timetable**, covering **what** and **how** you will revise, will help you organise your revision thoroughly.

3 **What is your learning style?** AM/PM? Little and often/long sessions? Evenings/ weekends?

4 **Do you have quality study time?** Unplug the phone. Let everybody know that you're studying and shouldn't be disturbed.

5 **Are you taking regular breaks?** Most people absorb more if they do not attempt to study for long uninterrupted periods of time. A five minute break every hour (to make coffee, watch the news headlines) can make all the difference.

6 **Are you rewarding yourself for your hard work?** Are you leading a **healthy lifestyle?**

What to revise

Key topics

You need to spend most time on, and practise full questions on, **key topics**.

Key topics

- Recur regularly
- Underpin whole paper
- Appear often in compulsory questions
- Discussed currently in press
- Covered in recent articles by examiner
- Shown as high priority in study material
- Tipped by lecturer

PROFESSIONAL EDUCATION

Difficult areas

You may also still find certain areas of the syllabus difficult.

Difficult areas

- Areas you find dull or pointless
- Subjects you highlighted as difficult when taking notes
- Topics that gave you problems when you answered questions or reviewed the material

DON'T become depressed about these areas; instead do something about them.

- Build up your knowledge by **quick tests** such as the quick quizzes in your BPP Study Text.

- Work carefully through **numerical examples** and **questions** in the Text, and refer back to the Text if you struggle with computations in the Kit.

- **Note down weaknesses** that your answers to questions contained; you are less likely to make the same mistakes if you highlight where you went wrong.

Breadth of revision

Make sure your revision has sufficient **breadth**. You need to be able to answer all the compulsory questions and enough optional questions on the paper. On certain papers all major topics in the syllabus will be tested, through short answer questions or longer questions. On some papers it will be impossible to predict which topics will be examined in compulsory questions, which topics in optional questions.

Paper P7

The examiner has stated that tax will not be tested in Section C of the paper, but it was tested in the pilot paper in both sections A and B. Section C is likely to have an accounts preparation question, so make sure you know the Income statement and Balance sheet formats. Make sure you understand the basics of working capital and cash management.

How to revise

There are four main ways that you can revise a topic area.

Write it!
Read it!
Teach it!
Do it!

Write it!

The Course Notes and the Study Text are too bulky for revision. You need a slimmed down set of notes that summarise the key points. Writing important points down will help you recall them, particularly if your notes are presented in a way that makes it easy for you to remember them.

Read it!

You should read your notes or BPP Passcards actively, testing yourself by doing quick quizzes or Kit questions while you are reading.

Teach it!

Exams require you to show your understanding. Teaching what you are revising to another person helps you practise explaining topics. Teaching someone who will challenge your understanding, someone for example who will be taking the same exam as you, can help both of you.

Do it!

Remember that you are revising in order to be able to answer questions in the exam. Answering questions will help you practise **technique** and **discipline**, which examiners emphasise over and over again can be crucial in passing or failing exams.

1 A bank of **multiple choice questions** is included for each syllabus area. Attempt all of these banks and use them as a **diagnostic tool**: if you get lots of them wrong go back to your BPP Study Text or look through the Paper P7 Passcards and do some revision. Additional guidance on how to tackle multiple choice questions is given on page (xviii). These provide you with a firm foundation from which to attempt Section B and C questions.

2 The more exam-standard questions you do, the more likely you are to pass the exam. At the very least, you should attempt the **key questions** that are highlighted from page (xi) onwards.

3 You should produce **full answers** under **timed conditions,** and don't cheat by looking at the answer! Look back at your notes or at your BPP Study Text instead if you are really struggling. Produce answer plans if you are running short of time.

4 Always read the **Pass marks** in the answers. They are there to help you, and will show you which points in the answer are the most important.

5 **Don't get despondent** if you didn't do very well. Refer to the **topic index** and try another question that covers the same subject.

6 When you think you can successfully answer questions on the whole syllabus, attempt the **two mock exams** at the end of the Kit. You will get the most benefit by sitting them under strict exam conditions, so that you gain experience of the four vital exam processes.

- Selecting questions
- Deciding on the order in which to attempt them
- Managing your time
- Producing answers

BPP's Learning to Learn Accountancy gives further valuable advice on how to approach revision. BPP has also produced other vital revision aids.

- **Passcards** – Provide you with clear topic summaries and exam tips
- **Success CDs** – Help you revise on the move
- **i-Pass CDs** – Offer you tests of knowledge to be completed against the clock

You can purchase these products by completing the order form at the back of this Kit or by visiting www.bpp.com/cima

---

Detailed revision plan

The table below gives you one possible approach to your revision for *Financial Accounting and Tax Principles*. There are of course many ways in which you can tackle the final stages of your study for this paper and this is just a suggestion: simply following it is no guarantee of success. You or your college may prefer an alternative but equally valid approach.

The BPP plan below requires you to devote a **minimum of 28 hours** to revision of Paper P7. Any time you can spend over and above this should only increase your chances of success.

Suggested approach

1 For each section of the syllabus, **review** your **notes** and the relevant chapter summaries in the Paper P7 **Passcards**.

2 Then do the **key questions** for that section. You should answer all questions that are identified in the table below as key questions by a box round the question number 1 . Even if you are short of time you must attempt these questions if you want to pass the exam. Try to complete your answers without referring to our solutions.

3 Once you have worked through all of the syllabus sections attempt **mock exam 1** under strict exam conditions. Then have a go at **mock exam 2** (pilot paper), again under strict exam conditions.

Syllabus section	2005 Passcards chapters	Questions in this Kit	Comments	Done ☑
General principles of taxation	1	1 2 3	Answer all of these MCQs. There will be more than one question on each topic, so you will get lots of practice.	☐
		6, 7	These are Section B-type questions. Make sure you do not spend more than 9 minutes on each.	☐
Company taxation	2	4, 5	Answer all of these MCQs. Make sure you really understand the adjustments necessary to get from accounting profit to taxable profit and can do it easily.	☐
		8, 9	These are Section B questions on company tax. Deferred tax is the most difficult aspect. Just make sure you understand the basics.	☐
The regulatory framework	3	10, 12	The MCQs are fairly simple here. The Section B questions invite you to spend a lot of time, so *don't do it* – practice answering these question with notes and bullet points.	☐
External audit	4	11, 13	External audit did not feature in the pilot paper, so it should appear in the first exam. Make sure you know the different types of audit report qualification and be very strict and to the point on the Section B questions.	☐
Financial accounts – presentation	5	14 15	This area is very important – IAS 1 and IAS 8. Do all of the MCQs and practice 15(b) until you can get it right – you may well need this for Section C.	☐
Financial accounts – presentation	5	16	This is the first Section C question. Make sure you only give yourself 36 minutes, then check the answer and try it again.	☐

Syllabus section	2005 Passcards chapters	Questions in this Kit	Comments	Done ✓
Cash flow statements	6	17	These MCQs are good revision for the various components of the cash flow, so do them before attempting the longer questions.	☐
Cash flow statements	6	18 19	These are two Section C questions on cash flow statements. Section C of the pilot paper had a cash flow statement and it could come up again. This is not a difficult topic. Do both of these questions and make sure you can produce *net cash flow from operating activities* using both methods.	☐
Non-current assets, inventories and construction contracts	8, 9, 11	20 21	These are fairly complex topics. If you have trouble with the MCQs, go back to the study text and revise the area. On the discursive questions in 21, try writing just a plan with all the main points.	☐
Construction contracts	9	22	Geneva is a Section C length question on construction contracts. This is not a simple topic, but it is likely to come up somewhere in the paper. See what you can do in 36 minutes and then go through the answer and make sure you understand it.	☐
Distributable profits and capital transactions	10	23	These MCQs cover most of the important issues in this area. Make sure you understand how to deal with redemption of capital and purchase of own shares.	☐
Accounting standards	12, 13	24 25 26	These questions cover IAS 10, IAS 24, IAS 37 and IAS 17. These are all important because they are relatively *easy* to learn and apply, so if they come up they will be easy marks. Make sure you can calculate finance lease interest payments using both methods.	☐
Leasing	13	27	This is a Section C question on leasing and is probably harder than what you will meet in the exam, but make sure you understand how leasing transactions are presented.	☐
Related parties	23	28	This is a Section C length question on related parties. Probably a longer question than you will meet in the exam, but it covers all aspects, so go through it carefully.	☐
Financial statements	5	29 30	It seems probable that Section C will have an accounts preparation question, so practice on these two.	☐

Syllabus section	2005 Passcards chapters	Questions in this Kit	Comments	Done ☑
Short-term finance	15, 16, 20, 21, 22	31 32 33	Make sure you do these three MCQ questions in the time allocated and look over anything you were unable to deal with.	☐
		34	Try all of these. Question (a) is harder than you will get, but good practice. Learn how to apply Baumol and Miller-Orr. You will be given these formulae in the exam, so there is nothing difficult to remember.	☐
		35	A Section C question on this part of the syllabus is not likely, but this covers a lot of useful ground. The answer is longer than you could probably produce in the time, but do part (b) in bullet points and see how many of the important points you can get.	☐
Working capital management	14, 17, 18, 19	36 37 38	Make sure you can do all of these. Working capital is an important part of the syllabus and it is not difficult. Make sure you can calculate receivables days/payables days etc	☐
		39	Do all of these. They are all useful questions and these issues are quite likely to appear in Section B.	
		40	This is a good question covering the EOQ and purchasing issues. Make sure you understand the EOQ. You will be given the formula in the exam, so make sure you can use it.	☐

The exam paper

Format of the paper

		Number of marks
Section A:	Around 20 multiple choice and other objective test questions, 2–4 marks each	50
Section B:	6 compulsory questions, 5 marks each	30
Section C:	1 out of 2 questions, 20 marks	20
		100

Time allowed: 3 hours

Section A will always contain some multiple choice questions but will not consist solely of multiple choice questions. Section A may contain types of objective test question that are different from those included in the pilot paper.

Further guidance on objective test questions and multiple choice questions is included on pages (xx) and (xxi)

Section B questions will be mainly written discussion, although some calculations may be included. This section will require breadth of syllabus knowledge and also good time management skills.

Section C questions will be in various different styles including more complex calculations and analysis of data. Most questions will require calculation and written evaluation. Questions may include issues from a number of areas of the syllabus. Careful planning of answers will be essential.

Pilot paper

Section A

1   21 objective test questions ranging from 2 to 4 marks each.

Section B – Six short answer questions – 5 marks each

2   Depreciation, change to estimated useful economic life

3   Treatment of decommissioning costs

4   Cash flow forecast

5   Income statement and balance sheet extracts to reflect entries in respect of tax on profits and deferred tax

6   Explain definition of provision as per IAS 37

7   Income statement and balance sheet extracts to show entries for leased asset

Section C – One question out of 2–20 marks

8   Income statement, balance sheet and statement of changes in equity

9   Cash flow statement in accordance with IAS 7.

Exam technique

Passing professional examinations is half about having the knowledge, and half about doing yourself full justice in the examination. You must have the right approach at the following times.

> **Before the exam**
>
> **Your time in the exam hall**

Before the exam

1   Set at least one **alarm** (or get an alarm call) for a morning exam.

2   Have **something to eat** but beware of eating too much; you may feel sleepy if your system is digesting a large meal.

3   Allow plenty of **time to get to the exam hall**; have your route worked out in advance and listen to news bulletins to check for potential travel problems.

4   **Don't forget** pens, pencils, rulers, erasers, watch. Also make sure you remember **entrance documentation** and **evidence of identity**.

5   Put **new batteries** into your calculator and take a spare set (or a spare calculator).

6   **Avoid discussion** about the exam with other candidates outside the exam hall.

Your time in the exam hall

1   **Read the instructions (the 'rubric') on the front of the exam paper carefully**

Check that the exam format hasn't changed. Examiners' reports often remark on the number of students who attempt too few – or too many – questions, or who attempt the wrong number of questions from different parts of the paper.

2   **Select questions carefully**

Read through the paper once, underlining the key words in the question and jotting down the most important points. Select the optional questions that you feel you can answer best. You should base your selection on:

- The **topics** covered

- The **requirements of the whole question** (see page (xxi) for the guidance on what the examiner means)

- How easy it will be to **apply the requirements** to the details you are given

- The availability of **easy marks**

Make sure that you are planning to answer the **right number of questions,** all the compulsory questions plus the correct number of optional questions.

3   **Plan your attack carefully**

Consider the **order** in which you are going to tackle questions. It is a good idea to start with your best question to boost your morale and get some easy marks 'in the bag'.

4   Check the time allocation for each question

Each mark carries with it a **time allocation** of 1.8 minutes (including time for selecting and reading questions, and checking answers). A 5 mark question therefore should be selected, completed and checked in 9 minutes. When time is up, you **must** go on to the next question or part. Going even one minute over the time allowed brings you a lot closer to failure.

5   Read the question carefully and plan your answer

Read through the question again very carefully when you come to answer it. Plan your answer taking into account how the answer should be **structured**, what the **format** should be and **how long** it should take.

Confirm before you start writing that your plan makes **sense**, covers **all relevant points** and does not include **irrelevant material.** Two minutes of planning plus eight minutes of writing is virtually certain to earn you more marks than ten minutes of writing.

6   Answer the question set

Particularly with written answers, make sure you **answer the question set**, and not the question you would have preferred to have been set.

7   Gain the easy marks

Include the obvious if it answers the question and don't try to produce the perfect answer.

Don't get bogged down in small parts of questions. If you find a part of a question difficult, get on with the rest of the question. If you are having problems with something, the chances are that everyone else is too.

8   Produce an answer in the correct format

The examiner will **state in the requirements** the format in which the question should be answered, for example in a report or memorandum.

9   Follow the examiner's instructions

You will **annoy** the examiner if you ignore him or her.

10   Lay out your numerical computations and use workings correctly

Make sure the layout fits the **type of question** and is in a style the examiner likes. Show all your **workings** clearly and explain what they mean. **Cross reference** them to your solution. This will help the examiner to follow your method (this is of particular importance where there may be several possible answers).

11   Present a tidy paper

You are a professional, and it should show in the **presentation of your work**. Students are penalised for poor presentation and so you should make sure that you write legibly, label diagrams clearly and lay out your work neatly. Markers of scripts each have hundreds of papers to mark; a badly written scrawl is unlikely to receive the same attention as a neat and well laid out paper.

12   Stay until the end of the exam

Use any spare time **checking and rechecking** your script. This includes checking:

- You have **filled out** the **candidate details correctly.**
- Question parts and workings are **labelled clearly.**
- Aids to navigation such as **headers and underlining** are used effectively.
- **Spelling, grammar** and **arithmetic** are correct.

13   Don't discuss an exam with other candidates afterwards

There's nothing more you can do about it so why discuss it?

14   **Don't worry if you feel you have performed badly in the exam**

It is more than likely that the other candidates will have found the exam difficult too. Don't forget that there is a competitive element in these exams. As soon as you get up to leave the exam hall, **forget that exam** and think about the next – or, if it is the last one, celebrate!

BPP's *Learning to Learn Accountancy* gives further valuable advice on how to approach the day of the assessment.

Tackling multiple choice questions

The MCQs in your exam will contain four or five possible answers. You have to **choose the option that best answers the question**. The three or four incorrect options are called distracters. There is a skill in answering MCQs quickly and correctly. By practising MCQs you can develop this skill, giving yourself a better chance of passing the exam.

You may wish to follow the approach outlined below, or you may prefer to adapt it.

Step 1   Skim read all the MCQs and identify which appear to be the easier questions.

Step 2   Work out **how long** you should allocate to each MCQ bearing in mind the number of marks available and any guidance the examiner has given about how long they should take in total. Also remember that the examiner will not expect you to spend an equal amount of time on each MCQ; some can be answered instantly but others will take time to work out.

Step 3   Attempt each question – **starting with the easier questions** identified in Step 1. Read the question thoroughly. You may prefer to work out the answer before looking at the options, or you may prefer to look at the options at the beginning. Adopt the method that works best for you.

You may find that you recognise a question when you sit the exam. Be aware that the detail and/or requirement may be different. If the question seems familiar, read the requirement and options carefully – do not assume that it is identical.

Step 4   Read the four options and see if one matches your own answer. Be careful with numerical questions, as the distracters are designed to match answers that incorporate **common errors**. Check that your calculation is correct. Have you followed the requirement exactly? Have you included every stage of the calculation?

Step 5   You may find that none of the options matches your answer.

- Re-read the question to ensure that you understand it and are answering the requirement
- Eliminate any obviously wrong answers
- Consider which of the remaining answers is the most likely to be correct and select that option

Step 6   If you are still unsure, make a note and continue to the next question. Likewise if you are nowhere near working out which option is correct, leave the question and come back to it later.

Step 7   Revisit unanswered questions. When you come back to a question after a break, you often find you can answer it correctly straightaway. If you are still unsure, have a guess. You are not penalised for incorrect answers, so **never leave a question unanswered!**

Step 8   Make sure you show your **workings** clearly on calculation of MCQs, as you may gain some credit for workings even if your final answer is incorrect.

Tackling objective test questions

What is an objective test question?

An objective test (**OT**) question is made up of some form of **stimulus**, usually a question, and a **requirement** to do something.

- **MCQs.** Read through the information on page (xxii) about MCQs and how to tackle them.

- **True or false**. You will be asked if a statement is true or false.

- **Data entry**. This type of OT requires you to provide figures such as the answer to a calculation, words to fill in a blank, single word answers to questions, or to identify numbers and words to complete a format.

- **Word-limited answers**. You may be asked to state, define or explain things in no more than a certain number of words or within a single line in the answer booklet.

- **Hot spots**. This question format may ask you to identify specific points on a graph or diagram.

- **Interpretation.** You may be asked to interpret or analyse graphical data.

- **Multiple response.** These questions provide you with a number of options and you have to identify those that fulfil certain criteria.

- **Listing**. You may be asked to list items in rank order.

- **Matching.** This OT question format could ask you to classify particular costs into one of a range of cost classifications provided, to match descriptions of variances with one of a number of variances listed, and so on.

OT questions in your exam

Section A of your exam will contain different types of OT questions. It is not certain how many questions in your exam will be MCQs and how many will be other types of OT, nor what types of OT you will encounter in your exam. Practising all the different types of OTs that this Kit provides will prepare you well for whatever questions come up in your exam.

Dealing with OT questions

Again you may wish to follow the approach we suggest, or you may be prepared to adapt it.

Step 1   Work out **how long** you should allocate to each OT, taking into account the marks allocated to it. Remember that you will not be expected to spend an equal amount of time on each one; some can be answered instantly but others will take time to work out.

Step 2   **Attempt each question**. Read the question thoroughly, and note in particular what the question says about the **format** of your answer and whether there are any **restrictions** placed on it (for example the number of words you can use).

You may find that you recognise a question when you sit the exam. Be aware that the detail and/or requirement may be different. If the question seems familiar read the requirement and options carefully – do not assume that it is identical.

Step 3   Read any options you are given and select which ones are appropriate. Check that your calculations are correct. Have you followed the requirement exactly? Have you included every stage of the calculation?

Step 4   You may find that you are unsure of the answer.

- Re-read the question to ensure that you understand it and are answering the requirement
- Eliminate any obviously wrong options if you are given a number of options from which to choose

Step 5   If you are still unsure, **continue to the next question**.

Step 6   Revisit questions you are uncertain about. When you come back to a question after a break you often find you are able to answer it correctly straight away. If you are still unsure have a guess. You are not penalised for incorrect answers, so **never leave a question unanswered!**

Step 7   Make sure you show your **workings** clearly on calculation OTs, as you may gain some credit for workings even if your final answer is incorrect.

What the examiner means

The table below has been prepared by CIMA to help you interpret exam questions.

Learning objective	Verbs used	Definition	Examples in the Kit
1 Knowledge What you are expected to know	• List • State • Define	• Make a list of • Express, fully or clearly, the details of/facts of • Give the exact meaning of	6 7 6
2 Comprehension What you are expected to understand	• Describe • Distinguish • Explain • Identify • Illustrate	• Communicate the key features of • Highlight the differences between • Make clear or intelligible/state the meaning of • Recognise, establish or select after consideration • Use an example to describe or explain something	12 9 8
3 Application How you are expected to apply your knowledge	• Apply • Calculate/compute • Demonstrate • Prepare • Reconcile • Solve • Tabulate	• To put to practical use • To ascertain or reckon mathematically • To prove the certainty or to exhibit by practical means • To make or get ready for use • To make or prove consistent/ compatible • Find an answer to • Arrange in a table	26 18 22 8
4 Analysis How you are expected to analyse the detail of what you have learned	• Analyse • Categorise • Compare and contrast • Construct • Discuss • Interpret • Produce	• Examine in detail the structure of • Place into a defined class or division • Show the similarities and/or differences between • To build up or complete • To examine in detail by argument • To translate into intelligible or familiar terms • To create or bring into existence	39 17 26 15
5 Evaluation How you are expected to use your learning to evaluate, make decisions or recommendations	• Advise • Evaluate • Recommend	• To counsel, inform or notify • To appraise or assess the value of • To advise on a course of action	35 40

Exam update

Since the publication of the Study Text, CIMA has provided further guidance on the content of this paper. We are therefore giving additional guidance below on certain areas of the syllabus.

Although It appeared in the official answer to one of the mock exam questions, EPS is not specifically mentioned in the syllabus. We would advise that there is not likely to be any question on EPS and, if there were, only very basic knowledge would be required.

Formulae to learn

For Paper 7 you are given most of the formulae that you need and they are in the 'Mathematical tables' section at the back of this revision pack.

The formula you *will* need to learn is the formula for the percentage cost of an early settlement discount to the company giving it.

Formula to learn

$$\left[\frac{100}{100-d} \right]^{\frac{365}{t}} - 1$$

Where: d is the discount offered (5% = 5 etc.)
         t is the reduction in payment period in days

Useful websites

The websites below provide additional sources of information of relevance to your studies for *Management Accounting – Decision Management*.

- BPP   www.bpp.com

  For details of other BPP material for your CIMA studies

- CIMA   www.cimaglobal.com

  The official CIMA website

- *Financial Times*   www.ft.com

- *The Economist*   www.economist.com

- *Wall Street Journal*   www.wsj.com

Questions

Part A: Principles of Business Taxation

Questions 1 to 9 cover Principles of Business Taxation, the subject of Part A of the BPP Study Text for Paper P7.

1 Objective test questions: General principles of taxation

36 mins

1   Which of the following is a direct tax?

    A   Sales tax ~ *VAT*

    B   *Ad valorem* tax – *Adding value*

    C   Unit tax – *no|qty of items being tax ie Cigarettes ie Excise*

  ✓ (D) Employee tax *ie Paye (direct-taxed on Individual).*   **(2 marks)**

2   Company J pays a dividend of $400,000. The rate of advanced tax is 20%. What is the advanced tax payable?

    A $80,000   *X ¼ by 400,000*

    B $85,000   *So $\frac{20}{100-20} = \frac{2}{8} = \frac{1}{4}$ of 400,000*

 ✓ (C) $100,000   *= 100,000 ✓*

    D $110,000   **(2 marks)**

3   Where is employee tax recorded in a set of financial accounts? *PAYE – were talking about*

    A   Charged to employee costs in the income statement *Part of wages charge in I.C.*

    B   Charged to cost of sales in the income statement *if not Paid over to Inland Rev*

 ✓ (C) Included as a creditor in the balance sheet *it's a CIL in the BIS*

    D   Included as a debtor in the balance sheet *Once paid over to* **(2 marks)**

4   Which of the following powers is *not* available to tax authorities. *Tax Authority it doesn't remaina liability.*

    A   Power to review and query filed returns *– Tax Authorities Can't do this obviously*

  (B) Power to detain company officials *they aren't the Police.*

    C   Power to request special returns

    D   Power to enter and search premises **(2 marks)**

5   Complete the blanks: *(– Tax Person   Entity*

    Direct taxation is charged directly on the ......*Individual*...... or ......*Company*...... that is intended to pay the tax. **(2 marks)**

6   Complete the following equation. ① *Disallowable Expenditure*

    Accounting profit + ?① – non-taxable income – tax allowable expenditure = ? *taxable Profit* **(2 marks)**

7   Complete the blanks:

    ...*Group Relief*...... (two words) in the UK treats the members of a group as one ...*Entity*...... for tax purposes. **(2 marks)**

8   Tax evasion is legal. True or(false?) *– Illegal ie don't disclose your Income.* **(2 marks)**

    – Tax Avoidance – Legal.

9   Complete the blanks:

The person liable to pay tax is called a ...taxable..Person...... (2 words). This includes an individual, an

..estate...of a deceased person, a ...Trust.................... fund, a partnership, a ....limited.....................

company and any other .....body..................... set up to carry out trade for profit.   **(2 marks)**

10   Sometimes interest payments may be treated for tax purposes as if they were dividends. What is the name
of this rule?   Recharacterisation Rule.   **(2 marks)**

- Shareholld lend money to Company, they get in
  Payments and get tax relief on taxable Payments.   **(Total = 20 marks)**
  ie If they feel i is to high they may feel dividends are Included In here.

2 Objective test questions: International tax   **36 mins**

1   Company Z has a factory in Malaysia with retail outlets in Hong Kong. The company's registered office is in
London but the head office is located in the Cayman Islands. All board meetings take place in the Cayman
Islands. Where is Company Z's country of residence?

     A   Malaysia   Board   Meetings
     B   Hong Kong
     C   England
     D   Cayman Islands   **(2 marks)**

2   Which of the following is a source of tax rules?   3 nICing Rules

     A   International accounting standards   1 Tax Rule.
     B   Local company legislation
     C   International tax treaties   Treaties
     D   Domestic accounting practice   - Where the rules came from.   **(2 marks)**

3   Which of the following statements most closely defines double taxation relief?

     A   The group is treated as one entity for tax purposes — Group Relief
     B   Losses of one group member can be offset against the profits of another. — "   "   - aspect of
     C   Capital gains tax is deferred until an asset is sold outside the group.   "   "   "   "
     D   Tax paid by a company in one country is offset against the tax due in another country.   **(2 marks)**

4   A company is resident in Country B. It has a branch in Country C. The branch has taxable profits of $50,000,
on which tax of $5,000 is paid. The tax rate in Country B is 20% and there is a double taxation treaty
between Countries B and C that allows tax relief on the full deduction basis. If the company has total taxable
profits, including those of the branch of $100,000, how much tax will it pay in Country B?

     A $5,000   100,000 × 20% = 20,000
     B $10,000   5,000
     C $15,000
     D $20,000   15,000   **(2 marks)**

5   A company is resident in Country B. It has a branch in Country C. The branch has taxable profits of $50,000,
on which tax of $15,000 is paid. The tax rate in Country B is 20% and there is a double taxation treaty
between Countries B and C that allows tax relief on the credit basis. If the company has total taxable profits,
including those of the branch of $100,000, how much tax will it pay in Country B?

     A $5,000   Credit basis - use % for both
     B $10,000   Ignore the $15,000. Paid
     C $15,000
     D $20,000   So   100,000 × 20% = 20,000.   **(2 marks)**

                       50,000 × 20% = 10,000

                                B - 10,000 .

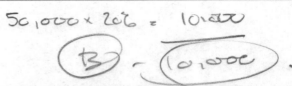

6   The European Union (EU) is an example of a supranational body. In not more than 20 words, describe the effect the EU has on its member states' tax rules.   **(2 marks)**

7   In countries such as the UK, different types of income are taxed according to different rules. What is the name of this system?   *Scheduleur System.*   **(2 marks)**

8   In the UK, a company is resident in the place of incorporation. True or false?   **(2 marks)**

9   Name four payments that are usually affected by withholding tax.   *Rayalties, dividends, PayE, Interest.*   **(2 marks)**

10   Name three methods of giving double taxation relief.   *- See Pages + deduction basis.*   **(2 marks)**

(Total = 20 marks)

3 Objective test questions: Indirect taxes   **36 mins**

1   Company Y has sales of $250,000, excluding sales tax, in a period. Its purchases, including sales tax, total $225,600. It has no zero-rated sales but 20% of its purchases are zero-rated. Sales tax is 17.5%. What is the sales tax payable for the period?

    ↳ no tax on these Purchases.
    Total monetary Amount of Purchases Including UAT

    A $5,650
    B $10,354   *180,480*
    C $12,166   *31,584.*   *225.600 × 80% = - then extract UAT.*
    D $16,870   **(2 marks)**

2   Which of the following is an indirect tax?

    A   Withholding tax
    B   Advanced tax
    C   Sales tax
    D   Company income tax   **(2 marks)**

3   Company T has sales of $230,000, including sales tax, in a period. Its purchases, excluding sales tax, total $180,000, of which $20,000 are zero-rated. Sales tax is 15%. What is the sales tax payable for the period?

    A $6,000   *10%.*   *230,000*   *× 15% = 30,000.*
    B $6,522   *Includes sales tax*   *―――*
    C $10,500   *115*
    D $11,022   *180,000 - 20,000 × 15% = 24,000*
    (2 marks)
    6000.

4   The cost of a sales tax is borne by which person?

    A   The supplier of raw materials   *As long as the Companys In the Chain*
    B   The end consumer   *are registered for UAT.*
    C   The retailer   *they (company) Acts as*
    D   The wholesaler   **(2 marks)**

    a Collector.

5   Company Q has sales of $700,000, excluding sales tax, in a period. Its purchases, including sales tax, total $550,000. The rate of sales tax is 10%. If 25% of all sales are zero rated, what is the sales tax payable for the period?

700,000 × 75% × 10% = 52500.

550,000 / 110 × 10 = 50000.

=2500

    A $2,500

    B $15,000

    C $20,000

    D $32,500   **(2 marks)**

6   Company K has sales of $250,000, excluding sales tax, in a period. Its purchases, including sales tax, total $225,600. However, 20% of its sales are exempt. Sales tax is 15%. What is the sales tax payable for the period?

    A $2,547

    B $2,928

    C $6,460

    D $16,870   **(2 marks)**

7   An *ad valorem* tax is an example of a direct tax. True or false?   **(2 marks)**

8   Company J has sales of $1,000,000, excluding sales tax, in a period. Its purchases, including sales tax, total $575,000. Sales tax is 15%. What is the sales tax payable for the period?

    A $44,185

    B $47,000

    C $75,000

    D $150,000   **(2 marks)**

9   Company W has sales of $500,000, excluding sales tax, in a period. Its purchases, including sales tax, total $345,000. It has no zero-rated sales but 25% of its purchases are zero-rated. Sales tax is 15%. What is the sales tax payable for the period?

75,000.

    A $26,405

    B $30,000

    C $31,465

    D $41,250   **(2 marks)**

10 Company A has sales of $250,000, excluding sales tax, in a period. Its purchases, including sales tax, total $225,600. It has exempt sales of 20%. Sales tax is 17.5%. What is the sales tax payable for the period?

    A $8,120

    B $10,354

    C $12,166

    D $16,870   **(2 marks)**

(Total = 20 marks)

4 Objective test questions: Company taxation

36 mins

1   Company G makes an accounting profit of $350,000 during the year. This includes non-taxable income of $25,000 and depreciation of $30,000. In addition, $15,000 of the expenses are disallowable for tax purposes. If the tax allowable depreciation totals $32,000, what is the taxable profit?

    A $323,000
    B $338,000
    C $352,000
    D $362,000

Handwritten: AICProfit = 350,000 . − 25,000 . + 30,000 . + 15,000 − 32,000

(2 marks)

2   Company G makes a taxable profit of $350,000 during the year. This includes adjustments for non-taxable income of $25,000, depreciation of $30,000 and $15,000 disallowed expenses. If the tax allowable depreciation totals $32,000, what is the accounting profit?

    A $323,000
    B $338,000
    C $352,000
    D $362,000

Handwritten: Same Calculation only do it backwards. + 32% − 15,000 − 30,000 + 25,000 TP 350.

(2 marks)

3   Company G makes an accounting loss of $350,000 during the year. This includes non-taxable income of $25,000 and depreciation of $30,000. In addition, $400,000 of the expenses are disallowable for tax purposes. If the tax allowable depreciation totals $32,000, what is the taxable amount?

    A $23,000 profit
    B $23,000 loss
    C $123,000 profit
    D $123,000 profit

(2 marks)

4   Company D pays a dividend of $360,000. The rate of advanced tax is 10%. What is the advanced tax payable?

    A $36,000
    B $40,000
    C $42,000
    D $44,444

Handwritten: $\frac{10}{90} = \frac{1}{9}$. Remember $\frac{1}{9}$. -

(2 marks)

5   Company P makes an accounting loss of $320,000 during the year. This includes non-taxable income of $20,000 and depreciation of $33,000. In addition, $40,000 of the expenses are disallowable for tax purposes. If the tax allowable depreciation totals $45,000, what is the taxable amount?

    A $182,000 loss
    B $300,000 loss
    C $312,000 loss
    D $328,000 loss

Handwritten: (320,000). − 20,000 + 33,000 + 40,000 − 45,000

(2 marks)

6   Company W makes a taxable profit of $50m during the year. This is after adjustments for non-taxable income of $3m, depreciation of $15m and $1m disallowed expenses. If the tax allowable depreciation totals $4m, what is the accounting profit?

    A $38m
    B $41m
    C $58m
    D $59m

(2 marks)

7   Company M makes an accounting profit of $250,000 during the year. This includes depreciation of $45,000 and disallowable expenses of $20,000. If the tax allowable depreciation totals $30,000 and the tax rate is 30%, what is the tax payable?

    A $64,500
    B $75,000
    C $79,500
    D $85,500   **(2 marks)**

8   Company B makes an accounting profit of $360,000 during the year. This includes non-taxable income of $35,000 and depreciation of $40,000. In addition, $10,000 of the expenses are disallowable for tax purposes. If the tax allowable depreciation totals $30,000 and the tax rate is 20%, what is the tax payable?

    A $60,000
    B $65,000
    C $69,000
    D $72,000   **(2 marks)**

9   Company X makes an accounting profit of $500,000 during the year. This includes non-taxable income of $25,000 and depreciation of $50,000.

    The finance director finds that $5,000 of the expenses are disallowable for tax purposes. If the tax allowable depreciation totals $60,000 and the tax rate is 25%, what is the tax payable?

    A $116,250
    B $117,500
    C $123,750
    D $132,500   **(2 marks)**

*mean you x the taxable Profit * tax rate*

10   Company G makes an accounting profit of $250,000 during the year. This is after charging depreciation of $40,000 and tax disallowable expenses of $2,000. If the tax allowable depreciation totals $30,000 and the tax rate is 30%, what is the tax payable?

    A $71,400
    B $72,000
    C $77,400
    D $78,600   **(2 marks)**

(Total = 20 marks)

[handwritten: overprovision for the yr.]

[handwritten: ↑ def tax ↑ Prov.]

5 Objective test questions: Deferred tax

36 mins

1 A company had a credit balance brought forward on current tax of $20,000. During the year it paid tax of $18,000 and it has a provision for the current year of $50,000. It has increased the deferred tax provision by $5,000. What is the total charge to tax for the year in the income statement?

- (A) $53,000
- B $55,000
- C $57,000
- D $68,000

[handwritten: Under Provision for the yr.]

*[handwritten:
over Provided by 20,000
Tax Paid   18,000.
(2,000) overprovide
Provision 50,000
↑ Provision 5,000   = 53,000]*

(2 marks)

2 A company had a debit balance brought forward on current tax of $2,000. During the year it has paid no tax and received a tax refund of $1,800. It has a provision for the current year of $30,000. It has decreased the deferred tax provision by $5,000. What is the total charge to tax for the year in the income statement?

- A $23,200
- B $24,800
- (C) $25,200
- D $35,200

[handwritten: ✓]

*[handwritten:
200
30,000 = 25,200.
(5,000)]*

(2 marks)

[handwritten: difference between dep & Capital allowances (main reason for deferred tax).]

3 In accounting for deferred tax, which of the following items can give rise to temporary differences?

[handwritten left margin: Did give rise to temp differences]

- ✓1 Differences between accounting depreciation and tax allowances for capital expenditure
- ✗2 Expenses charged in the income statement but disallowed for tax – *[handwritten: never going to reverse so]*
- ✓3 Revaluation of a non-current asset – *[handwritten: you will get a temp differences Permanate here.]*
- ✓4 Unrelieved tax losses – *[handwritten: temp diff.]*

[handwritten: └ If you make losses & can't carry them back Just forward.]

- (A) 1, 3 and 4 only
- B 1 and 2 only ✗.
- C 3 and 4 only ✗.
- D All four items ✗.

[handwritten: ✓]

(2 marks)

[handwritten: Give rise to a deferred tax liability.]

4 Which of the following items are taxable temporary differences, according to IAS 12 *Income taxes?*

- ✓1 Capitalised development costs being amortised in the income statement, but deducted in full from taxable profit as incurred - *[handwritten: Getting tax Advantage first, tax charge will be low In Comparison to Accounting Profit]*
- ✓2 Interest received in arrears and time apportioned for accounting purposes, but included in taxable profit on a cash basis – *[handwritten: if Interest Paid it will be the other way around no tax relief as it hadn't been Paid.]*
- ✓3 Tax allowances for capital expenditure exceeding depreciation charged in accounts – *[handwritten: Straight forward.]*

- (A) All three items
- B 1 and 2 only ✗
- C 1 and 3 only ✗
- D 2 and 3 only ✗

[handwritten: ✓]

(2 marks)

*[handwritten:
4)   Interest receivable: 100.]*

*[handwritten:
Tax once received:
low to the
Interest
receivable.
Deferred tax charge: 30]*

1 & 3 are Perm differences.

5   Which of the following are examples of assets or liabilities whose carrying amount is always equal to their
     tax base?

Carrying Value is = Tax base.   *never worry about deferred tax*

1   Accrued expenses that will never be deductible for tax purposes *- Disallowable exp.*

2   Accrued expenses that have already been deducted in determining the current tax liability for current
     or earlier periods *- does this create a temp. difference.*
     ↳ Advertising - no temp diff between AlCing Profit & Taxable Profit.

Same as 1   3   Accrued income that will never be taxable   *Base.*

temp.

4   A loan payable in the balance sheet at the amount originally received, which is also the amount
     eventually repayable *no difference ↳ loan not doing*

     Anything to
     AlCing or Tax
     Profit.

     A   1 and 3 only ✗
     B   1 and 2 only ✗
     C   2 and 4 only ✗
     D   All four items ✓   **(2 marks)**

6   Which of the following statements about IAS 12 *Income taxes* are correct?
     ↓ doesn't allow discounting deferred tax / Assets / liabilities.

✗ 1   Companies may discount deferred tax assets and liabilities if the effect would be material.

2   The financial statements must disclose an explanation of the relationship between tax expense and
     accounting profit. *- Does ask this off you in IAS12*

3   Deferred tax may not be recognised in respect of goodwill unless any impairment of that goodwill is
     deductible for tax purposes. *- IAS12 does agree with this.*

4   The tax base of an asset or liability is the amount attributed to that asset or liability for tax purposes.
     ↳ Again Correct.

     A ✗ All the statements are correct
     B   2, 3 and 4 only are correct
     C ✗ 1 and 4 only are correct
     D ✗ None of the statements is correct.   **(2 marks)**

7   The following information relates to an entity.

     •   At 1 January 20X8, the net book value of non-current assets exceeded their tax written down value by
         $850,000.

     •   For the year ended 31 December 20X8, the entity claimed depreciation for tax purposes of $500,000 and
         charged depreciation of $450,000 in the financial statements.

     •   During the year ended 31 December 20X8, the entity revalued a freehold property. The revaluation
         surplus was $250,000. The entity has no plans to sell the property and realise the gain in the
         foreseeable future.

     •   The tax rate was 30% throughout the year.

     What is the provision for deferred tax required by IAS 12 *Income taxes* at 31 December 20X8?

     A $240,000   850,000
     B $270,000   -   500,000
     C $315,000   (450,000).
     D $345,000   250,000   **(2 marks)**

                                                  _____
                                                  1,150,000

                                        Deferred tax   315,000.
                                        @ 30% =.

8   A company had a credit balance brought forward on current tax of $25,000. During the year it has paid no tax and received a tax refund of $2,500. It has a provision for the current year of $30,000. It has decreased the deferred tax provision by $10,000. What is the total charge to tax for the year in the income statement?

   A $5,000 debit
   B $5,000 credit
   C $7,500 debit
   D $7,500 credit   (2 marks)

9   A country had a current tax regime whereby advanced tax is paid on dividends. What system of tax is this?   (2 marks)

10 A company has a credit balance brought forward on current tax of $25,000. During the year it has paid tax of $27,800. It has a provision for the current year of $28,000. It has increased the deferred tax provision by $5,000. What is the total charge to tax for the year in the income statement?

   A $31,200
   B $33,000
   C $33,800
   D $35,800   (2 marks)

                                                                    (Total = 20 marks)

6 Section B questions: Taxation I   45 mins

(a) Define a taxable person and give three examples. What is a competent jurisdiction for tax purposes? (5 marks)

(b) Tax rules arise from four main sources. List the sources and describe two of these in detail.   (5 marks)

(c) (i)   A has an accounting profit of $50,000,000. This total is after charging depreciation of $1,250,000, formation expenses of $250,000 and entertaining expenses of $750,000. The figure also includes government grants received of $2,500,000.

          The tax rate is 25%. Under A's tax regime, government grants are tax-free. If the tax allowable depreciation is $1,350,000, calculate the tax due for the current period.   (2 marks)

     (ii) A has paid a dividend during the accounting period of $1,700,000. The advanced tax rate is 15%. Calculate the following.

           –   The advanced tax payable on the dividend.   (2 marks)

           –   How much tax remains to be paid to the tax authorities at the end of the accounting period.   (3 marks)

(d) (i)   Give a definition of an indirect tax and explain how it works.   (3 marks)

     (ii) There are two types of indirect taxes. State what these are and give two examples of each. (2 marks)

(e) F has sales of $587,500 including sales tax. Its purchases for the same period were $350,000 excluding sales tax. The sales tax rate is 17.5%. Calculate the tax payable to the tax authorities if 20% of B's sales are exempt and its deductible input tax is to be apportioned accordingly.   (5 marks)

                                                                    (Total = 25 marks)

7 Section B questions: Taxation II

45 mins

(a)   D has an accounting period ending on 31 December each year. It is resident in the UK. D is reviewing its record keeping and retention policies. What does it need to consider from a tax viewpoint?   **(5 marks)**

(b)   An employee feels that she is paying too much tax. What is a business' position with regard to employee tax? How should it deal with this query?   **(5 marks)**

(c)   Tax authorities have various powers to enforce compliance with the tax rules.

State what these powers are and give examples of each.   **(5 marks)**

(d)   What is withholding tax and why do tax authorities use it? Give two examples of payments affected by withholding tax.   **(5 marks)**

(e)   Why do countries need to enter into double taxation agreements? What are the three main methods of giving double taxation relief?   **(5 marks)**

(Total = 25 marks)

---

8 Section B questions: Taxation III

45 mins

(a)   H is a major manufacturing entity. According to the entity's records, temporary differences of $2.00 million had arisen at 30 April 20X4 because of differences between the carrying amount of non-current assets and their tax base, due to H claiming accelerated tax relief in the earlier years of the asset lives.

At 30 April 20X3, the temporary differences attributable to non-current assets were $2.30 million.

H's tax rate has been 30% in the past. On 30 April 20X4, the directors of H were advised that the rate of taxation would decrease to 28% by the time that the temporary differences on the non-current assets reversed.

Required

Prepare the note in respect of deferred tax as it would appear in the financial statements of H for the year ended 30 April 20X4. (Your answer should be expressed in $ million and you should work to two decimal places.)   **(5 marks)**

(b)   B is a retail entity. Its tax rate is 30%. It has a current tax payable brought forward from the year ended 30 April 20X3 of $750,000 and a deferred tax payable of $250,000.

On 30 April 20X4, the estimated tax charge for the year ended 30 April 20X4 was $1,400,000. The actual tax charge for the year ended 30 April 20X3 was agreed with the tax authority and settled with a payment of $720,000. The deferred tax payable needs to be increased to $300,000 as at 30 April 20X4.

Required

Prepare the notes in respect of current and deferred tax as they would appear in the financial statements of B for the year ended 30 April 20X4. (Your answer should be expressed in $ million and you should work to two decimal places.)   **(5 marks)**

(c)   IAS 12 *Income taxes* requires entities to publish an explanation of the relationship between taxable income and accounting profit. This can take the form of a numerical reconciliation between the tax expense and the product of the accounting profit and the applicable tax rate. Explain why this explanation is helpful to the readers of financial statements.   **(5 marks)**

(d)   Identify the external auditor's duties with respect of the disclosure of specific items in the financial statements, such as those in respect of deferred taxation or current tax.

Do **not** describe any of the detailed audit tests that the auditor would conduct.   **(5 marks)**

(e)   Explain how the audit report would be affected by any disagreement over the current and deferred tax disclosures made.

(5 marks)

(Total = 25 marks)

9 Section B questions: Taxation IV *— they haven't updated the answer they still talk about the old IAS12.* **45 mins**

(a)   IAS 12 *Income taxes* requires that the full provision basis be used to account for deferred tax, and therefore rejects the two alternative bases of accounting for deferred tax – the nil provision (or 'flow-through') basis and the partial provision basis. IAS 12 requires that (subject to certain exceptions) the full provision approach should be applied to all temporary differences. There is an alternative view held that under the full provision approach, deferred tax is not required unless the temporary difference is a timing difference. Such an approach implies that entities are not normally required to provide for deferred tax on revaluation surpluses or fair value adjustments arising on consolidation of a subsidiary for the first time.

Required

Explain why the IASB rejected the nil provision and partial provision bases when developing IAS 12.

(5 marks)

(b)   Discuss the logic underlying the IAS 12 approach to recognition of deferred tax and explain why this can lead to deferred tax being provided on revaluation surpluses and fair value adjustments. **(5 marks)**

Scenario for questions (c) and (d)

You are the management accountant of Pay It. Your assistant is preparing the consolidated financial statements for the year ended 31 March 20X5. However, he is unsure how to account for the deferred tax effects of certain transactions, as he has not studied IAS 12. These transactions are given below. In each case, compute the effect of both transactions on the deferred tax amounts in the consolidated balance sheet of Pay It at 31 March 20X5. You should provide a full explanation for your calculations and indicate any assumptions you make in formulating your answer

(c)   During the year, Pay it sold goods to a subsidiary for $10 million, making a profit of 20% on selling price. Of these goods, 25% were still in the inventories of the subsidiary at 31 March 20X5. The subsidiary and Pay It are in the same tax jurisdiction and pay tax on profits at 30%. **(5 marks)**
— deferred tax asset. (not getting relief for a while).

(d)   An overseas subsidiary made a loss adjusted for tax purposes of $8 million ($ equivalent). The only relief available for this tax loss is to carry it forward for offset against future taxable profits of the overseas subsidiary. Taxable profits of the overseas subsidiary suffer tax at a rate of 25%. **(5 marks)**

(e)   What criticisms can be made of IAS 12? **(5 marks)**

(Total = 25 marks)

Part B: Principles of Regulation of Financial Reporting

Questions 10 to 13 cover Principles of Regulation of Financial Reporting, the subject of Part B of the BPP Study Text for Paper P7.

10 Objective test questions: The regulatory framework 36 mins

1   Which of the following characteristics of financial information contribute to reliability, according to the International Accounting Standards Board's *Framework for the Preparation and Presentation of Financial Statements?*

    1   Freedom from bias
    2   Freedom from material error
    3   Faithful representation
    X 4   Consistency – Comparability

    A   All four characteristics
    (B)   1, 2 and 3 only
    C   1, 2 and 4 only
    D   3 and 4 only   **(2 marks)**

2   Guidance on the application and interpretation of International Financial Reporting Standards is provided by:

    A   The IASB
    B   The IASC Foundation
    (C)   The IFRIC International Financial Reporting Interpretations Committee
    D   The Standards Advisory Council   **(2 marks)**

3   Which of the following is *not* an advantage of global harmonisation of accounting standards?

    (A)   Priority given to different user groups in different countries barrier to harmonisation
    You aren't gas B →   Easier transfer of accounting staff across national borders – for much-national Companies.
    to a different   C   Ability to comply with the requirements of overseas stock exchanges
    Standard entire D   Better access to foreign investor funds ✓   **(2 marks)**

4   The IASB has recently revised and improved a number of standards. One of the major purposes of these revisions has been:

    A   To make the standards more relevant to developing countries
    (B)   To eliminate alternative treatments of items in accounts
    C   To give preparers of accounts more choice
    D   To comply with the demands of pressure groups   **(2 marks)**

5   Conceptual basis.

    Which of these is not a purpose of the *Framework for the preparation and presentation of financial statements?*

    A   To assist preparers of accounts in the application of IASs
    B   To overrule any individual IAS in case of conflict
    Book.   (C)   To assist in the development of national standards – not a Purpose of the framework.
    D   To assist auditors in forming an opinion regarding whether financial statements conform with IASs   **(2 marks)**

(handwritten top margin: Prudence & Consistency not really seen fundamental to the whole — fundamental Concepts as fundamental Process)

6   Which two of the following, per the *Framework*, are *underlying assumptions* relating to financial statements?

1   The accounts have been prepared on an accruals basis
2   Users are assumed to have sufficient knowledge to be able to understand the financial statements
3   The accounting policies used have been disclosed
4   The business is expected to continue in operation for the foreseeable future
5   The information is free from material error or bias

(handwritten left margin: Going Concern)
(handwritten right: − Going Concern, − Accruals/left)

A   1 and 3
B   2 and 3
C   1 and 4
D   3 and 5   **(2 marks)**

---

7.   The four principal qualitative characteristics of financial information *per* the *Framework* are:

A   Fair presentation; relevance, reliability, comparability
B   Relevance, comparability, materiality, understandability
C   Relevance, reliability, comparability, understandability
D   Materiality, comparability, reliability, fair presentation   **(2 marks)**

---

8   Which two of the following are not elements of financial statements *per* the *Framework*?

1   Profits
2   Assets   *− B.S*
3   Income   *− I.S*
4   Equity   *− B.S*
5   Losses
6   Expenses   *− I.S*

A   2 and 4
B   1 and 5   *— aren't an element in your financial statements.*
C   3 and 4
D   5 and 6   **(2 marks)**

---

9   According to the *Framework*, the income statement measures:

A   Financial position *− B.S*   *Income statement*
B   Performance *− I.S*   *Measures Performance*
C   Profitability
D   Financial adaptability *− Cash flow statement|B.S|I.S*   **(2 marks)**

---

10   An asset has to meet two recognition criteria before being recognised in financial statements. One of these is the probability that future economic benefits will flow to the enterprise. The other criterion is:

A   The asset has a cost or value that can be measured reliably
B   The future economic benefits will be received within the current accounting period
C   The future economic benefits can be reliably measured
D   The asset has an open market value   **(2 marks)**

(Total = 20 marks)

(handwritten bottom: Asset derive from Past events, expected to bring about future economic benefits.)

11 Objective test questions: External audit

36 mins

1   Which of these statements about auditors are correct?

    1   The auditors of a large company are likely to place emphasis on checking the operation of the company's systems of internal control.

    2   The prevention and detection of fraud are primarily the responsibility of a company's directors.

    3   Auditors should have the right of access to the records and vouchers of a client company at all times.

    A   All three statements are correct.
    B   1 and 2 only
    C   1 and 3 only
    D   2 and 3 only

    (2 marks)

2   Which of the following statements about the auditors of a limited liability company are correct?

    1   The auditors must carry out their work so as to have a reasonable expectation of detecting material misstatements in the financial statements arising from error or fraud.

    2   The auditors carry out walk-through tests to confirm their understanding of the client's accounting system.

    3   At the end of their audit, the auditors report to the directors expressing their opinion of the financial statements.

    4   Substantive tests are designed to confirm that internal controls operated effectively throughout the relevant period.

    A   3 and 4 only
    B   2 and 3 only
    C   1 and 2 only
    D   All four statements are correct

    (2 marks)

3   Which of the following are normally rights of the auditors of a limited liability company?

    1   Right of access to the company's records at all times

    2   Right to attend all meetings of directors

    3   Right to attend all general meetings of the company

    4   Right to obtain any information and explanations they think necessary for their audit from the company's officers

    A   All four are statutory rights
    B   1, 2 and 3 only
    C   1, 3 and 4 only
    D   1, 2 and 4 only

    (2 marks)

4   Which of the following are covered by the auditors' report?

    1   Cash flow statement
    2   Statement of recognised income and expense
    3   Notes to the income statement and balance sheet

    A   All three are covered.
    B   1 and 2 only
    C   2 and 3 only
    D   1 and 3 only

    (2 marks)

BPP
PROFESSIONAL EDUCATION

5   There is a major uncertainty facing Z, a limited liability company. Actions are pending against the company for allegedly supplying faulty goods, causing widespread damage.

The directors have fully described the circumstances of the case in a note to the financial statements.

What form of audit report is appropriate in this case?

A   Qualified opinion – limitation on auditors' work
B   Disclaimer of opinion
C   Unqualified report with an additional explanatory paragraph – re true & fair view
D   Qualified opinion – disagreement   (2 marks)

6   Which of the following matters are normally covered by the auditors' report?

1   Whether the company has kept proper accounting records

2   Whether the accounts are in agreement with the accounting records

3   Whether the accounts have been prepared in accordance with the relevant legislation and accounting standards
      – responsibility to do this:
4   Whether other information presented with the financial statements is consistent with them

A   1 and 2 only
B   1, 2 and 3 only
C   3 and 4 only
D   All four matters are normally covered   (2 marks)

7   A company's auditors find insufficient evidence to substantiate the company's cash sales, which are material in amount.

What form of qualification of the audit report would normally be appropriate in this situation?

A   Qualified opinion – disagreement
B   Qualified opinion – limitation on auditors' work
C   Disclaimer of opinion
D   Qualified opinion – adverse opinion   (2 marks)

8   A company's accounting records were largely destroyed by fire shortly after the balance sheet date. As a result, the financial statements contain a number of figures based on estimates.

What form of qualification of the audit report would be appropriate in this situation?

A   Qualified opinion – disagreement
B   Qualified opinion – limitations on auditors' work
C   Disclaimer of opinion
D   Qualified opinion – adverse opinion   (2 marks)

9   An auditor forms the opinion that a company's trade receivables are overstated by a material amount because of the company's failure to provide for a balance due from a company that has ceased trading.

What form of qualification of the audit report would normally be appropriate in this case?

A   Qualified opinion – disagreement   – In a Certain Area of Accounts.
B   Qualified opinion – limitation on auditors' work
C   Disclaimer of opinion
D   Qualified opinion – adverse opinion   (2 marks)

10   When carrying out an audit an external auditor must satisfy himself of a number of matters. Which of the following are not one of those matters?

   A   The accounts have been prepared by a qualified accountant ✓ *Answer.*

   B   Proper accounting records have been kept ✓

   C   The accounts have been prepared in accordance with local legislation and relevant accounting standards ✓

   D   The accounts are in agreement with accounting records ✓   **(2 marks)**

(Total = 20 marks)

---

12 Section B questions: Regulation   36 mins

(a)   Explain and give an example of the effect on a set of published financial statements of a company, if the going concern convention is held *not* to apply.   **(5 marks)**

(b)   Explain in general terms what the IASB Framework is trying to achieve.   **(5 marks)**

(c)   Describe the advantages and disadvantages of offering companies the option of departing from the detailed requirements of International Accounting Standards in order to achieve a fair presentation.   **(5 marks)**

(d)   Discuss briefly the problems encountered in attempting to regulate financial reporting in the absence of a conceptual framework.   **(5 marks)**

- There are a no. of users to Satisfy.
- Even with a Conceptual framework **(Total = 20 marks)**
  it's still difficult to Apply A/Cing treatments.

13 Section B questions: External audit   27 mins

- You may need different standards for different Purposes.

(a)   Explain what you understand by the 'expectations gap'? What problems has this caused for the auditing profession? ✓   **(5 marks)**

(b)   Explain the circumstances in which an audit report will express each of the following:

   (i)   A qualified opinion
   (ii)   A disclaimer of opinion
   (iii)   An adverse opinion   **(5 marks)**

(c)   An auditor, in carrying out his statutory duty, may sometimes find himself to be in conflict with the directors of the company. What statutory rights does he have to assist him in discharging his responsibility to the shareholders?   **(5 marks)**

(Total = 15 marks)

- Right to Access of Info.
- Rights to attend general Meets.
- Right to Ask officers for Any further Explanations
- Right In Relation to Written Resolution.
- Right to Speak at the meetings.

Part C: Single company financial accounts

Questions 14 to 30 cover Single Company Financial Accounts, the subject of Part C of the BPP Study Text for Paper P7.

14 Objective test questions: Presentation

36 mins

1   Which, if any, of the following statements about limited liability companies are correct, according to IAS1?

- Six months within

1   ✗ Companies must produce their financial statements within one year after their balance sheet date.

2   ✓ The accounting policies adopted by a company must be disclosed by note.

3   ✗ The accounting records of a limited liability company must be open to inspection by a member of the company at all times. *— Auditors do this*

A   2 only
B   2 and 3 only
C   1 and 3 only
D   None of the statements is correct

(2 marks)

2   IAS 1 *Presentation of financial statements* defines the classification of liabilities as current or non-current.

Which of the following liabilities should be included within current liabilities in the balance sheet?

C.L. 1   Loan notes issued five years ago, due for repayment within one year, which have been agreed to be refinanced on a long-term basis before the financial statements are approved *but after the B/S date.*

C.L. 2   Trade payables due for settlement more than twelve months after the balance sheet date, within the normal course of the operating cycle *~ Still a C.L even after it's 12mths as long as it's in the normal course of the operating cycle*

C.L. 3   Trade payables due for settlement within twelve months after the balance sheet date, within the normal course of the operating cycle

C.L 4   Bank overdrafts *— Must always be a C.L. as the bank can call it in any day*

A   All four items
B   1, 3 and 4 only
C   1 and 2 only
D   2, 3 and 4 only

(2 marks)

3   Which of the following items can appear in a company's statement of changes in equity, according to IAS 1 *Presentation of financial statements*?

↳ how did you get from opening S/holders balances to the Closing S/holders balance.

✓ 1   Net profit or loss for the period
✓ 2   Dividends paid *— statement of*
✓ 3   Surplus on revaluation of properties *— revaluation Surplus.*
✓ 4   Proceeds of issuance of share capital

Dividends Proposed: + B/S if it's before IAS10: Has to go in here; the year end after year end - don't go in Just notes

A   All four items
B   1, 2 and 3 only
C   1, 3 and 4 only
D   2 and 4 only

Share Proceeds Issued Lunder 2 col-

Share K + Share Premium

(2 marks)

4 Which of the following statements about company financial statements are true?

[handwritten: doesn't Include Share Issues — take to Reserves / Changes in Equity / Recognised statement of Expenses]

1 ✗ The statement of recognised income and expense must not include unrealised gains.

[handwritten: Not true Any more!]

2 ✗ The number of employees at the end of the period or the average number of employees for the period must be disclosed by note. *[handwritten: —Under IAS 1 did one this was true not any more]*

3 ✓ Investments may appear in the balance sheet as either non-current assets or current assets.

4 ✓ When a revalued asset is sold, the revaluation surplus may be transferred from revaluation reserve to retained earnings in the balance sheet.

A 2, 3 and 4
B 3 and 4
C 1 and 2
D 1 and 4

(2 marks)

5 Which of these items may appear in a company's statement of total recognised income and expense, according to IAS 1 *Presentation of financial statements*?

1 ✓ Profit for the financial year
2 ✗ Dividends paid
3 ✓ Unrealised revaluation gains and losses
4 ✗ New share capital subscribed

[handwritten: Excludes dist/share Issue/shareholders / All 4 appear in Changes of Equity Statements.]

A 1, 2 and 4
B 1, 3 and 4
C 1 and 3 only
D All four items

(2 marks)

6 Which of the following items are required by IAS 1 *Presentation of financial statements* to be disclosed in the financial statements of a limited liability company?

1 ✓ Authorised share capital *[handwritten: — N·B to B·S]*
2 ✓ Finance costs *[handwritten: — I·S]* *[handwritten: I·S by Function :- Heading]*
3 ✓ Staff costs *[handwritten: — " "]* *[handwritten: I > Functional headings buried So Put in N·B]*
4 ✓ Depreciation *[handwritten: — " "]*

A 1 and 4 only
B 1 , 2 and 3 only
C 2, 3 and 4 only
D All four items

(2 marks)

7 Which of the following constitute a change of accounting policy according to IAS 8 Net profit or loss for the period, fundamental errors and changes in accounting policies?

[handwritten: — Weighted Avs/Avco = change in Alcing Policy]

1 ✓ A change in the basis of valuing inventory *[handwritten: Life — not allowed Under IAS2.]*

2 ✗ A change in depreciation method *[handwritten: — Change In Alcing Estimate. Not Alcing Policy]*

3 ✓ A decision to capitalise borrowing costs relating to the construction of non-current assets, rather than writing them off as incurred *[handwritten: A change In Alcing Policy As you change the way you deal with the asset.]*

4 ✗ Adopting an accounting policy for a new type of transaction not previously dealt with *[handwritten: ↳ Not a change In Alcing Policy.]*

A 1 and 2
B 2 and 3
C 1 and 3
D 2 and 4

(2 marks)

8   Which of the following items would qualify for treatment as a change in accounting estimate, according to IAS 8 (revised) *Accounting policies, changes in accounting estimates and errors?*

1   Provision for obsolescence of inventory
2   Correction necessitated by a material error
3   A change as a result of the adoption of a new International Accounting Standard
4   A change in the useful life of a non-current asset

A   All four items
B   2 and 3 only
C   1 and 3 only
D   1 and 4 only

(2 marks)

9   A change in accounting policy is accounted for by:

A   Changing the current year figures but not previous year's figures
B   Retrospective application   — *Restate our opening balance sheet.*
C   No alteration of any figures but disclosure in the notes
D   No alteration of any figures nor disclosure in the notes

(2 marks)

10   Shah changes the depreciation method for its motor vehicles from the straight line method to the reducing balance method. How would this be treated in the financial statements?

A   Changing the current year figures but not previous year's figures   — *Change in estimation technique.*
B   Retrospective application
C   No alteration of any figures but disclosure in the notes
D   No alteration of any figures nor disclosure in the notes

(2 marks)

(Total = 20 marks)

15 Section B questions: Presentation   27 mins

(a)   IAS 1 (revised) states that there are overall considerations that ensure the fair presentation of financial statements and compliance with International Accounting Standards.

Required

Explain briefly these overall considerations:

(i)   Materiality and aggregation
(ii)   Offsetting
(iii) Consistency

as the terms are used in IAS 1 (Revised).   (5 marks)

(b)   IAS 1 sets out the components of financial statements and minimum requirements for balance sheet and income statement disclosure. Two income statements are presented: with income and expenses by nature and by function.

Required

Set out a pro-forma balance sheet and a pro-forma income statement; the latter to be set out with classification of expenses by function.   (5 marks)

(c)   Suggest reasons why companies should be expected to publish accounts using standard formats saying why and to whom the specific information shown in the formats would be useful.   (5 marks)

(Total = 15 marks)

16 Leonardo

36 mins

(a) IAS 8 *Accounting policies, changes in accounting estimates and errors* deals with a number of matters important in the presentation of the income statement of an enterprise. IFRS 5 deals with discontinued operations.

Required

State the treatments in IAS 8 and IFRS 5 as regards accounting for the following in relation to the income statement of an enterprise.

[handwritten: Face of the I.S.
- Including total net Profit/loss of discontinued ops]

(i) Discontinuing operations **(3 marks)**

[handwritten: - The Profit/loss to the measurement of fair values less Cost to sell on disposal assets/discontinued ops.]

(ii) The correction of prior period errors **(3 marks)**

(iii) Changes in accounting policies, other than those resulting from the adoption of an International Accounting Standard **(3 marks)**

(b) The trial balance (list of account balances) of Leonardo, a limited liability company, at 30 September 20X8 included the following items:

	Dr $'000	Cr $'000
Revenue		6,840
Opening inventory	1,200	
Purchases	3,670	
Distribution costs	880	
Administrative expenses	590	
Interest payable	300	
Costs of a fundamental reorganisation of the company's operations	560	
Profit on sale of head office building (the company plans to move its central administration into a rented building)		1,200
Allowance for doubtful debts 1 October 20X7		150

In preparing the company's income statement the following further information is to be taken into account.

(i) The closing inventory was taken on 27 September 20X8 (all valued at cost) and amounted to $950,000. Between that date and the close of business on 30 September 20X8, goods costing $68,000 were sold and there were no further receipts of goods. These sales are included in the revenue total of $6,840,000.

(ii) During the year a debt of $400,000 proved to be irrecoverable and is to be written off. The allowance for doubtful debts is to be increased to $200,000.

(iii) The income tax expense on the profit for the year was $300,000.

Required

Prepare the company's income statement for the year ended 30 September 20X8 for inclusion in the company's annual report and complying, so far as the information permits, with the requirements of IAS 1 (Revised) *Presentation of financial statements*. **(11 marks)**

Note. In part (b) marks are awarded for layout and style as well as for the correct calculation of figures required for the answer. **(Total = 20 marks)**

17 Objective test questions: Cash flow statements   36 mins

1   The following is an extract from a cash flow statement prepared by a trainee accountant.

Reconciliation of operating profit to net cash flow from operating activities

[handwritten: Indirect Method]

	$'000
Cash flows from operating activities	
Net profit before taxation –	3,840
Adjustments for	
Depreciation	(1,060)
Loss on sale of building	210
	2,990
Increase in inventories	(490)
Decrease in trade payables	290
Net cash inflow from operating activities	2,790

Which of the following criticisms of this extract are correct?

1 T Depreciation should have been added, not deducted. ✓
2 F Loss on sale of building should have been deducted, not added. ✗ *Loss on sales of building added*
3 F Increase in inventories should have been added, not deducted. ✗ – *Increase in Inventories deducted*
4 T Decrease in trade payables should have been deducted, not added. ✓ *T.P - should be deducted.*

A   1 and 4   *– 1 & 4 are valid.*
B   2 and 3
C   1 and 3
D   2 and 4   **(2 marks)**

---

2   In the year ended 31 December 20X4 a company sold some plant which had cost $100,000 for $20,000. At the time of sale the net book value of the plant was $18,000.   *$2,000 - Profit Made.*

Which of the following correctly states the treatment of the transaction in the company's cash flow statement?

[handwritten: 20000 Cash Inflow]

	Proceeds of sale	Profit on sale
A	Cash inflow under financing activities	Deducted from profit in calculating cash flow from operating activities.
B	Cash inflow under investing activities	Added to profit in calculating cash flow from operating activities.
C	Cash inflow under financing activities	Added to profit in calculating cash flow from operating activities.
D	Cash inflow under investing activities	Deducted from profit in calculating cash flow from operating activities.

[handwritten: deducted in here if a Profit]   **(2 marks)**

---

3   Which of the following items should not appear in a company's cash flow statement?

1   Proposed dividends   *no cash flow so can't appear on Cash flow.*
2   Dividends received   *– yes it's Cash flow.*
3   Bonus issue of shares   *no cash flow again (no cash)*
4   Surplus on revaluation of a non-current asset   *no Cash flow again.*
5   Proceeds of sale of an investment not connected with the company's trading activities   *– yes it's Cash flow.*

A   1, 2, 3 and 5
B   3 and 4 only
C   1, 3 and 4
D   2 and 5   **(2 marks)**

4   Which, if any, of the following statements about cash flow statements are correct according to IAS 7 Cash flow statements?

Maybe a different way → of getting the figure but we get the same figure

1   The direct and indirect methods produce different figures for operating cash flow. *– Incorrect*

2   In calculating operating cash flow using the indirect method, an increase in inventory is added to operating profit. *↑ I.C.A is Neg – Incorrect.*

3   Figures shown in the cash flow statement should include sales taxes. *– Incorrect*

4   The final figure in the cash flow statement is the increase or decrease in cash at bank. *– Incorrect It's left out Cash Equ.*

A   1 and 4
B   2 and 3
C   2 only
D   None of the statements is correct.   **(2 marks)**

---

5   A company's balance sheets at 31 December 20X4 and 20X5 included the following items.

No I.S. Just 2 Bal. sheets. So workbackwards:

| | Balance sheets at | |
| | 31.12.X5 | 31.12.X4 |
	$'000	$'000
Taxation payable	840	760
Retained earnings	1,660	1,470

The company paid no interest or interim dividends during these years, and the tax provision of $760,000 in the 20X4 balance sheet was the amount paid in 20X5. Using this information, what is the company's operating profit for 20X5 for inclusion in its cash flow statement?

A $190,000
B $1,030,000
C $ 950,000
D $1,660,000   **(2 marks)**

---

6   The balance sheets of R, a limited liability company, at 31 December 20X3 and 20X4 included these figures.

| | 31 December | |
| | 20X3 | 20X4 |
	$m	$m
Property, plant and equipment: cost	40	50
Accumulated depreciation	(10)	(14)
	30	36

The income statement for the year ended 31 December 20X4 showed the following figures.

Depreciation charge for year	$6m
Loss on sales of property, plant and equipment	$1m

The company purchased new property, plant and equipment costing $16m during the year.

What figure should appear in the company's cash flow statement for 20X4 for receipts from the sale of property, plant and equipment?

A $3m
B $5m
C $4m
D   The figure cannot be calculated from the information provided.   **(2 marks)**

Short term, Highly liquid

7 A cash flow statement shows the increase or decrease in cash and cash equivalents in the period.

Which of the following items are included in this movement?

1   Cash at bank ✓

2   Overdraft at bank ✓

– if they Conform with the definition of CashEqu.

3   Current asset investments readily convertible into known amounts of cash and which can be sold without disrupting the company's business. ✓

4   Equity investments. ✗ *– Subject to Sign risk in Change In Value* *Significant.* *So not highly liquid.*

    A   All four items

    (B)   1, 2 and 3 only

    C   1 and 2 only

    D   1 and 3 only

(2 marks)

---

8 Which of the following should appear in a cash flow statement according to IAS 7 Cash flow statements?

1   ✓ Dividends paid on preference shares

2   ✓ Interest capitalised as part of the cost of a non-current asset *– as Cashflaw waved be there.*

3   ✓ Cash flows resulting from share issues

    (A)   All three items

    B   1 and 2 only

    C   1 and 3 only

    D   2 and 3 only

(2 marks)

---

9 The IAS 7 format for a cash flow statement using the indirect method opens with adjustments to net profit before taxation to arrive at cash flow from operating activities.

Which of the following lists consists only of items that would be deducted in that calculation? *ie which of the below are negative:*

    A   Loss on sale of non-current assets, increase in inventories, decrease in trade payables

    B   Depreciation, increase in trade receivables, decrease in trade payables

    ✓ C   Increase in trade receivables, profit on sale of non-current assets, decrease in trade payables

    D   Profit on sale of non-current assets, increase in trade payables, decrease in trade receivables

(2 marks)

---

10 A company's accounting records contain the following figures.

	$'000	
Sales for year	3,600	1200
Purchases for year	2,400	
Receivables: 31 December 20X2	600	(100)
31 December 20X3	700	
Payables: 31 December 20X2	300	+150
31 December 20X3	450	
Salaries and other expenses paid during 20X3, excluding interest	760	(760)

Rec↑ –   *Pay↑.*

What figure should appear in the company's cash flow statement for 20X3 for cash generated from operations, based on these figures?

    (A) $490,000

    B $390,000

    C $1,250,000

    D   None of these figures

(2 marks)

(Total = 20 marks)

18 Cee Eff

— Noi.S given Just 2.B.S.

36 mins

The balance sheet of CF Co for the year ended 31 December 20X4, together with comparative figures for the previous year, is shown below (all figures $'000).

	20X4		20X3	
	$'000	$'000	$'000	$'000
Assets				
Property, plant and equipment	270	*(a. ~s)*	180	
Less depreciation	(90)		(56)	
		180		124
Current assets				
Inventory	50		42	
Receivables	40		33	
Cash	–		11	
		90		86
Total assets		270		210
Equity and liabilities				
Equity				
Ordinary share capital $1 shares		25		20
Share premium		10		8
Retained earnings		65		55
		100		83
Non-current liabilities				
15% loan stock repayable 20X8		80		60
Current liabilities				
Trade and operating payables	33		24	
Taxation	19		17	
Dividend payable	28		26	
Bank overdraft	10		–	
		90		67
Total liabilities and capital		270		210

You are informed that:

(a) There were no sales of property, plant and equipment during 20X4

(b) The company does not pay interim dividends

(c) New loan stock and shares issued in 20X4 were issued on 1 January

Required

(a) Show your calculation of the operating profit of CF Co for the year ended 31 December 20X4. **(4 marks)**

(b) Prepare a cash flow statement for the year, in accordance with IAS 7 Cash flow statements. **(9 marks)**

(c) Show the note required in respect of cash and cash equivalents. **(3 marks)**

(d) Comment on the implications of the information given in the question plus the statements you have prepared, regarding the financial position of the company. **(4 marks)**

(Total = 20 marks)

Retained

19 T cash flow

36 mins

The following information has been extracted from the draft financial statements of T, a manufacturing company.

T: Income statement for the year ended 30 September 20X1

	$'000
Revenue	15,000
Cost of sales	(9,000)
Gross profit	6,000
Other operating expenses	(2,400)
	3,600
Finance cost	(24)
Profit before taxation	3,576
Income tax expense	(1,040)
Profit for the period	2,536

T: Balance sheet as at 30 September 20X1

	20X1 $'000	20X1 $'000	20X0 $'000	20X0 $'000
Assets				
Property, plant and equipment		18,160		14,500
Current assets				
Inventories	1,600		1,100	
Trade receivables	1,500		800	
Bank	150		1,200	
		3,250		3,100
Total assets		21,410		17,600
Equity and liabilities				
Equity:				
Issued capital		10,834		7,815
Retained earnings		5,836		4,400
		16,670		12,215
Non-current liabilities				
Interest-bearing borrowing	1,700		2,900	
Deferred tax	600		400	
		2,300		3,300
Current liabilities				
Trade payables	700		800	
Dividend payable	700		600	
Taxation	1,040		685	
		2,440		2,085
		21,410		17,600

Property, plant and equipment

	Property $'000	Plant $'000	Total $'000
Cost			
30 September 20X0	8,400	10,800	19,200
Additions	2,800	5,200	8,000
Disposals	–	(2,600)	(2,600)
30 September 20X1	11,200	13,400	24,600
Depreciation			
30 September 20X0	1,300	3,400	4,700
Disposals	–	(900)	(900)
Charge for year	240	2,400	2,640
30 September 20X1	1,540	4,900	6,440
Net book value			
30 September 20X1	9,660	8,500	18,160
30 September 20X0	7,100	7,400	14,500

The plant that was disposed of during the year was sold for $730,000.

All additions to property, plant and equipment were purchased for cash.

Dividends were declared before the balance sheet dates. The dividend declared for 20X1 was $1,100,000.

Required

(a) Prepare T's cash flow statement and associated notes for the year ended 30 September 20X1. These should be in a form suitable for publication. **(15 marks)**

(b) After the publication of the balance sheet at 30 September 20X0, the directors of T were criticised for holding too much cash. The annual report for the year ended 30 September 20X1 claims that the company has managed its cash more effectively.

Required

Explain whether T's cash management appears to have been any more effective this year. **(5 marks)**

(Total = 20 marks)

20 Objective test questions: Non-current assets, inventories and construction contracts

36 mins

2 excluded

1   The components of the cost of a major item of equipment are given below.

	$
Purchase price *-bring Into Cost ✓*	780,000
Import duties *"*	117,000
Irrecoverable Sales tax (refundable) *ie recouerable VAT ✗ goes to VAT instead.*	78,000
it would have been Site preparation ✓	30,000
Installation ✓	28,000
Pre-production costs *✓ ie tested - Assuming Costs were to get the Asset up Into operational Condition*	18,000
Hotel → Initial operating losses before the asset reaches planned performance *✗ ie As long as you*	50,000
not full capacity for ex. can't Capitalise it. Estimated cost of dismantling and removal of the asset, recognised as a provision *✓ Can use it* under IAS 37 *Provisions, contingent liabilities and contingent assets*	100,000
	1,201,000 *- 78 -50*

What amount may be recognised as the cost of the asset, according to IAS 16 *Property, plant and equipment?*

1073
1073 - 18 (= Preprodion Costs
1055
but they took of Pre-prod Costs as well

A	$956,000
(B)	$1,055,000
C	$973,000
D	$1,201,000

(2 marks)

2   Which of the following statements about IAS 36 *Impairment of assets* are correct? *< Carrying Value then you write down the Asset to the*

- at each reporting date.

ie you don't 1 ✓ Non-current assets must be checked annually for evidence of impairment. ✓
have to do an Impairment Calculation but you should Check them *recovering*

2 ✓ An impairment loss must be recognised immediately in the income statement, except that all or part *the* of a loss on a revalued asset should be charged against any related revaluation surplus.
If no Carrying Value it goes to I.S ie it's the 1st time *amount*

3 ✓ If individual assets cannot be tested for impairment, it may be necessary to test a group of assets as a unit. *- Very rare that Just 1 Asset Can be tested but Normally it's a Cash generating unit ie a group of Assets as Stated above.*

A	1, and 2 only ✗
B	1 and 3 only ✗
C	2 and 3 only ✗
(D)	1, 2 and 3 ✓

Carry Value 500   Rec Value 460   the 40 gets written Off (2 marks)

3   Which one or more of the following statements about IAS 38 *Intangible assets* are correct? *then remains of the remaining Assets.*

1 ✓ Research expenditure, other than capital expenditure on buildings and equipment for research purposes, must be written off as incurred. ✓

2 ✓ All companies must disclose in their financial statements the total amount spent on research and development and recognised as an expense during the period. *For all Companies ; ✓*

3 ✗ If development expenditure is capitalised, it must be amortised over a period not exceeding five years. *there is no time Period.* ✗

A	1 only
(B)	1 and 2
C	2 and 3
D	1 and 3

(2 marks)

[handwritten note at top: Negative Goodwill - take to the CR of I.S.
Pos " = B.S as Intangible Asset Only gets written down if Impairment review requires it]

4 Which of the following statements is corrects?

1 ✗ Negative goodwill should be shown on the balance sheet as a deduction from positive goodwill.

2 ✗ IAS 38 allows goodwill to be written off immediately against reserves as an alternative to capitalisation.

3 ✗ As a business grows, internally generated goodwill may be revalued upwards to reflect that growth.

4 ✓ Internally developed brands must not be capitalised. *— Same really as Internally Generated Goodwill.*

- A 1 and 4
- B 2 and 3
- C 3 only
- (D) 4 only

[handwritten: unacceptable.]

(2 marks)

5 Which of the following accounting policies would contravene International Accounting Standards if adopted by a company?

[handwritten left margin: Land isn't deprecnated]

1 ⁽ᶜᵒ⁾✓ Goodwill on acquisitions is written off immediately against reserves.

2 ✗ Land on which the company's buildings stand is not depreciated.

3 ✓ Internally generated brands are capitalised at fair value as advised by independent consultants.

4 ✓ In calculating depreciation, the estimated useful life of an asset is taken as half the actual estimated useful life as a measure of prudence.

- (A) 1, 3 and 4
- B 2 and 4 only
- C 1 and 3 only
- D All four are unacceptable

(2 marks)

6 Which of the following items should be included in arriving at the cost of the inventory of finished goods held by a manufacturing company, according to IAS 2 *Inventories*?

[handwritten left margin: Overall Cost of Inventory]

1 ✓ Carriage inwards on raw materials delivered to factory

2 ✗ Carriage outwards on goods delivered to customers *— Can't Include:*

3 ✓ Factory supervisors' salaries

4 ✓ Factory heating and lighting

5 ✗ Cost of abnormally high idle time in the factory *— abnormal Costs aren't allow to be Included they get written off*

6 ✓ Import duties on raw materials

- (A) 1, 3, 4 and 6
- B 1, 2, 4, 5 and 6
- C 3, 4 and 6
- D 2, 3 and 5

(2 marks)

7   Which of the following statements about IAS 2 *Inventories* are correct?

Normal.

1 ✗ Production overheads should be included in cost on the basis of a company's actual level of activity
   in the period. *It's the normal level of Activity.*

Trade discounts not settlement dis.

2 ✗ In arriving at the net realisable value of inventories, trade discounts and settlement discounts must
   be deducted. *you can deduct trade discounts but not settlement discounts*

3 ✗ In arriving at the cost of inventories, FIFO, LIFO and weighted average cost formulas are acceptable.
   ← Banned *LIFO has been banned.*

4 ✗ It is permitted to value finished goods inventories at materials plus labour cost only, without adding
   production overheads.

A   1 only
B   2 only
C   3 only
D   None of them

✓

(2 marks)

8   The position of a construction contract at 30 June 20X6 is as follows.

	$
Contract price	900,000
At 30 June 20X6	
Costs to date	720,000
Estimated costs to completion	480,000
Progress payments invoiced and received	400,000
Percentage complete	60%

What figures should appear for this contract in the accounts at 30 June 20X6, according to IAS 11
Construction contracts?

		Income statement		Balance sheet	
A	Sales revenue	$540,000		Receivables	$140,000
	Costs	$840,000			
B	Sales revenue	$540,000			
	Costs	$720,000			
C	Sales revenue	$540,000		Amount due from customer	$20,000
	Costs	$840,000			
D	Sales revenue	$540,000		Receivables	$140,000
	Costs	$720,000			

(2 marks)

9   According to IAS 16 *Property, plant and equipment*, which, if any, of the following statements about depreciation are correct?

    1 ✕ The main purpose of depreciation is to reflect the fall in value of an asset in the balance sheet over its useful life. *– Really Just an allocation Process.*

    2 ✕ When an asset is revalued, depreciation relating to the revaluation surplus should be debited to the revaluation reserve rather than the income statement.

    3 ✕ Provision for depreciation ensures that there are funds available to replace an asset when this becomes necessary, though in times of inflation additional amounts may need to be set aside.

    4 ✕ A change in depreciation method constitutes a change in accounting policy and must be accounted for as such. *it's a change In alCing estimate.*

    From no dep to start dep - change In AKus Policy end make a .. ⟶Prior Period adjustment

    A   1 and 4
    B   2 and 3
    C   4 only
    (D) None of the statements is correct   **(2 marks)**

10   IAS 38, *Intangible assets* allows internally developed intangible assets to be capitalised where

    A   Reasonable records have been maintained to ensure that its value can be measured reliably
    B   A reasonable estimate can be made of its useful life   ✕
    C   There is a readily ascertainable market value for the asset
    D   It relates to generally accepted intangible items such as brands and publishing titles   **(2 marks)**

Ignore this and Use notes.

                                                            (Total = 20 marks)

21 Section B questions: Non-current assets, inventories and construction contracts

27 mins

(a)   (i)   Discuss the criteria which IAS 38 *Intangible assets* states should be used when considering whether research and development expenditure should be written off in an accounting period or carried forward.

       (ii) Discuss to what extent these criteria are consistent with the fundamental accounting assumptions within IAS 1.   **(5 marks)**

(b)   Jedders Co has three long leasehold properties in different parts of the region each of which had an original life of 50 years. As at 1 January 20X0, their original cost, accumulated depreciation to date and carrying (book) values were as follows.

	Cost	Depreciation	Carrying value 1.1.20X0
	$'000	$'000	$'000
Property in North	3,000	1,800	1,200
Property in Central	6,000	1,200	4,800
Property in South	3,750	1,500	2,250

On 1 January an independent surveyor provided valuation information to suggest that the value of the South property was the same as book value, the North property had fallen against carrying value by 20% and the Central property had risen by 40% in value against the carrying value.

The directors wish to show all their properties at a revalued amount in the accounts as at 31 December 20X0.

Required

Calculate the income statement charges and the non-current asset balance sheet extracts for all the properties for the year ended 31 December 20X0. You should follow the requirements of IAS 16 *Property, plant and equipment*. **(5 marks)**

(c) 'The cost of inventories should comprise all costs of purchase, costs of conversion and other costs incurred in bringing the inventories to their present location and condition' (IAS 2).

This statement results in problems of a practical nature in arriving at the amount at which inventories and short term work in progress are stated in the accounts.

Required

Comment on the above statement identifying and discussing both the accounting policy and the problems 'of a practical nature' that may arise when computing the amount at which inventories and short term work in progress are stated in financial accounts. **(5 marks)**

(Total = 15 marks)

22 Geneva ~ Likely to be In Exam: ~ Section B: 36 mins

3 Construction Contracts:

Geneva Co is a company involved in the building industry and often has a number of major construction contracts which fall into two or more accounting periods. *1 of these Contracts are likely to be loss making*

During the year ended 31 December 20X8, Geneva Co enters into three construction contracts as follows:

		Contract	
	Zurich	Bern	Lausanne
	$'000	$'000	$'000
Fixed contract price	2,000	2,000	2,000
Payments on account	800	950	1,080
Costs incurred to date	640	1,100	1,000
Estimated costs to complete the contract	1,160	1,100	600
Estimate percentage of work completed	35%	50%	60%

Total Costs.

When you arrive to perform the audit for the year ended 31 December 20X8, you find that the marketing director is in dispute with the other directors. He can not understand how unfinished buildings can be worth anything and included at a value in the financial statements. He believes that if any of the buildings were abandoned the company would probably end up having to pay demolition costs.

He also does not understand how the company can estimate completion percentage and value the contracts. He thinks it must be very easy to fool the auditor in these cases.

Required

(a) Show how each contract would be reflected in the Balance sheet and Income statement of Geneva Co for the year ended 31 December 20X8. **(13 marks)**

(b) Prepare notes for a discussion with the marketing director explaining why construction contracts should be valued. **(7 marks)**

(Total = 20 marks)

$$\frac{\text{Cost to date}}{\text{Total Costs}} = \text{to get Costs to date or } \% \text{ if not given to them.}$$

23 Objective test questions: Distributable profits and capital transactions

36 mins

1   A company made an issue of 100,000 ordinary shares of 50c at $1.10 each. The cash received was correctly recorded in the cash book but the whole amount was entered into ordinary share capital account.

Which of the following journal entries will correct the error made in recording the issue?

[handwritten: Share Capital > Split it into this / Share Premium]

		Debit $	Credit $
A	Share capital account	10,000	
	Share premium account		10,000
B	Cash	60,000	
	Share premium account		60,000
C	Share capital account	60,000	
	Share premium account		60,000
D	Share premium account	60,000	
	Share capital account		60,000

(answer C is circled)

(2 marks)

2   A company issued 1,000,000 $1 shares at $1.50 each payable as follows.   *[handwritten: $1 e / from 1.50 / 50c to S.PAIC]*

On application (including premium)	*[handwritten: 500,000,]*	70c
On allotment	*[handwritten: + 6,000]*	30c
First and final call		50c

All monies were received except for the call due from a holder of 10,000 shares. These shares were subsequently forfeited and reissued at $1.60 per share.

What *total* will be credited to share premium account as a result of this issue?

A $501,000
B $506,000
C $511,000
D   None of the above

(answer C is circled)

(2 marks)

3   At 1 January 20X4, a company's share capital consisted of 1,000,000 ordinary shares of 50c each, and there was a balance of $800,000 on its share premium account.

During 20X4, the following events took place.

1 March	The company made a bonus issue of 1 share for every 2 held, using the share premium account.
1 July	The company issued 600,000 shares at $2 per share.
1 October	The company made a rights issue of 1 share for every 3 held at $1.80 per share.

What are the balances on the company's share capital and share premium accounts at 31 December 20X4?

	Share capital $	Share premium $
A	1,400,000	2,860,000
B	2,800,000	1,460,000
C	1,800,000	2,320,000
D	1,400,000	2,360,000

(answer D is circled)

(2 marks)

BPP
PROFESSIONAL EDUCATION

4   A company has forfeited shares for non-payment of calls, but has not yet reissued them.

How, if at all, will the forfeited shares be shown in the company's balance sheet?

A   As a deduction from called up share capital
B   As an asset under investments
C   As a current asset under receivables
D   No item appears in the balance sheet for the shares   **(2 marks)**

5   Which of the following are normally permitted uses for a company's share premium account? *Can we use the S. Premium Alc for any of these.*

1   ✓ Issuing fully paid bonus shares
2   ✓ Being repaid to members as part of an authorised reduction of share capital
3   ✓ Writing off preliminary expenses of company formation
4   ✓ Writing off subsequent share issue expenses

A   1, 2 and 4 only
B   1, 3 and 4 only
C   2, 3 and 4 only
D   All four are permitted   **(2 marks)**

6   The balance sheet of X, a limited liability company, at 31 December 20X5 is shown below. *Pursuang UK legislation:*

	$m
Issued share capital: ordinary shares of 50c each, fully paid	10
Retained earnings	3
	13
Sundry net assets *- Partially making a replacement of shares with 300,000 shares.*	13

At this date X purchased 1,000,000 of its own ordinary shares at par. 300,000 $1 preferred shares were issued at $1.20 each to help finance the purchase.

What balance should appear on the company's capital redemption reserve account when these transactions have been correctly recorded?

1,000,000 x.5 = 500,000

A $140,000   *360,000 (300,000*
B $200,000   *x $1.20).*
C $500,000   *140,000.*
D   None of these figures   **(2 marks)**

The information below relates to questions 7 and 8.

The balance sheet of A, a limited liability company, is as follows.

	$
Issued share capital	
Ordinary shares of $1 each, fully paid	280,000
Retained earnings	80,000
	360,000
Sundry net assets	360,000

The company is to buy 50,000 of its own shares at $2 each.

Local legalisation allows small companies to purchase or redeem shares out of capital.

$20k Short.

7   What, if any, is the amount of the permissible capital payment in this share purchase?

    A   A permissible capital payment does not arise.
    B $20,000
    C $30,000
    D $50,000   **(2 marks)**

8   What transfer, if any, must be made to capital redemption reserve?

    A   No transfer is required   *-Maximum*
    B $20,000   *Possible*
    C $30,000
    D $50,000   *$30,000*   **(2 marks)**

9   Which of the following statements regarding share issues is incorrect?

    A   *Application* is where potential shareholders apply for shares in the company and send cash to cover their application

    B   *Allotment* is when the company allocates shares to the successful applicants and returns cash to unsuccessful applicants

    C   A *call* is where the purchase value is payable in instalments. The company will 'call' for instalments.

    D   If a shareholder fails to pay a call his allotment is cancelled and his money returned to him. His shares may then be reissued.   *Shares are forfeited and the Company don't have*   **(2 marks)**
    to return his money

10   A company had 1,000,000 ordinary shares of 50c each in issue on 1 January 20X2. On 1 July 20X2 the company made a bonus issue of one share for every two held. Its profit for the year ended 31 December 20X2 was $120,000. What will the company's earnings per share (EPS) be for the year ended 31 December 20X2?

Basic EPS = $\frac{E}{N}$ - Earnings - shares.

    A   12c per share.
    B   10c per share.   *But with a bonus Issue =*
    C   8c per share.
    D   16c per share.   *$\frac{E}{N+B}$*   **(2 marks)**

(Total = 20 marks)

$E = \dfrac{120,000}{1,500,000} = 8c$ per share.

Multiply last years repated EPS $\times \dfrac{N}{N+B}$

For last year.

Which would Give / Generate Comparative figure

BPP PROFESSIONAL EDUCATION

24 Objective test questions: Accounting standards I   36 mins

1   A company leases some plant on 1 January 20X4. The cash price of the plant is $9,000, and the company leases it for four years, paying four annual instalments of $3,000 beginning on 31 December 20X4.

The company uses the sum of the digits method (Rule of 78) to allocate interest.

What is the interest charge for the year ended 31 December 20X5?

     A $900
     B $600
     C $1,000
     D $750

                                                                                              (2 marks)

2   A company leases some plant on 1 January 20X4. The cash price is $9,000, and the company leases it for four years, paying four annual instalments of $3,000, beginning on 1 January 20X4.

The company uses the sum of the digits method (Rule of 78) to allocate interest.

What is the interest charge for the year ended 31 December 20X5?

     A $750
     B $500
     C $900
     D $1,000

                                                                                              (2 marks)

3   Which of the following statements about IAS 17 *Leases* are correct?

     1   A finance lease is one which transfers substantially all the risks and rewards of the ownership of an asset to a lessee.

     2   A leased asset should be depreciated over the shorter of the lease term and the useful life of the asset.

     3   All obligations under finance leases will appear in the balance sheet under the heading of 'Current liabilities'.

     4   An asset held on an operating lease should appear in the lessee's balance sheet as a non-current asset and be depreciated over the term of the lease.

     A   1 and 3 only
     B   1 and 2 only
     C   2 and 4 only
     D   All four statements are correct

                                                                                              (2 marks)

4   Which of the following statements about IAS 10 *Events after the balance sheet date* are correct?

     1   Notes to the financial statements must give details of all material adjusting events reflected in those financial statements.

     2   Notes to the financial statements must give details of non-adjusting events affecting users' ability to understand the company's financial position.

     3   Financial statements should not be prepared on a going concern basis if after the balance sheet date the directors have decided to liquidate the company.

     A   All three statements are correct.
     B   1 and 2 only
     C   1 and 3 only
     D   2 and 3 only

                                                                                              (2 marks)

5   A company's income statement showed a profit before tax of $1,800,000

After the balance sheet date and before the financial statements were authorised for issue, the following events took place.

1   The value of an investment held at the balance sheet date fell by $85,000. *– If event took Place after BIS date don't Adjust for this*

2   A customer who owed $116,000 at the balance sheet date went bankrupt owing a total of $138,000. *↳ Adjusting event.*

3   Inventory valued at cost $161,000 in the balance sheet was sold for $141,000. *↳ lower Cost NRV – Adjusting event write down by 20*

4   Assets with a carrying value at the balance sheet date of $240,000 were unexpectedly expropriated by government. *Not an adjusting event.*

What is the company's profit after making the necessary adjustments for these events?

A $1,399,000
B $1,579,000
C $1,664,000
D   None of these figures   **(2 marks)**

---

6   Which of the following events after the balance sheet date would normally be classified as *adjusting*, according to IAS 10 *Events after the balance sheet date*?

Adjusting events: These Conditions would have existed at balance sheet date & you've Just discovered them.

X 1   Destruction of a major non-current asset
X 2   Issue of shares and debentures
✓ 3   Discovery of error or fraud
✓ 4   Evidence of impairment in value of a property as at the balance sheet date
X 5   Purchases and sales of non-current assets

Purchases/ Sales/ floods Nonadjusting

A   1, 2 and 5 only
B   3 and 4 only
C   3, 4 and 5 only
D   1, 3 and 4 only   **(2 marks)**

The other happened Since/ after B.S date.

---

7   Which of the following events after the balance sheet date would normally be classified as *non-adjusting*, according to IAS 10 *Events after the balance sheet date*?

1   ✓ Opening new trading operations
2   X Sale of goods held at the balance sheet date for less than cost
3   X A customer is discovered to be insolvent
4   ✓ Announcement of plan to discontinue an operation
5   ✓ Expropriation of major assets by government

A   2 and 3 only
B   1, 2 and 3 only
C   2, 3, 4 and 5 only
D   1, 4 and 5 only   *– Conditions didn't exist at BIS date.*   **(2 marks)**

BPP))
PROFESSIONAL EDUCATION

8   In compiling its financial statements, the directors of a company have to decide on the correct treatment of the following items. *should they be disclosed in note.*

1   An employee has commenced an action against the company for wrongful dismissal. The company's solicitors estimate that the ex-employee has a 40 per cent chance of success in the action. *less than 50% only a contingent so just provide a note.*

2   The company has guaranteed the overdraft of another company, not at present in any financial difficulties. The possibility of a liability arising is thought to be remote. *— nothing at all, no disclosure — not even a note.*

3   Shortly after the balance sheet date, a major installation owned by the company was destroyed in a flood. The company's going concern status is not affected. *— disclosed by a note.*

What are the correct treatments for these items, assuming all are of material amount?

A   ✗   All three should be disclosed by note.
B   ✗   A provision should be made for item 1 and items 2 and 3 disclosed by note.
C   ✓   Items 1 and 3 should be disclosed by note, with no disclosure for item 2.
D   ✗   Item 1 should be disclosed by note. No disclosure is required for items 2 and 3.   **(2 marks)**

9   Which of the following statements about IAS 37 *Provisions, contingents liabilities and contingent assets* are correct?   *Constructive liabilities can lead to a provision*

1   ✓   Provisions should be made for constructive obligations (those arising from a company's pattern of past practice) as well as for obligations enforceable by law.

2   ✓   *— under IAS37 — decommissioning* Discounting may be used when estimating the amount of a provision if the effect is material. *you can use discounting*

3   ✗   A restructuring provision must include the estimated costs of retraining or relocating continuing staff. *(Any ongoing costs you aren't allowed to provide for.*

4   ✓   A restructuring provision may only be made when a company has a detailed plan for the reconstruction and a firm intention to carry it out.   *They have a constructive obligation. Here is they can't get out of it.*

A   ✗   All four statements are correct
B   ✓   1, 2 and 4 only
C   ✗   1, 3 and 4 only
D   ✗   2, 3 and 4 only   **(2 marks)**

10   Which of the following criteria must be present in order for a company to recognise a provision?

1   There is a present obligation as a result of past events.
2   It is probable that a transfer of economic benefits will be required to settle the obligation.
3   A reliable estimate of the obligation can be made.

A   All three criteria must be present.   *Really all 3 are the definition of a provision.*
B   1 and 2 only
C   1 and 3 only
D   2 and 3 only   **(2 marks)**

(Total = 20 marks)

25 Objective test questions: Accounting standards II   36 mins

1   IAS 37 *Provisions, contingent liabilities and contingent assets* governs the recognition of contingent items. Which of the following statements about contingencies, if any, are correct according to IAS 37?

    1   A contingent liability should be disclosed by note if it is probable that an obligation will arise and its amount can be estimated reliably. ~ *More likely to arise if Probable than you Should Provide for a Provision*

    2   A contingent asset should be disclosed by note if it is probable that it will arise. *↳ < than 50/50*

    3   An entity should not recognise a contingent asset. *– it's not Probable to happen.*

    A   None of the statements is correct.

    B   1 and 2

    (C)   2 and 3

    D   All of the statements are correct.   **(2 marks)**

---

2   IAS 24 *Related party disclosures* governs disclosures required for transactions between a company and parties deemed to be related to it.

Controlled by another Company then related Party.

Which of the following parties will normally be held to be related parties of a company?

    1   Its subsidiary companies

    2   Its directors

    3   Close family of the company's directors –

    4   Providers of finance to the company

    5   A customer or supplier with whom the company has a significant volume of business *– even if you only had One Customer ie Desmonds ∂MS wouldn't be a related Party .*

    A   All of the parties listed

    B   1, 2, 3 and 4 only

    (C)   1, 2 and 3 only

    D   3, 5 and 6 only   **(2 marks)**

---

3   Which of the following statements defines a finance lease?

    A   A short term hire agreement

    B   A long term hire agreement where the legal title in the asset passes on the final payment

    (C)   A long term hire agreement where substantially all the risks and rewards of ownership are transferred

    D   A long term hire agreement where the hirer is responsible for maintenance of the asset   **(2 marks)**

---

4   An asset is hired under a finance lease with a deposit of $30,000 on 1 January 20X1 plus 8 six monthly payments in arrears of $20,000 each. The fair value of the asset is $154,000. The finance charge is to be allocated using the sum of the digits method.

What is the finance charge for the year ending 31 December 20X3?

    (A) $7,000

    B $8,000

    C $10,000

    D $11,000   **(2 marks)**

$$\frac{N(N+1)}{2} \leftarrow \text{Sum of digits}$$

IF N = 8

$30 + (8 \times 20) - 154 = \underline{\underline{36}}$ then $\frac{8 \times 9}{2} = 36$.

$X1 = 36 \times {}^{8}/_{36}$ ${}^{7}/_{36}$ (– yr1

$X2 = 36 \times {}^{6}/_{36}$ ${}^{5}/_{36}$ (– yr2?

$X3 = 36 \times {}^{4}/_{36}$ ${}^{3}/_{36}$ ← yr3 = 7,000

$3.9. + 2.9$ ↳ $X3 = 36 \times {}^{7}/_{36} = 7,000.$

5   An asset with a fair value of $15,400 is acquired under a finance lease on 1 January 20X1 with a deposit on that date of $4,000 and four further annual payments in arrears of $4,000 each. The interest rate implicit in the lease is 15%.

What figure would appear in the balance sheet at 31 December 20X1 under the heading of current liabilities?

A $2,634
B $4,000
C $6,476
D $9,110

(2 marks)

6   The directors of Robin (year end 31 December 20X6) were informed on 27 February 20X7 that a serious fire at one of the company's factories had stopped production there for at least six months to come. On 3 March 20X7 the directors of Robin were informed that a major customer had gone into liquidation owing a substantial amount to Robin as at the year end. The liquidator was pessimistic about the prospect of recovering anything for unsecured creditors. The financial statements for the year ended 31 December 20X6 were approved on 20 March 20X7.

In accordance with IAS 10 *Events after the balance sheet date*, how should the two events be treated in the financial statements?

	Fire	*Liquidation*
A	Accrued in accounts	Disclosed in notes
B	Disclosed in notes	Disclosed in notes
C	Accrued in accounts	Accrued in accounts
D	Disclosed in notes	Accrued in accounts

~ if given extra Info
at the year end.

(2 marks)

7   Which of the following is a non-adjusting post balance sheet event in accordance with IAS 10 for financial statements prepared to 30 June 20X6 and approved on 3 October 20X6?

A   Final agreement of the price for the sale of a building which had been under contract since 28 June 20X6 − Adjusting events − Better View of the Price:

B   Receipt of the financial statements for the year ended 31 May 20X6 of an unlisted company in which the business owns 10% of the share capital showing that it is going into liquidation − Adjusting event
⤷ Write down your Investment Here.

C   A decision made on 1 July 20X6 to close a division of the business which made significant losses in the year ending 30 June 20X6

D   Information showing that a long-term contract on which profit had been taken in the year ending 30 June 20X6 will in fact not be profitable due a defect in materials used in January 20X6   (2 marks)
⤷ Adjusting events.

8   In which of the following circumstances would a provision be recognised under IAS 37 *Provisions, contingent liabilities and contingent assets* in the financial statements for the year ending 31 March 20X6?

1 ✗ A board decision was made on 15 March to close down a division with potential costs of $100,000. At 31 March the decision had not been communicated to managers, employees or customers.
⤷ you've not yet Communicated this decision - So you can reverse it.

2 ✓ There are anticipated costs from returns of a defective product in the next few months of $60,000. In the past all returns of defective products have always been refunded to customers. − Although legally
theren't required to but have done so in the future ie Constructive liability

3 ✗ It is anticipated that a major refurbishment of the company Head Office will take place from June onwards costing $85,000. − Only Anticipated no Present obligation.

A   1 and 2 only
B   2 and 3 only
C   2 only
D   3 only

(2 marks)

9   According to IAS 24 *Related party disclosures,* which of the following would not be a related party of Garo?

    A   An associated undertaking of Garo
    B   The managing director of Garo's parent company
    C   A company in which Garo holds a 10% investment   *- no Control or Significant Influence ie <20%.*
    D   Garo's pension fund for its employees   **(2 marks)**

10   According to IAS 24 *Related party disclosures,* which of the following would be presumed to be a related party of Fredo unless it can be demonstrated otherwise?

    A   The bank which has given a loan to Fredo
    B   The husband of the managing director of Fredo   *- Key Management | closely related to*
    C   Fredo's major supplier
    D   The assistant accountant of Fredo   *- not Part of Key Management*   **(2 marks)**

(Total = 20 marks)

26 Section B questions: Accounting standards   27 mins

(a)   Your firm is involved in four unrelated legal cases, P, Q, R and S. In case P the firm is suing for $10,000; in case Q the firm is suing for $20,000; in case R the firm is being sued for $30,000 and in case S the firm is being sued for $40,000. The firm has been advised by its expert and expensive lawyers that the chances of the firm winning each case are as follows.

Case	*Percentage likelihood of winning*
P	10
Q	90
R	10 *- Put down as an assumption.*
S	90

Required

(i)   State the required accounting treatment for each of the four cases in the published accounts
(ii)   Give journal entries for any necessary adjustments in the double-entry records   **(5 marks)**

(b)   IAS 10 distinguishes between 'adjusting' and 'non-adjusting' events.

Required

Explain what is meant by 'adjusting events' and 'non-adjusting events' and give three examples of each.
    (5 marks)

(c)   The following definitions have been taken from the International Accounting Standards Committee's *Framework for the Preparation and Presentation of Financial Statements.*

    •   'An asset is a resource controlled by the entity as a result of past events and from which future economic benefits are expected to flow to the entity.'

    •   'A liability is a present obligation of the entity arising from past events, the settlement of which is expected to result in an outflow from the entity of resources embodying economic benefits.'

IAS 17 *Leases* requires lessees to capitalise finance leases in their financial statements.

Required

Explain how IAS 17's treatment of finance leases applies the definitions of assets and liabilities.   **(5 marks)**

(Total = 15 marks)

27 Evans   36 mins

On 1 October 20X3 Evans Co entered into a non-cancellable agreement whereby Evans Co would lease a new rocket booster. The terms of the agreement were that Evans Co would pay 26 rentals of $3,000 quarterly in advance commencing on 1 October 20X3, and that after this initial period Evans Co could continue, at its option, to use the rocket booster for a nominal rental which is not material. The cash price of this asset would have been $61,570 and the asset has a useful life of 10 years. Evans Co considers this lease to be a finance lease and charges a full year's depreciation in the year of purchase of an asset. The rate of interest implicit in the lease is 2% per quarter.

On 1 July 20X2 Evans Co entered into another non-cancellable agreement to lease a Zarkov rocket for a period of 10 years at a rental of $5,000 half-yearly to be paid in advance, commencing on 1 July 20X2. Evans Co considers this lease to be an operating lease.

Required

Show how these transactions would be reflected in the financial statements for the year ended 31 December 20X3.

(20 marks)

28 Newcars   36 mins

Newcars is a vehicle dealership; it sells both new and good quality second-hand cars. The company is large and has a large number of shareholders. The only large block of shares is held by Arthur, who owns 25% of Newcars. Arthur is a member of Newcars' board of directors and he takes a keen interest in the day-to-day management of the company.

Arthur also owns 25% of Oldcars. Oldcars sells inexpensive second-hand cars which tend to be either relatively old or have a high mileage. Arthur is also a member of the board of directors of Oldcars.

Apart from Arthur, Newcars and Oldcars have no shareholders in common. The only thing that they have in common, apart from Arthur's interest in each, is that Newcars sells a large number of cars to Oldcars. This usually happens when a customer of Newcars has traded in a car that is too old to be sold from Newcars' showroom. Most of these cars are immediately resold to Oldcars and go into Oldcars' normal trading inventories. These sales account for approximately 5% of Newcars' turnover. Oldcars acquires approximately 20% of its cars from Newcars.

Required

— Control and Influence:

(a)   Explain whether Newcars and Oldcars are related parties in terms of the requirements of IAS 24 Related party disclosures.   **(7 marks)**

(b)   Assuming that Newcars and Oldcars are related parties, describe the related parties' disclosures that would have to be made in the companies' financial statements in respect of the sale and purchase of cars between the two companies.   **(6 marks)**

(c)   Explain why it is necessary to disclose such information in respect of transactions involving related parties.   **(7 marks)**

(Total = 20 marks)

[handwritten: - dep of plant in Cost of Sales,]

29 L Manufacturing

36 mins

L manufactures protective clothing and overalls for sale to specialist retailers. The following trial balance has been extracted from the company's financial records.

L: Trial balance at 30 June 20X1

	DR $m	CR $m
Retained earnings		38
Administration salaries	22 ✓	
Bank	45	
Cost of sales	208 ✓	
Distribution costs	51 ✓	
Dividend	96	
Equipment – cost	46	
Equipment – depreciation		14
Interest paid	5	
Inventory at 30 June 20X1 *- BS*	16	
Loans (repayable 20X5) *– BS – N.current.*		76
New process (University of Newtown)	8	
Plant – cost	282	
Plant – depreciation		99
Property – cost	534	
Property – depreciation		178
Revenue *= I.S. Revenue (Sales)*		755
Share capital *- BS*		160
Taxation *- did we overpay last yr.*		10
Trade payables *C ◣*		13
Trade receivables *C. A.*	57	
Warranties		27
	1,370	1,370

[handwritten left margin: Provision of 27 should - Cost of Sales. now be 35]

(a) The company gives a three year warranty on all of its products. The balance on the warranties account represents the provision for future warranty costs as estimated at 30 June 20X0. The balance at 30 June 20X1 should be modified to $35 million. *[handwritten: 27 liability]*

[handwritten: – But this is a change in AlCns Policy.]

[handwritten left margin: Reduces balance to Strangtl 1 line - charge In AlCns N.B. estimate not AlCns not AlCns policy]

(b) The directors have decided to change their method for charging depreciation on equipment. Previously, they had not depreciated certain categories of equipment on the grounds that this was a common industry practice. The directors have, however, decided that it would give a fairer presentation of the results of the business if depreciation was charged on all equipment. The figures in the trial balance are based on the old policy. If the company had used the new policy instead, it would have had a balance at 30 June 2000 of $26 million on the equipment depreciation account instead of the $14 million currently shown. *[handwritten: 14 goes up to 26.]*

[handwritten: - Sold for $23m - if B.V is $23m - no ∴ Profit or Loss]

(c) Plant which had cost $42 million was sold at its book value of $23 million during the year. New plant was purchased for $55 million. These transactions have been included in the above figures. There were no other transactions involving non-current assets.

(d) Depreciation for the year has still to be charged as follows.

[handwritten left margin: Non Current Assets {]

Property	2% of cost
Equipment	25% reducing balance
Plant	25% reducing balance

A whole year's depreciation is charged in the year of acquisition and none in the year of disposal. Plant depreciation is charged to cost of sales.

(e)   During the year, the company paid $8 million to the University of Newtown for work on a new process to make the company's clothing more durable. A new fabric has been produced, but this tends to cause a severe allergic reaction to wearers. The company is working to overcome this problem before test marketing can begin.

(f)   The directors have estimated the tax charge for the year at $30 million. The balance on the taxation account is the amount remaining after settling the liability for the year ended 30 June 20X0.
        – Have to Include in B.S if a liability (IAS10)

(g)   The directors declared a final dividend of $80 million before the balance sheet date. *– look out for this.   After Can't Include.*

(h)   L is a quoted company. Authorised share capital is 200 million shares of $1. Issued share capital is 100 million shares of $1, fully paid. This includes 40 million shares that were issued on 31 March 20X1 for a total consideration of $65 million.

Required

Prepare L's income statement for the year ended 30 June 20X1 and its balance sheet at that date. These should be in a form suitable for publication. Notes are not required.   **(20 marks)**

30 PW   **36 mins**

PW is a limited liability company. Its trial balance at 31 December 20X5 was as follows:

	$'000	$'000
Administrative expenses	2,300	
Loan interest paid	50	
Distribution expenses	696	
Purchases	8,662	
Sales		18,000
Rent and rates	700	
Interim ordinary dividend	32	
Equity shares $1 each, fully paid		800
10% preferred shares $1 each, fully paid		1,200
Provision for legal costs		300
Revaluation reserve		1,300 *-600.*
Retained earnings		1,100
5% loan notes		2,000
Patent	600	
Property – cost	9,200	
Property – accumulated depreciation		3,500
Plant and equipment – cost	3,000	
Plant and equipment – accumulated depreciation		1,200
Inventory	4,300	
Trade receivables	3,400	
Trade payables		3,500
Bank and cash	400	
Provision for doubtful trade receivables		200
Deferred taxation		240
	33,340	33,340

Additional information provided:

(i) Non-current assets are being depreciated as follows:

Property – 10% per annum straight line
Plant and equipment – 20% per annum reducing balance

Important. * An external revaluation of the property has been carried out and the carrying value is to be reduced by $600,000. This reverses part of a previous upward revaluation.

Plant and equipment depreciation is to be charged to distribution costs.

(ii) A bad debt of $40,000 is to be written off and the provision for doubtful receivables is to be adjusted to 5% of remaining trade receivables.

(iii) A final dividend of 12c per share was declared before the year end but has not yet been paid. The preferred dividend will be paid in full.

(iv) Tax due for the year to 31 December 20X5 has been estimated at $210,000. A transfer of $10,000 is to be made from deferred tax.

(v) The closing inventory at 31 December 20X5 was $3,900,000.

(vi) A legal case against the company has just been concluded. $450,000 damages were awarded, which exceeds the amount provided. This will be paid in the first week of the new year.

(vii) An impairment review has been carried out following changes in the market, and the value of the patent is to be written down by 10%.

Required

Prepare PW's income statement for the year to 31 December 20X5, a balance sheet at that date and a statement of changes in equity for the year. These should be in a form suitable for presentation to the shareholders, in accordance with the requirements of International Accounting Standards.

Notes to the financial statements are not required.   **(20 marks)**

Part D: Managing short term finance

Questions 31 to 40 cover Managing Short-term Finance, the subject of Part D of the BPP Study Text for Paper P7.

31 Objective test questions: Short-term finance I   36 mins

1   An amount of $10,000 is invested at a fixed rate of 10% per annum. What will be the value of the investment in three years' time if the interest is compounded every six months?

    A $11,576
    B $13,310
    C $13,400
    D $17,716

10,000 x 0.10
10,000 + (1 + 0.05)⁶

    (2 marks)

2   Which of the following could a company NOT use as a source of short-term credit?

    A   Trade credit from suppliers
    B   Bank overdraft
    C   Factoring of trade debts
    D   Mortgage on property

Greater than say 5 yrs is the Mortgage.

    (2 marks)

3   Which of the following statements is NOT a feature of an overdraft facility?

    A   Interest is paid on the full facility.
    B   Legal documentation is minimal in comparison with other types of loan.
    C   The facility is repayable on demand.
    D   An overdraft facility is often used to overcome a temporary cash shortage.

The rest are true.

↳ It's flexible for fluctuating balances.

~ Why it's always on C+ in Fin. Statements.

    (2 marks)

4   Of what is the following statement a definition?

'A document issued by a bank on behalf of a customer authorising a person to draw money to a specified amount from its branches or correspondents, usually in another country, when the conditions set out in the document have been met.'

    A   Bill of exchange *~ not necessarily with a bank.*
    B   Export guarantee
    C   Banker's draft *~ Person you are paying doesn't trust you ie Cae ~ It can't be stopped.*
    D   Letter of credit *~ Documentary Credit.*

    (2 marks)

5   Which of the following factors would a bank be LEAST LIKELY to take into account when deciding whether to lend money to a company?

    A   The purpose of the loan
    B   The amount of the loan
    C   The duration of the loan
    D   The currency in which the loan is denominated

Have Same effect on Credit Risk.

    (2 marks)

6   Which of the following is the LEAST IMPORTANT consideration when assessing how to invest a short-term cash surplus?

    A   Length of time for which the funds are available
    B   Maximising the return generated by the funds
    C   Ease of realisation
    D   Risk associated with calling in the investment early

Short-term - you want the money @ the end of it you want to minimise the risk.

    (2 marks)

7 Which of the following services is LEAST LIKELY to be offered by a factoring company?

- A Provision of finance by advancing, say 80% of invoice value immediately, and the remainder on settlement of the debt by the customer
- B Taking over responsibility for administration of the client's sales ledger *They can do this with/without customer knows.*
- C Deciding what credit limits customers should be given
- D Non-recourse finance, ie taking over responsibility for bad debts *Selling the debt and if they don't get money out of Cust, it's the factor's problem.*

(2 marks)

8 KEN is awaiting the go-ahead to start its new building programme. This is likely to take place within the next 90 days, but the precise start date and timing of the cash flows are still uncertain. The company has $150,000 available in cash in anticipation of the investment. Which of the following is the LEAST APPROPRIATE use of the funds in the interim period?

- A Investment in equities *high Risk. We don't want to take a risk.*
- B Treasury bills
- C Bank deposits
- D Local authority deposits

(2 marks)

9 Which of the following theories could NOT be used to explain the term structure of interest rates?

- A Expectations theory *~ Interest rates/short-term/long-term.*
- B Miller-Orr model *— odd one out. — when to replenish your cash.*
- C Liquidity preference theory *— Return.*
- D Market segmentation *— Is rates fixed In this market Segmentation*

(2 marks)

10 What is the present value to the nearest $10 of a five year annuity of $100, assuming interest rates are 8%?

- A $400 *Use P.V tables.*
- B $500 *Cum tables*
- C $850 *on Pg186.* *3.993*
- D $1,250

(2 marks)

(Total = 20 marks)

32 Objective test questions: Short-term finance II   36 mins

1 A company with large amounts of surplus cash may decide to invest it in short-term money market instruments. Which of the following money market investments would carry the LOWEST interest rate?

- A Sterling certificates of deposit (CDs)
- B Treasury bills *— Gout. — Less Risk.*
- C Finance house deposits
- D Local authority deposits *— Not Very Risky, but riskier than Gout.*

(2 marks)

2 An organisation invests $14,000 at an interest rate of 6% per annum, compounded monthly.

How much will be available in two years' time?

- A $14,840
- B $15,680
- C $15,730
- D $15,780

$14,000 (1+0.05)^{24}$

$= 14,000 \times 1.005^{24}$

$= 15,780$

(2 marks)

3   A manufacturer of china commemorating the Olympic Games is facing a short-term liquidity shortage. Which of the following assets could it sell in order to make good the cash shortfall while doing the minimum damage to its core activities?

[handwritten: – 10% is relatively small.]   *[handwritten: Sell of doing less damage to Core Activities.]*

    A   10% of its fleet of delivery vehicles

[handwritten left margin: Producing Product]

    B   The pigment blending plant

    C   The patent on a new design of china pouring device intended to commemorate the Olympic Games

    D   Its 60% equity stake in the company that supplies its gold leaf   **(2 marks)**

4   A person wishes to have $10,000 in savings in three years' time. She plans to make regular monthly payments into a saving account which offers monthly interest of 0.5% (compounded monthly).

How much should the monthly payments be, to the nearest $1?

[handwritten: Learn this formula!]

    A $254

    B $278

    C $304

    D $369

[handwritten: Formula you need to know!
$$S = A\left[\frac{R^m - 1}{R - 1}\right] \text{ where } R = 1 + r.$$
R = 0.005.
$$10,000 = ?\left[\frac{1.005^{36} - 1}{1.005 - 1}\right] = 254.$$
]   **(2 marks)**

5   Which of the following investments would not be appropriate for a company with a temporary cash surplus of approximately one week?

    A   Local authority deposits *[handwritten: – overnight]*   *[handwritten: The long-term Investment]*

    B   Money market lending arranged directly

    C   Treasury bills *[handwritten: – 91 days]* *[handwritten: nightly/daily or weekly]* *[handwritten: Is the Convertible loan Stock!]*

    D   Convertible loan stock   **(2 marks)**

6   What is the value of $3,000 per year in **perpetuity**, when the interest rate is 12%?

    A $8,333

    B $25,000

    C $36,000

    D $75,000

[handwritten:
$$P_V = \frac{1}{r} = \frac{1}{0.12} \text{ - of } \$1$$
$$= \frac{3000}{0.12} = \$25,000$$
Know this formula! (They give you this!) *]*   **(2 marks)**

7   An investor buys $11,000 (nominal value) of a bond with a coupon rate of 10%, for the current market value of $10,000. Average market returns are 12%. What is the interest yield to the nearest one percent?

[handwritten: Nothing to do with this question – it's a red herring]

    A   9%

    B   10%

    C   11%

    D   12%

[handwritten: Interest = 10% on $11,000 = 1100
$$\frac{1100}{10000} = 11\% \leftarrow \text{Answer!}$$
]   **(2 marks)**

8   If $2,000 is invested at an interest rate of 10% per annum, compounded quarterly, the sum it will give in four years' time is:

    A $2,772

    B $2,800

    C $2,928

    D $2,969

[handwritten:
$$2000(1 + .025)^{16}$$
$$= \$2969$$
Eg. Too right! *]*   **(2 marks)**

[handwritten: divide by 4 to get quarterly rate!]

[handwritten: High Inflation – Paid to be a borrower Not a Saver.]

9   Which of the following statements about inflation is UNTRUE?

A   Inflation introduces uncertainty into a company's financial projections.

B   Inflation makes it more difficult to appraise company performance accurately.

C   Because inflation erodes the capital value of amounts borrowed, it favours lenders at the expense of borrowers.

D   With very low inflation, or deflation, negative interest rates are possible. *[handwritten: – Has happened in Japan.]*   (2 marks)

10   Suppose that the yield curve has been steeply inverted and, as a consequence of the persistently high short-term interest rates, the bond market eventually comes under pressure and bond prices start to fall. What is the likely consequence for equity share prices and equity yields?

[handwritten: Short-term yields ↑ than longterm yields]

A   Equity prices will fall; equity yields will rise.

B   Equity prices will fall; equity yields will fall.

C   Equity prices will be unaffected; equity yields will be unaffected.

D   Equity prices will rise; equity yields will fall.   (2 marks)

[handwritten: If bond prices go ↓ ↑ rates remain same equity yields will rise]

(Total = 20 marks)

33 Objective test questions: Short-term finance III   36 mins

1   A perpetuity series of cash flows of $10,000 each year commences in two years. The relevant rate of interest is 10% each year.

What is the present value, to the nearest $1, of the cash flows?

A $100,000

B $90,909   *[handwritten: books]*

C $82,645

D $110,000   (2 marks)

2   The following money and real rates of interest are expected over the next two years:

	Year 1	Year 2
Money rate	9%	10%
Real rate	4%	5%

Calculate the average rate of inflation expected over the 2 years as implied by the stated money and real rates (to 2 decimal places).

[handwritten: Inflation of 5% in yr 1 & yr 2. ie 9-4=5   10-5=5%]

A   4.76%

B   4.78%   *[handwritten: Formula to use:]*

C   4.81%

D   5.00%

$$\frac{1 + \text{Money rate}}{1 + \text{Inflation rate}} = 1 + \text{real rate}$$ *[handwritten: See page for rest of formula]*   (2 marks)

3   The yield curve for bonds shows the relationship between the redemption yield and the term to maturity.

If the yield curve for a series of government bonds is upward sloping, this is MOST LIKELY to indicate that

A   The coupon interest rate declines over time.

B   Market interest rates are expected to fall in future.

C   Short-term bonds offer a higher redemption yield than long-term bonds.

D   Long-term bonds offer a higher redemption yield than short-term bonds.   (2 marks)

[handwritten: More risk on 10yrs than 5yrs. The longer you go for]

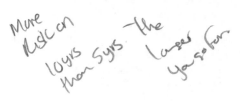
BPP
PROFESSIONAL EDUCATION

4   Examine the validity of the following statements with respect to the yield curve showing the term structure of interest rates.

Statement 1   When interest rates are expected to fall consistently, short-term interest rates are likely to be higher than long-term interest rates.

Statement 2   When interest rates are expected to fall consistently, a yield curve would normally be downward sloping.

	Statement 1	*Statement 2*
A	True	False
B	True	True
C	False	False
D	False	True

(2 marks)

5   What is the present value of an amount of $100, receivable in 10 years from now, at an interest rate of 10% each year (to the nearest $1)?

A $39
B $42
C $259
D $614

(2 marks)

6   Which one of the following would MOST APPROPRIATELY describe commercial paper?

A   Secured long-term loan notes issued by companies
B   Secured short-term loan notes issued by companies
C   Unsecured long-term loan notes issued by companies
D   Unsecured short-term loan notes issued by companies

(2 marks)

7   In two years from now, $100,000 will be invested for a further 5 years at an annual compound rate of 8%. What will be the terminal value of the investment at the end of this period (that is, 7 years from now)?

A $85,734
B $146,933
C $171,382
D $586,703

(2 marks)

8   Which one of the following MOST APPROPRIATELY describes forfaiting?

A   It is a method of providing medium-term export finance.
B   It provides long-term finance to importers.
C   It provides equity finance for the redemption of shares.
D   It is the surrender of a share because of the failure to make a payment on a partly-paid share.

(2 marks)

9   Which of the following statements about certificates of deposit is FALSE?

A   Certificates of deposit are negotiable instruments issued by banks.
B   Certificates of deposit will typically have maturity periods of between one month and five years.
C   Certificates of deposit are non-negotiable.
D   Certificates of deposit are issued in bearer form.

(2 marks)

51

10   Which of the following statements about venture capital is correct?

    A   Venture capital would not be appropriate to finance a management buyout.

    B   Venture capital organisations may provide loan finance as well as equity finance to a company.

    C   Secured medium-term bank loans are a form of venture capital.

    D   Companies with a stock market quotation would have no difficulty raising finance from a venture capital organisation.   (2 marks)

(Total = 20 marks)

---

34 Section B questions: Short-term Finance   45 mins

(a)   TR has forecast the following cash movements for the next six months.

	$
Cash available now	2,000,000
Inflow in two months	4,000,000
Outflow in four months	2,000,000
Outflow in six months	4,000,000

Assume that all movements of cash take place on the last day of each two-month period.

The structure of short-term interest rates is as follows.   *Rates are Improving In 2/4 mths time.*

Current		Expected in 2 months		Expected in 4 months	
Maturity period	Annual yield	Maturity period	Annual yield	Maturity period	Annual yield
	%		%		%
2 months	7.3	2 months	8.0	2 months	8.3
4 months	7.4	4 months	8.1	4 months	8.4
6 months	7.5	6 months	8.2	6 months	8.3

The company invests surplus cash balances in marketable securities. Company policy is to hold such securities to maturity once they are purchased. Every purchase transaction of marketable securities costs $100.

Required

Calculate which securities should be purchased to maximise before-tax income.   (10 marks)
(This is equivalent to two Section B questions)

(b)   The treasurer of a local government department is reviewing her cash management procedures. The following information is available.

    (i)   The department has agreed with its bank that it will maintain a minimum daily cash balance of $15,000. Severe financial penalties will apply if this balance is not maintained.

    (ii)   A forecast of daily cash movements for the next twelve months shows a standard deviation of daily cash flows of $3,000. *– need a variance here. √ it.*

    (iii) The daily interest rate is at present 0.0236% and this is not expected to change for the foreseeable future.

    (iv)   The transaction cost for each sale or purchase is $25.

Required   *– don't have number to remember this model. – Spread.*

Using the Miller-Orr model calculate the spread between the upper and lower cash balance limits. Explain what is meant by the **return point** and calculate what it will be in this case.   (5 marks)

(c) Official statistics show that over the past four to five years, overdraft usage has been falling by around 5% per annum and is being replaced by other forms of asset-based lending.

Required

Explain the main uses of overdraft facilities as part of a company's working capital management policy.

(5 marks)

(d) Discuss the alternative sources of finance which are available to companies which do not want to run an overdraft. **(5 marks)**

(Total = 25 marks)

35 DF

36 mins

DF is a manufacturer of sports equipment. All of the shares of DF are held by the Wong family.

The company has recently won a major 3-year contract to supply FF with a range of sports equipment. FF is a large company with over 100 sports shops. The contract may be renewed after 3 years.

The new contract is expected to double DF's existing total annual sales, but demand from FF will vary considerably from month to month.

The contract will, however, mean a significant additional investment in both non-current and current assets. A loan from the bank is to be used to finance the additional non-current assets, as the Wong family is currently unable to supply any further share capital. Also, the Wong family does not wish to raise new capital by issuing shares to non-family members.

The financing of the additional current assets is yet to be decided. In particular, the contract with FF will require orders to be delivered within two days. This delivery period gives DF insufficient time to manufacture items, thus significant inventories need to be held at all times. Also, FF plc requires 90 days' credit from its suppliers. This will result in a significant additional investment in receivables by DF.

If the company borrows from the bank to finance current assets, either using a loan or an overdraft, it expects to be charged annual interest at 12%. Consequently, DF is considering alternative methods of financing current assets. These include debt factoring, invoice discounting and offering a 3% cash discount to FF for settlement within 10 days rather than the normal 90 days.

Required

(a) Calculate the annual equivalent rate of interest implicit in offering a 3% discount to FF for settlement of debts within 10 days rather than 90 days.

Briefly explain the factors, other than the rate of interest, that DF would need to consider before deciding whether to offer a cash discount. **(5 marks)**

(b) Write a report to the Wong family shareholders explaining the various methods of financing available to DF to finance the additional current assets arising from the new FF contract. The report should include the following headings:

Bank loan
Overdraft
Loan note issue
Debt factoring
Invoice discounting **(15 marks)**

(Total = 20 marks)

36 Objective test questions: Working capital management I

36 mins

1   HMP has decided to adopt a moderate working capital policy. It has fluctuating current assets of $1m, permanent current assets of $5m, and non-current assets of $9m. Which of the following mixes of finance is the company MOST LIKELY to choose?

   Ⓐ   Short-term financing of $1m; permanent financing of $14m *- Rule of thumb - moderate.*
   B   Short-term financing of $0.5m; permanent financing of $14.5m *- Conservative.*
   C   Short-term financing of $2m; permanent financing of $13m *-*
   D   Short-term financing of $4m; permanent financing of $11m *- Less Conservative*

                                                             (2 marks)

2   The following figures are taken from the balance sheet of GEN:

	$m
Inventories	2
Receivables	3
Cash	1
Payables	3
5 year bank loan *✗ doesn't Come Into it*	3

What is the current ratio? $\frac{6}{3} = 2.$

   A   1.33
   Ⓑ   2.00
   C   1.00
   D   0.33

                                                             (2 marks)

3   The following figures are taken from the accounts of GRE Ltd:

	$
Inventories	400,000
Receivables	600,000
Cash	200,000
Payables	800,000
Loan stock redeemable in three years time	800,000

$\dfrac{C.A}{C.L}$ $\dfrac{800}{800} = 1$

What is the quick ratio?

   A   0.75
   B   1.50
   C   0.50
   Ⓓ   1.00

                                                             (2 marks)

4   You have been given the following extracts from the accounts of NQ.

Sales	$600,000
Fixed assets to capital employed	80%
Current ratio	2:1
Current assets	$100,000

What is the ratio of sales to capital employed?

   C.L = 50,000.
   Working Capital = 20%.

   A   0.6:1
   B   1.2:1   *So W.C is 100,000 - 50,000*
   C   1.8:1   *= 50,000.*
   Ⓓ   2.4:1   **(2 marks)**

5   Which ONE of the following is NOT a stage in the credit cycle?

A   Negotiation of the price of the goods — *Earlier stage before you set to Credit Cycle.*
B   Receipt of the customer order
C   Checking the credit limit
D   Goods despatched with delivery note   **(2 marks)**

6   The following figures have been extracted from the accounts of WI:

	$
Total sales	200,000
Cash sales	20,000
Credit sales	180,000
Year end receivables	25,000
Bad debts	5,000

year end — $\frac{25,000}{180,000} \times 365 = 50.7$

What is the average debt collection period in days (based on 365 days per year)?

A   50.7
B   60.8
C   54.8
D   45.6   **(2 marks)**

So save on bad debts. If factor's can't get money it's their problem

7   DEN is considering whether to factor its sales ledger. It has been offered a 'without recourse' package by the factor at a cost of 2% sales, plus an administration fee of $5,000 per year. Annual sales are currently $1m, with bad debts of 1%. What is the annual cost of the package to DEN likely to be?

A $5,000   *Our Answer 15*
B $20,000
C $24,800   *Their's is $25.*
D $25,000   **(2 marks)**

8   GOR is considering changing its credit policy. It currently allows customers 90 days credit, but suffers bad debts amounting to 3% of its annual sales of $2m. It is proposing to reduce the credit period to 30 days, which should cause the bad debts to fall to 1% of turnover. However, it expects that this will result in a reduction in sales of 20%. This reduction will also be reflected in the level of purchases and inventory holding. What will be the effect of this on the annual financing cost? Current figures are:

Inventories (raw materials and finished goods)	$500,000
Annual purchases	$360,000
Payables	$30,000
Cost of capital	10%

A   Saving of $46,000
B   Increase of $46,000
C   Saving of $36,000
D   Increase of $36,000   **(2 marks)**

9   A company has a current ratio of 1:5. It has decided to offer credit customers 60 days credit rather than 30 days.   *1.5:1*

What will be the effect of this change on the company's current ratio, assuming the policy does not involve any interest cost?

A   Increase
B   Decrease
C   Neither increase nor decrease
D   Either increase or decrease   **(2 marks)**

If Cash doesn't come In you Still have your Creditors. Or do you make more Sales ∴ More Creditors.

Formula : Learni

10   Z requires a rate of return of 13% each year.

Two of Z's suppliers, Y and X are offering the following terms for immediate cash settlement.

Company	Discount	Normal settlement period
X	3%	3 months
Y	4%	4 months

Which of the following discounts should be accepted to achieve the required rate of return?

A   X's
B   Y's
C   Both X's and Y's
D   Neither X's nor Y's   **(2 marks)**

(Total = 20 marks)

37 Objective test questions: Working capital management II

discount, within 10 days

36 mins

1   PAL has been offered credit terms of 2.5/10, net 60. If the company refuses the discount, what is the implied cost in interest per annum?

A   15.2%
B   15.6%
C   20.3%
D   30%   **(2 marks)**

2   Which of the following payments would NOT normally be made by standing order?

A   Hire purchase payments
B   Insurance premiums
C   Property rental payments
D   Trade supplier payments   **(2 marks)**

3   What is the MAIN WAY in which a payment made by direct debit differs from one made by standing order?

A   The person who makes the payment initiates each payment.
B   The person who receives the payment initiates each payment.
C   The payment is made at regular intervals.
D   The payment goes directly from the customer's bank account to the supplier's bank account.
                                                                 (2 marks)

4   (a)   A company's sales are made up of 75% on credit and 25% for cash.

(b)   Bad debts are 2% of credit sales on average.

(c)   Half the company's credit customers pay in the month following the sale and the remainder who pay, pay in the month after that.

(d)   Sales have grown at a constant rate of 10% per month for every month since October 20X0 and are expected to grow at this rate throughout 20X1.

(e)   Sales for January 20X1 were $220,000.

The cash received during February 20X1 was:

A $214,850
B $215,000
C $216,700
D $218,000   **(2 marks)**

5   KEN manufactures shopping trolleys. It produces 2,500 trolleys per year, each of which has four wheels. The wheels are purchased from a single supplier, and it costs $25 to place an order. The cost of holding a single wheel in inventory for a year is 50c. How many wheels should be ordered each time to minimise stock costs (answer to the nearest 10)?

A   350
B   500
C   710
D   1,000   **(2 marks)**

6   FIN manufactures shopping trolleys. It produces 10,000 trolleys per year, each of which has four wheels. The wheels are purchased from a single supplier, and it costs $100 to place an order. The cost of holding a single wheel in inventory for a year is $2. How many orders should be placed each year to minimise inventory costs?

A   3
B   10
C   14
D   20   **(2 marks)**

7   STAN manufactures shopping trolleys. It produces 40,000 trolleys per year, each of which has four wheels. The wheels are purchased from a single supplier, and it costs $400 to place an order. The cost of holding a single wheel in inventory for a year is $8. How long is it between each order?   EOQ

 A   1.3 weeks
B   2.6 weeks
C   3.9 weeks
D   5.2 weeks   **(2 marks)**

8   Which of the following would NOT NORMALLY form part of the purchasing manager's responsibilities?

A   Liaising with the R & D department to find suppliers for materials which are to the specifications required by the designers

B   Locating and selecting suppliers

C   Agreeing prices, discounts and lead times with suppliers

D   Issuing payments to suppliers   **(2 marks)**

9   FRA is a small restaurant business. It has just acquired a new van under a lease agreement, and it must make a monthly payment to the finance company of $276.53. Which of the following payment methods is the MOST APPROPRIATE for FRA to use?

 A   Cheque
B   Standing order
C   Direct debit
D   Banker's draft   **(2 marks)**

10 AYS is a small domestic cleaning business. It has just acquired a new van for $12,750, which is needed urgently since the old one has been written off in an accident. The garage will not accept a company cheque on collection of the vehicle. Which of the following payment methods is the MOST APPROPRIATE for AYS to use?

A Cash
B Standing order
C Direct debit
D Banker's draft

(2 marks)

(Total = 20 marks)

38 Objective test questions: Working capital management III

36 mins

1 A company has a current ratio of 1.5:1. It decides to use surplus cash balances to settle 30% of its total current liabilities.

The current ratio will

A Decrease by more than 30%
B Decrease by less than 30%
C Increase by more than 30%
D Increase by less than 30%

(2 marks)

2 A company buys goods on credit and then, before payment is made, it is forced to sell all of these goods on credit for less than the purchase price. What is the consequence of these two transactions immediately after the sale has taken place?

A Inventory decreases and cash decreases.
B Cash decreases and payables increase.
C Inventory decreases and receivables increase.
D Receivables increase and payables increase.

(2 marks)

3 Which one of the following would NOT NORMALLY be considered a cost of holding inventory?

A Inventory obsolescence
B Insurance cost of inventories
C Lost interest on cash invested in inventories
D Loss of sales from running out of inventory

(2 marks)

4 The following items were extracted from a company's budget for next month:

	$
Purchases on credit	360,000
Expected decrease in inventories over the month	12,000
Expected increase in trade payables over the month	15,000

What is the budgeted payment to trade payables for the month?

A $333,000
B $345,000
C $357,000
D $375,000

(2 marks)

BPP
PROFESSIONAL EDUCATION

5   Y Co has funding requirements of $10,000 per month. Money on deposit earns 2% per annum, while the interest cost of new funds is 5% per annum. Transaction costs are $50.

Using the Baumol model what is the optimum amount of securities to transfer into cash in each transaction?

(2 marks)

6   A retailing company has an annual turnover of $36 million. The company earns a constant margin of 20% on sales. All sales and purchases are on credit and are evenly distributed over the year. The following amounts are maintained at a constant level throughout the year.

	$m
Inventories	6
Receivables	8
Payables	3

What is the company's cash cycle to the nearest day (that is, the average time from the payment of a supplier to the receipt from a customer)?

A   81 days
B   111 days
C   119 days
D   195 days

(2 marks)

7   A company uses the economic order quantity model (EOQ model). Demand for the company's product is 36,000 units each year and is evenly distributed each day. The cost of placing an order is $10 and the cost of holding a unit of stock for a year is $2.

How many orders should the company make in a year?

A   60
B   120
C   300
D   600

(2 marks)

8   Working capital is MOST LIKELY to increase when

A   Payments to suppliers are delayed.
B   The period of credit extended to customers is reduced.
C   Non-current assets are sold.
D   Inventory levels are increased.

(2 marks)

9   BACS (Bankers Automated Clearing Services) is an example of an electronic funds transfer system.

Which of the following BEST describes the system?

A   Provides same-day settlement for large sums of money

B   Is mostly concerned with processing payrolls and transactions involving standing orders and direct debits

C   Is a network for rapid transmission of international remittances between participating banks

D   Requires cheques to be completed to ensure settlement of a transaction

(2 marks)

10 A company maintains a minimum cash holding of $1,000. The variance of its daily cash flows has been measured as $250,000. The transaction cost for each sale or purchase of treasury bills is $20. The daily interest rate is 0.025% per day and is not expected to change in the foreseeable future. Using the Miller-Orr cash management model, the maximum cash holding level would be:

A $1,594
B $2,594
C $7,400
D $8,400

(2 marks)

(Total = 20 marks)

39 Section B questions: Working capital management 36 mins

(a)   Extracts from the financial statements of PRT for the years ended 31 March are as follows.

	20X6 $'000	20X7 $'000
Raw material inventories	55	80
Finished goods inventories	185	185
Purchases of raw materials	600	850
Cost of sales	1,570	1,830
Administrative expenses	45	65
Sales	1,684	1,996
Trade receivables	114	200
Trade payables	50	70
Overdraft	400	950
Additions to non-current assets	700	900

Cost of sales includes all relevant production costs including manufacturing overheads and labour.

Required

Calculate the length in days of the company's operating cycle for the year ended 31 March 20X7. **(5 marks)**

(b)   Discuss the main factors that a company should consider when determining the appropriate mix of long-term and short-term debt in its capital structure. **(5 marks)**

(c)   AAD is a newly-created subsidiary of a large listed company. It commenced business on 1 October 20X2, to provide specialist contract cleaning services to industrial customers. All sales are on credit.

More favourable credit terms are offered to larger customers (class A) than to smaller customers (class B). All sales are invoiced at the end of the month in which the sale occurs. Class A customers will be given credit terms requiring payment within 60 days of invoicing, while class B customers will be required to pay within 30 days of invoicing.

Since it is recognised, however, that not all customers comply with the credit terms they are allowed, receipts from customers have prudently been estimated as follows:

Customer type	Within 30 days	31 to 60 days	61 to 90 days	91 to 120 days	Bad debts
Class A		50%	30%	15%	5%
Class B	60%	25%	10%		5%

The above table shows that customers are expected either to pay within 60 days of the end of the credit period, or not at all. Bad debts will therefore be written off 60 days after the end of the credit period.

Budgeted credit sales for each class of customer in the first 4 months of trading are as follows:

Customer type	October $'000	November $'000	December $'000	January $'000
Class A	100	150	200	300
Class B	60	80	40	50

Assume all months are of 30 days.

Required

Prepare a statement showing the budgeted cash to be received by AAD from customers in each of the three months of November 20X2, December 20X2 and January 20X3, based upon the prudently estimated receipts from customers. **(5 marks)**

(d) Discuss:

(i) The significance of trade payables in a firm's working capital cycle
(ii) The dangers of over-reliance on trade credit as a source of finance **(5 marks)**

(Total = 20 marks)

40 STK   36 mins

STK sells bathroom fittings throughout England. In order to obtain the best price, it has decided to purchase all its annual demand of 10,000 shower units from a single supplier. After investigation, it has identified two possible manufacturers – SSS and RRR. Each has offered to provide the required number of shower units each year under an exclusive long-term contract.

Demand for shower units is at a constant rate all year. The cost to STK of holding one shower unit in inventory for one year is $4 plus 3% of the purchase price.

SSS is located only a few miles from the STK main showroom. It has offered to supply each shower unit at $400 with a transport charge of $200 per delivery. It has guaranteed such a regular and prompt delivery service that STK believes it will not be necessary to hold any safety inventory (that is buffer inventory) if it uses SSS as its supplier.

RRR is located in the Far East. It has offered to supply each shower unit at $398 but transport charges will be $500 per delivery. There is also a minimum order size of 1,000 shower units. Deliveries will be by ship and will therefore take some time to arrive. There is also significant uncertainty about the lead time which means that STK will need to hold a safety inventory of 600 shower units.

Required

(a) Using the economic order quantity model (EOQ model), calculate the optimal order size, assuming that SSS is chosen as the sole supplier of shower units for STK. **(5 marks)**

(b) (i) Prepare calculations to determine whether SSS or RRR should be chosen as the sole supplier of shower units for STK. **(10 marks)**

(ii) Describe any further factors that STK should consider before making a final choice of supplier. **(5 marks)**

(Total = 20 marks)

Answers to Questions

PROFESSIONAL EDUCATION

1 Objective test answers: General principles of taxation

1   D   An employee tax is charged directly on the employee and so is a direct tax.

           Ad valorem tax and unit tax are indirect taxes. A sales tax is an example of an ad valorem tax.

2   C   The dividend is 80% of the total payment and so the advanced tax is $^{20}/_{80}$ or $^{1}/_{4}$.

$$\frac{\$400,000}{4} = \$100,000$$

3   C   The company acts as a tax collector on behalf of the tax authority. Therefore any tax deducted is put in a creditor account until the money is actually paid to the tax authority. The balance on the creditor account represents the amount collected but not yet paid over.

4   B   The tax authorities do not have the power to detain company officials. Their powers relate to documents and information (eg information held on computer).

5   Direct taxation is charged directly on the **person** or **entity** that is intended to pay the tax.

6   Accounting profit + disallowable expenditure – non-taxable income – tax allowable expenditure = taxable profit

7   **Group relief** in the UK treats the members of a group as one **entity** for tax purposes.

8   False. Tax evasion is illegal; it is tax avoidance that is legal.

9   The person liable to pay tax is called a **taxable person**. This includes an individual, an **estate** of a deceased person, a **trust** fund, a partnership, a **limited** company and any other **body** set up to carry out trade for profit.

10   This is called the recharacterisation rule.

2 Objective test answers: International tax

1   D   The head office is located, and all board meetings take place in, the Cayman Islands. Therefore the place of management is in the Cayman Islands.

2   C   International tax treaties (eg double taxation treaties) are a source of tax rules.

           The other options are all sources of accounting rules.

3   D   Option A is the definition of group relief and options B and C show aspects of group relief.

4   C   Total tax due is $20,000 ($100,000 × 20%) less double taxation relief for $5,000, leaves $15,000 to pay.

5   B   Total tax due is $20,000 ($100,000 × 20%) less double taxation relief of $10,000 ($50,000 × 20%), leaves $10,000 to pay.

6   The EU issues rules on sales taxes, which must be applied by all member states.

7   It is called the schedular system.

8   False. In the UK, a company is treated as taxable in its place of management.

9   •   Interest payments
           •   Dividends
           •   Royalties
           •   Capital gains accruing to non-residents

10 • Full deduction
   • Exemption
   • Credit

3 Objective test answers: Indirect taxes

1   D

	$
Output tax (250,000 × 17.5%)	43,750
Input tax $\left(\dfrac{(225,600 \times 80\%)}{117.5} \times 17.5\right)$	26,880
Payable	16,870

2   C   The sales tax is an indirect tax, all the others are direct taxes.

3   A

	$
Output tax $\left(\dfrac{230,000}{115} \times 15\right)$	30,000
Input tax ((180,000 − 20,000) × 15%)	24,000
Payable	6,000

4   B   As long as they are registered for sales tax, options A, C and D merely act as tax collectors, it is the end consumer who suffers the tax.

5   A

	$
Output tax (700,000 × 75% × 10%)	52,500
Input tax $\left(\dfrac{550,000}{110} \times 10\right)$	50,000
Payable	2,500

The important point to remember is that zero rated sales are still taxable supplies; they just pay tax at 0%. Therefore the purchases do not need to be restricted.

6   C

	$
Output tax (250,000 × 80% × 15%)	30,000
Input tax $\left(\dfrac{(225,600 \times 80\%)}{115} \times 15\right)$	23,540
Payable	6,460

7   False. An *ad valorem* tax is an indirect tax.

all exclude Sales tax in Sales.

8   C

	$
Output tax (1,000,000 × 15%)	150,000
Input tax $\left(\dfrac{575,000}{115} \times 15\right)$	75,000
Payable	75,000

9   D

	$
Output tax (500,000 × 15%)	75,000
Input tax $\left(\dfrac{(225,600 \times 75\%)}{115} \times 15\right)$	33,750
Payable	41,250

10	A			$
		Output tax (250,000 × 80% × 17.5%)		35,000
		Input tax $\left(\dfrac{(225,600 \times 80\%)}{117.5} \times 17.5\right)$		26,880
		Payable		8,120

4 Objective test answers: Company taxation

1	B		$	$
		Accounting profit		350,000
		Add: depreciation	30,000	
		disallowed expenses	15,000	
				45,000
				395,000
		Less: non-taxable income	25,000	
		tax allowable depreciation	32,000	
				(57,000)
		Taxable profit		338,000

2	D		$	$
		Taxable profit		350,000
		Less: depreciation	30,000	
		disallowed expenses	15,000	
				(45,000)
				305,000
		Add: non-taxable income	25,000	
		tax allowable depreciation	32,000	
				57,000
		Accounting profit		362,000

3	A		$	$
		Accounting loss		(350,000)
		Add: depreciation	30,000	
		disallowed expenses	400,000	
				430,000
				80,000
		Less: non-taxable income	25,000	
		tax allowable depreciation	32,000	
				(57,000)
		Taxable profit		23,000

4   B   The dividend is 90% of the total payment and so the advanced tax is $^{10}/_{90}$ or $^{1}/_{9}$.

$$\frac{\$360,000}{9} = \$40,000$$

			$	$
5	C			(320,000)
		Accounting loss		
		Add: depreciation	33,000	
		disallowed expenses	40,000	
				73,000
				(247,000)
		Less: non-taxable income	20,000	
		tax allowable depreciation	45,000	
				(65,000)
		Taxable loss		(312,000)

			$m	$m
6	B			50
		Taxable profit		
		Less: depreciation	15	
		disallowed expenses	1	
				(16)
				34
		Add: non-taxable income	3	
		tax allowable depreciation	4	
				7
		Accounting profit		41

			$	$
7	D			250,000
		Accounting profit		
		Add: depreciation	45,000	
		disallowed expenses	20,000	
				65,000
				315,000
		Less: tax allowable depreciation		(30,000)
		Taxable profit		285,000

Tax payable = $285,000 × 30% = $85,500.

			$	$
8	C			360,000
		Accounting profit		
		Add: depreciation	40,000	
		disallowed expenses	10,000	
				50,000
				410,000
		Less: non-taxable income	35,000	
		tax allowable depreciation	30,000	
				(65,000)
		Taxable profit		345,000

Tax payable = $345,000 × 20% = $69,000.

			$	$
9	B			500,000
		Accounting profit		
		Add: depreciation	50,000	
		disallowed expenses	5,000	
				55,000
				555,000
		Less: non-taxable income	25,000	
		tax allowable depreciation	60,000	
				(85,000)
		Taxable profit		470,000

Tax payable = $470,000 × 25% = $117,500.

10	D		$	$
		Accounting profit		250,000
		Add: depreciation	40,000	
		disallowed expenses	2,000	
				42,000
				292,000
		Less: tax allowable depreciation		(30,000)
		Taxable profit		262,000

Tax payable = $262,000 × 30% = $78,600.

5 Objective test answers: Deferred tax

1	A		$
		Over provision for prior period	(2,000)
		Provision for current period	50,000
		Increase in deferred tax charge	5,000
		Charge to income statement	53,000

2	C		$
		Under provision for prior period	200
		Provision for current period	30,000
		Decrease in deferred tax charge	(5,000)
		Charge to income statement	25,200

3   A   Item 2 consists of permanent differences, all the rest are temporary differences.

4   A   All three items are taxable temporary differences.

5   D   All four items have a carrying amount equal to their tax base.

6   B   IAS 12 states that deferred tax assets and liabilities should not be discounted.

7	D		$
		Taxable temporary differences b/f	850,000
		Depreciation for tax purposes	500,000
		Depreciation charged in the financial statements	(450,000)
		Revaluation surplus	250,000
		Taxable temporary differences c/f	1,150,000
		Deferred tax at 30%	345,000

8	D		$
		Over provision for prior period	(27,500)
		Provision for current period	30,000
		Decrease in deferred tax charge	(10,000)
		Credit to income statement	(7,500)

9   It is an imputation system.

10	D		$
		Under provision for prior period	2,800
		Provision for current period	28,000
		Increase in deferred tax charge	5,000
		Charge to income statement	35,800

6 Section B answers: Taxation I

(a)   The person liable to pay tax is called a **taxable person**.

Examples include the following. (You only need to give three examples.)

- An individual
- An estate of a deceased person
- A trust fund
- A partnership
- A limited company
- Any other body set up to carry out a trade for profit (eg the bar at a golf club).

A taxable person usually pays tax in the country where he or she is resident. The tax authority able to charge tax is called the **competent jurisdiction**.

(b)   The four main sources are as follows.

- Domestic tax legislation and court rulings
- Domestic tax authority practice
- Supranational bodies
- International tax treaties

You need to give **two** out of the following four answers.

(i)   Domestic tax legislation and court rulings

The main source of tax rules arises from the domestic tax legislation of the country, eg in the UK, the annual Finance Act. Although the legislators try to think of all possible situations, business is always changing and so the law may have to be interpreted by the courts. This gives rise to court rulings that have the force of law.

(ii)   Domestic tax authority practice

Every tax authority develops its own practice on how the law is applied. For example, UK tax law states that employees should be taxed on all 'benefits' supplied by the employer. However, in practice, certain benefits are exempted from the rules because it would be too time consuming and yield little in the way of tax.

(iii)   Supranational bodies

Supranational bodies, such as the European Union (EU), can affect tax rules. The EU has a number of rules on value added or sales tax, which have to be applied by all members of the EU.

(iv)   International tax treaties

Some businesses trade in many different countries of the world, so called 'multi-national' companies. This means that their profits will be subject to tax in the local countries they trade in, as well as the country where the company has its headquarters. This could mean that the company pays tax on certain profits twice. In order to avoid this 'double tax', countries enter into tax treaties which set out which country taxes the profits. These treaties also allow relief for local taxes paid, for example withholding taxes.

			$'000	$'000
(c)	(i)	Accounting profit		50,000
		Add: disallowable expenditure: entertaining	750	
		formation costs	250	
		book depreciation	1,250	
				2,250
				52,250
		Less: non-taxable income	2,500	
		tax allowable depreciation	1,350	
				(3,850)
		Taxable profit		48,400

The tax rate is 25%, so the tax due is $12,100,000 (25% × $48,400,000).

(ii) — Advanced tax

As the advanced tax rate is 15%, the dividend paid is 85%.

$$\text{Advanced tax} = \frac{\$1,700,00}{85} \times 15$$

$$= \$300,000$$

— The tax due for the current period is unaffected by the advanced tax paid, it remains at $12,100,000.

However, the tax payable is reduced by the advanced tax paid.

Tax payable = $12,100,000 – $300,000
= $ 11,800,000

(d) (i) **Indirect taxation** is charged indirectly on the final consumer of the goods or services. An example is a sales tax (eg VAT in the UK; TVA in France). As value is added, the tax increases cumulatively.

Indirect taxes are not actually paid by the business. Instead, the business acts as a tax collector on behalf of the tax authorities. For example, a business charges sales tax on its sales (output tax) and it pays sales tax on its purchases (input tax). The difference between output tax and input tax is paid over to the tax authorities.

(ii) The two types of indirect tax are as follows.

- Unit taxes
- *Ad valorem* taxes

Unit taxes are based on the number or weight of items, eg excise duties on the number of cigarettes or on the weight of tobacco.

Ad valorem taxes are based on the value of the items, eg a sales tax or value added tax.

(e)

	$
Output tax $\dfrac{(587,500 \times 80\%)}{117.5} \times 17.5$	70,000
Input tax (350,000 × 80%) × 17.5%	49,000
Tax payable	21,000

7 Section B answers: Taxation II

(a) D's accounting period ends on 31 December but the UK tax year-end is 5 April. Therefore, records may need to be kept for different periods and retained for longer intervals than required for normal accounting purposes.

Obviously a business needs to keep records of the tax it pays. It makes no difference if the tax is a cost to the business (eg tax on business profits) or whether the business acts merely as a tax collector (eg sales tax).

However, tax records usually need to be kept in more detail than is strictly necessary for pure accounting purposes. For example, records of employee taxation will need to be kept in great detail for every employee. This is so that the business can satisfy the tax authority that it has complied with the law.

Most tax authorities have the power to inspect business records to ensure compliance. If mistakes are made, the tax authority may be able to re-open earlier years and collect back taxes owed. In the UK, the Inland Revenue have the power to go back six tax years if errors are found. Therefore tax records may need to be kept longer than normal, eg payroll records are usually kept for at least six years after the end of the tax year.

(b) The main point to remember here is that employee taxation is personal tax. The employer acts strictly as a tax collector on behalf of the tax authorities and in accordance with their instructions. Therefore, any queries arising must be sent to the tax authorities.

In this case, provided that the employer is correctly applying the instructions given to him, the employer is powerless to deal with the employee's query. The employee must be told to raise the query with the tax authorities. She should be given details of the tax office and her personal tax reference number. It may be wise to tell the employee that the employer cannot change the tax deductions until new instructions are received from the tax authorities.

(c) Tax authorities have the power to enforce compliance with the tax rules. These powers include the following.

(i) Power to review and query filed returns.
(ii) Power to request special reports or returns.
(iii) Power to examine records (generally extending back some years).
(iv) Powers of entry and search.
(v) Exchange of information with tax authorities in other jurisdictions.

Regarding point (i), the tax authorities usually have the power to ask for further information if they are not satisfied with a filed return. These queries must be answered or there may be legal penalties.

With regard to (ii), the special report may take the form of asking for details of pay and tax deducted from an individual employee, where there are indications that the tax rules have been broken. There have been instances of casual employees having a number of jobs but using a number of false names, so that the tax authority has been defrauded.

Most tax authorities have the power to inspect business records to ensure compliance (point (iii)). If mistakes in returns have been made, the tax authority may be able to re-open earlier years and collect back taxes owed.

However, where the tax authority believes fraud has occurred, it can obtain warrants to enter a business's premises and seize the records (iv).

Point (v) has become very important as a counter-terrorism measure in recent years. One tax authority may become aware of funds being moved to another country in suspicious circumstances. It will then warn the tax authority in that other jurisdiction. Exchange of information is also useful in dealing with drug smuggling and money laundering.

(d)   If a company makes payments to an individual or another company resident in a different tax jurisdiction, it may have to pay **withholding tax** to the tax authority of its own jurisdiction.

The reason for this is to stop companies paying all their earnings abroad and then stopping trading without paying any tax to the tax authorities of the country where they are resident. Therefore the local tax authority will take a payment on account of the final tax liability by deducting at source a withholding tax from all payments sent abroad. The withholding tax can be as low as 5% or as high as 40%.

Payments affected are usually the following. (*You were only asked to give two examples.*)

- Interest payments
- Dividends
- Royalties
- Capital gains accruing to non-residents

(e)   In order to establish more clearly which tax authority has jurisdiction, countries enter into **double taxation treaties**. These treaties seek to avoid a business having to pay tax twice on its income simply because it deals with two tax authorities.

A double taxation treaty (eg that between the UK and the USA) sets out which tax authority has jurisdiction. So a company incorporated in the UK that trades with the USA will be taxed primarily in the UK. The treaty defines a **permanent establishment** and directs that the business will be taxed in the country where it has its permanent establishment.

Where a double taxation treaty exists, provisions are usually made to reduce withholding taxes, or even to avoid paying withholding tax at all.

Another feature of a double taxation treaty is that where a company pays tax in Country A, but is resident in Country B, the tax authorities of Country B will give relief for the tax paid in Country A.

Methods of giving relief

One way is to give full **deduction** for foreign taxes paid. However this is not always appropriate, particularly if the country where the tax is paid has a high tax rate and the other has a low rate.

Relief may be given by **exemption**. In this case, if income is taxed in Country A, then it will not be taxed in Country B.

Another way of giving relief is by **credit**. This usually occurs where the tax rate in Country A is higher than that in Country B. Instead of deducting the full amount of tax paid in Country A, Country B credits the amount it would have paid in Country B. For example, the income is $10,000 and the tax rate in Country A is 30%, while that in Country B is 20%. The tax paid in Country A will be $3,000 but the double tax relief allowed in Country B will be $2,000 (20% × $10,000).

8 Section B answers: Taxation III

(a) **Deferred tax – balance sheet disclosure and note**

	$m
Temporary differences on non-current assets	0.56
Provision at 30 April 20X3	0.69
Deferred tax credit in income statement	(0.13)
Provision at 30 April 20X4	0.56

Working: Deferred tax

	$m
Temporary difference at 30 April 20X3	2.30
Temporary difference at 30 April 20X4	2.00
Deferred tax at 30 April 20X3 (2.30 × 30%)	0.69
Deferred tax at 30 April 20X4 (2.00 × 28%)	0.56
Reduction in deferred tax provision	0.13

Alternative working. The reduction in provision is made up of two elements

	$m
Reversal of temporary differences ((2.30 – 2.00) × 30%)	0.09
Change in tax rate (2.00 × (30% – 28%))	0.04
	0.13

(b) **Tax on profit on ordinary activities – note to income statement**

	$m
Current tax	
Tax on profit for the period	1.40
Overprovision for previous period ($750,000 – $720,000)	(0.03)
Deferred tax	
Increase in provision ($300,000 – $250,000)	0.05
Total tax charge	1.42

Balance sheet

	$m
Payables	
Current tax	1.40
Deferred tax	0.30

(c) In many sets of financial statements, there may appear to be little relationship between the figure reported as the profit before tax and the actual tax charge that appears in the income statement. In a simple tax system, the tax charge would be the reported profit multiplied by the tax rate. However this will not normally be the case in real life, due to the complexities of the tax system and the estimates and subjective decisions that the directors must make in estimating the tax charge for the year.

The purpose of the reconciliation between the actual tax charge and the reported profit multiplied by the standard rate of tax is to highlight to the users of the financial statements these estimates and judgements. This reconciliation should clarify the effect of adjustments such as changes in tax rates, estimated tax charges differing from final agreed tax liabilities and other factors that have affected the amount that appears as the tax charge in the income statement.

(d)   The **main duty** of the external auditor is to **express an opinion** on whether the financial statements as a whole **present fairly** the entity's position. Therefore the auditor has to decide whether, in his opinion, each item in the financial statements has been accurately accounted for and shown on a fair basis.

With regard to the **deferred tax disclosures**, the auditor must satisfy himself that the calculation of the deferred tax balance is **technically** and **mechanically accurate**:

- Regarding the facts
- According to the requirements of the relevant accounting standard, IAS 12.

The external auditor must ensure that the company's accounting policy with regard to deferred tax is in line with the requirements of IAS 12 and that all of the disclosures required by IAS 12 have been made. Any **departures** from the **IAS** must be **disclosed** in the **notes** to the accounts.

With regard to the current taxes the auditor will be concerned with the calculation of the tax charge and its correct disclosure according to IAS 12.

(e)   **Impact of disagreement over disclosures**

If the external auditor **disagrees** with the disclosures or calculations made concerning any figure in the financial statements, including deferred tax and current tax, then he should **firstly inform** the **directors** of his concerns.

In most cases in practice, the external auditor should be able to convince the directors of his arguments and in consequence the financial statements will be suitably amended, thereby securing **auditor and client satisfaction**.

If the directors are not prepared to change the financial statements then the auditor must consider whether to give a qualified audit report. A **qualification** of an audit report will **only** be made **if** the **matter is material.**

Therefore the auditor must consider whether the amounts involved are material. If not, then no further action needs to be taken.

If the auditor considers that the amounts involved are material and that users of the financial statements will be misled by the disclosures that the directors are making then his audit report must make this quite clear.

If the disagreement is regarding the deferred tax balance or current taxes then the audit response will be:

- Describe the nature of the problem

- Quantify its effects as far as possible

- State that the financial statements give a true and fair view except for the disagreement over the treatment of the deferred tax balance or current taxes.

9 Section B answers: Taxation IV

(a)   Under the **nil provision or flow through method**, the tax liability recognised is the expected legal tax liability for the period, ie **no provision is made for deferred tax.** This method has the advantage of being easy to understand, but it was rejected by the IASB for several reasons.

(i)   This method can lead to large **fluctuations** in the tax charge.

(ii)   It does not allow **tax relief** for liabilities to be recognised until those liabilities are settled.

(iii)   The method is **not used internationally.** The IASB is committed to convergence of international accounting standards.

(iv)   The full provision method accords better with the **definitions of liabilities** in the *Framework.*

(v)   The flow through method **does not match income and expenditure.**

The IASB also rejected the **partial provision** method, for the following reasons.

(a)   It is also **inconsistent with international practice.**

(b)   Deferred tax recognised at the balance sheet date includes the tax effect of future transactions that have not been recognised in the financial statements, and to which the undertaking is not yet committed. This is **difficult to reconcile with the *Framework* definition of a liability.**

(c)   The method is **too subjective**.

> **Pass marks.** This question requires more depth of knowledge – you need to discuss the incremental liability approach in the standard and explain that revaluations or fair value adjustments do not normally create separate tax assets or liabilities.

(b)   IAS 12 uses the **incremental liability** approach to accounting for deferred tax. This means that deferred tax is recognised only when it can be viewed as **meeting the definition of a liability in its own right.** Revaluing a non-current asset does not usually create an unavoidable, incremental tax liability because the entity does not have to realise the revaluation gain by selling the asset. The tax liability will only crystallise when the asset is sold. Accordingly, deferred tax is **not recognised** on timing differences arising from revaluing assets unless the entity has:

– Under old IAS12.

(a)   Entered into a **binding agreement to sell** the revalued assets

(b)   **Recognised the gains and losses** expected to arise on the sale

However, deferred tax **must be provided** when the timing difference arises on assets that are **marked to market** with gains or losses **recognised in the income statement**. Because the gain/loss has been recognised, it is appropriate to recognise the deferred tax effect.

Fair value adjustments made in consolidated accounts **do not** give rise to deferred tax assets or liabilities. This is because the amount of tax payable when the asset is sold will be determined by the profit made by the new subsidiary, and the fact that it has been consolidated is irrelevant. An exception might be where, on acquisition, the entity entered into a binding agreement to sell the asset that was revalued on consolidation.

> **Pass marks.** It is important to appreciate that the timing difference creates potential tax assets.

(c)   This intra-group sale will give rise to a **provision for unrealised profit** on the unsold inventory of $10,000,000 \times 20\% \times 25\% = \$500,000$. This provision must be made in the consolidated accounts.

However, this profit has already been taxed in the financial statements of Pay It. In other words there is a **timing difference**. In the following year when the inventory is sold outside the group, the provision will be released, but the profit will not be taxed. The timing difference therefore gives rise to a **deferred tax asset**. The asset is $30\% \times \$500,000 = \$150,000$.

Deferred tax assets are recognised to the extent that they are **recoverable**. This will be the case if **it is more likely than not** that **suitable tax profits** will exist from which the reversal of the timing difference giving rise to the asset can be deducted. The asset is carried forward on this assumption.

BPP
PROFESSIONAL EDUCATION

> **Pass marks.** It is important to consider whether the loss is recoverable.

(d) An unrelieved tax loss gives rise to a **timing difference** because the loss is recognised in the financial statements but not yet allowed for tax purposes. When the overseas subsidiary generates sufficient taxable profits, the loss will be offset against these in arriving at taxable profits.

The amount of the deferred tax asset to be carried forward is 25% × $8m = $2m.

Deferred tax assets are recognised to the extent that they are **recoverable.** This will be the case if **it is more likely than not** that **suitable tax profits** will exist from which the reversal of the timing difference giving rise to the asset can be deducted.

(e) (i) ~~The provisions on **discounting** are somewhat **confusing.**~~ *Wrong!* The full reversal basis of discounting deferred tax liabilities may turn them into assets in the early years of an asset's life because capital allowances exceed depreciation before the timing differences reverse.

(ii) The standard is **complicated,** and there is **scope for manipulation and inconsistency**, since discounting is optional.

(iii) It is **open to question whether deferred tax is a liability** as defined in the *Framework*. It is not, strictly speaking, a present obligation arising as a result of a past event. However, it is being recognised as such under the IAS.

— does it meet a liability (the meaning of this).

10 Objective test answers: The regulatory framework

1 B Consistency contributes to comparability.

2 C Guidance on application and interpretation of IASs/IFRSs is provided by the International Financial Reporting Interpretations Committee (IFRIC).

3 A The priority given to different user groups in different countries (eg. investor groups in the US and employees in Europe) is actually a **barrier** to harmonisation.

4 B Many of the older IASs permitted **two** accounting treatments for like transactions or events – the benchmark treatment and the allowed alternative. As these are revised allowed alternative treatments are being eliminated. This gives preparers of accounts **less** choice.

5 C The *Framework* provides a conceptual basis for the formulation of **International** standards. It is not relevant to the development of national standards.

6 C The *Framework* cites two underlying assumptions:

The accounts have been prepared on an accruals basis (accruals).
The business is expected to continue in operation for the foreseeable future (going concern).

7 C The four principle qualitative characteristics are relevance, reliability, comparability and understandability.

8 B The elements of financial statements are assets, liabilities and equity in the balance sheet and income and expenses in the income statement. Profits and losses are not elements.

9 B The income statement measures **performance**. Financial position is measured in the balance sheet and financial adaptability in the cash flow statement.

10 C The future economic benefits can be reliably measured.

11 Objective test answers: External audit

1	A	All three statements are correct.	
2	C	Item 3	The auditors report to the shareholders not the directors.
		Item 4	Compliance tests test that the internal controls are operating effectively, not substantive tests.
3	C	Auditors have the right to attend meetings of the **company**, not of the directors.	
4	A	A statement of recognised income and expense may be replaced by a statement of changes in equity.	
5	C	No qualification is needed as the directors have made full disclosure.	
6	D	The auditors report covers all of these matters.	
7	B	This is a limitation of scope.	
8	C	The auditors will be unable to give an opinion in this case.	
9	A	This will be an 'except for' qualification.	
10	A	In order to state that the financial statements show a true and fair view the auditor must satisfy himself that the other three matters are valid.	

12 Section B answers: Regulation

(a) The **going concern assumption** is that an entity will continue in operational existence for the foreseeable future. This means that the financial statements of an entity are prepared on the assumption that the entity will **continue** trading. If this were not the case, various adjustments would have to be made to the accounts: provisions for losses; revaluation of assets to their possible market value; all non-current assets and liabilities would be reclassified as current; and so forth.

Unless it can be assumed that the business is a going concern, other accounting assumptions cannot apply.

For example, it is meaningless to speak of consistency from one accounting period to the next when this is the final accounting period.

The **accruals basis** of accounting states that revenue and expenses which are related to each other are matched, so as to be dealt with in the same accounting period, without regard to when the cash is actually paid or received. This is particularly relevant to the purchase of non-current assets. The cost of a non-current asset is spread over the accounting periods expected to benefit from it, thus matching costs and revenues. In the absence of the going concern convention, this cannot happen, as an example will illustrate.

Suppose a company has a machine which cost $10,000 two years ago and now has a net book value of $6,000. The machine can be used for another three years, but as it is obsolete, there is no possibility of selling it, and so it has no market value.

If the going concern assumption applies, the machine will be shown at **cost less depreciation** in the accounts (ie $6,000), as it still has a part to play in the continued life of the entity. However, if the assumption cannot be applied, the machine will be given a nil value and other assets and liabilities will be similarly revalued on the basis of winding down the company's operations.

(b)   The IASB Framework seeks to provide a basis for effective regulation of financial reporting.

One of the ideas behind such a framework is to **avoid the fire-fighting approach**, which had previously characterised the development of accounting standards and instead develop an underlying philosophy as a basis for consistent accounting principles so that each standard fits into the whole framework. Research began from an analysis of the fundamental objectives of accounting and their relationship to the information needs of accounts users. The framework has gone behind the requirements of existing accounting standards, which define accounting treatments for particular assets, liabilities, income and expenditure, to define the nature of assets, liabilities, income and expenditure.

In this way, the Framework seeks to ensure that there are no conflicts between different standards. Any issue that arises with a standard can be resolved by reference to the basic principles set out in the Framework.

(c)   International Accounting Standards are designed to be applicable **to companies in general** and are not tailored to the specific circumstances of individual companies. Therefore one **advantage** of offering companies the option of departing from the detailed requirements of International Accounting Standards in order to achieve a fair presentation is that **if the treatment required** by an International Accounting Standard **does not suit** the circumstances of a particular company then they can **depart** from that standard.

The **disadvantage** of offering companies the option of departure from the requirements of International Accounting Standards is that this option could be used to **manipulate financial statements** or to show the financial statements in the best light by the directors of the company even though the accounting treatment chosen is not allowed by International Accounting Standards.

The aim of the IASB is that ultimately fair presentation will be synonymous with compliance with IAS/IFRS, so the possibility of departure from standards will not arise. Recent revisions to IASs have been carried out to eliminate allowed alternative treatments in accounts, so the general trend is towards more uniformity and less choice.

(d)   A conceptual framework provides the theoretical basis upon which financial reporting can be regulated. It establishes generally agreed-upon principles and accounting standards can be developed in accordance with this. Lack of a conceptual framework can lead to the following problems:

(i)   Standards being developed in a firefighting fashion, in response to problems or abuses as they arise. Standards developed in this way are unlikely to be well thought-out and may need further revision as more problems are identified.

(ii)   Because standards are not being developed as part of a consistent whole, there may be conflicts and inconsistencies between different standards. Also issues may be addressed in more than one standard, leading to duplication of effort and confusion.

(iii)   If there is no overall framework to which reference can be made, standard setters will feel the need to cover every eventuality. This can lead to standards becoming very detailed and prescriptive. This has already been observed in the USA with the FASB standards.

(iv)   A conceptual framework provides some sort of protection from political pressure from vested interests. A new standard developed as part of a conceptual framework cannot be amended in a way which will bring it into conflict with the conceptual framework.

13 Section B answers: External audit

(a)   The 'expectations gap' is the gap between the statutory duties and responsibilities of auditors and what the public perceive those duties and responsibilities to be. The 'gap' includes the following misconceptions:

    (i)   **The auditor is responsible for the detection of fraud and error**.

        This is not the case. While the auditor may uncover fraud and error in the course of the audit, and will certainly follow up any suspicions, the detection and prevention of fraud is the responsibility of the **directors**.

    (ii)   **The auditor is responsible for preparing the financial statements**.

        Again, this is the responsibility of the directors.

    (iii)   **The auditor is responsible for ensuring that the accounting system is secure and has the required internal controls**.

        The auditor will advise upon this, and his report does require him to report on the internal control system, but the responsibility for the system lies with the directors.

    (iv)   **The audit report guarantees that the accounts are free from fraud and error and that the company will continue as a going concern**.

        The auditor is unable to give any such guarantee. His statutory duty requires him only to state his *opinion*.

        Although the true nature of the auditor's position is becoming more widely understood, the problems caused by the expectations gap surface whenever there is a financial scandal. This is not helped by those instances such as Enron where the auditors were involved in the wrongdoing. Resistance to the idea of limited liability for auditors is based on the idea that auditors bear responsibility for whatever goes wrong and should not be allowed to escape responsibility for it.

(b)   (i)   An auditor will be unable to issue an unqualified audit report if he has disagreements with management regarding the treatment of one or more items in the accounts, or if the scope of his audit has been limited in some way, for instance certain records may not have been made available to him. When the auditor concludes that he cannot issue an unqualified report for one of these reasons, but that the effect of the disagreement or limitation of scope is not so material or pervasive as to require an adverse opinion or a disclaimer of opinion, then he will express a **qualified opinion**. The opinion will be expressed as being 'except for the effects of the matter to which the qualification relates'.

    (ii)   Where the possible effect of a limitation of scope is so material or pervasive that the auditor has not been able to obtain sufficient appropriate audit evidence and is therefore unable to express an opinion on the financial statements, a **disclaimer of opinion** will be expressed. This limitation may have arisen through circumstances, or may have been imposed by the client or may have arisen due to the inadequate nature of the company's accounting records. The auditor's report should give an explanation of the nature of the limitation of scope and quantify the effects on the financial statements where possible.

    (iii)   Where the effect of a disagreement is so material or pervasive that the auditor concludes that a qualified opinion is insufficient to disclose the misleading or incomplete nature of the financial statements an **adverse opinion** will be expressed. Such a disagreement may concern the selection of accounting policies, the application of accounting standards or the inadequacy of disclosures. The report must fully describe the circumstances leading to the adverse opinion. The opinion will state that, because of the effect of these circumstances, the financial statements do not present fairly the financial position of the company and its results.

(c) Because they have a statutory duty to carry out on behalf of the shareholders, auditors are also given certain statutory rights to enable them to carry out that duty.

Right of access to records

The auditor has a right of access at all times to the books, accounts and vouchers of the company.

Right to require information

The auditor has a right to require from the company's officers such information and explanations as he thinks necessary for the performance of his duties as auditor. It is an offence for a company's officer to make a statement to the auditor which is materially misleading, false or deceptive.

These rights make it possible for the auditor to carry out an audit. If these rights are violated, the auditor will qualify his report. If the situation is serious, for instance if the auditor believes the directors to be involved in a fraud, he has the following rights which enable him to communicate directly to the shareholders:

Right to attend/receive notice of general meetings

The directors cannot keep the auditor away from the AGMs by not informing him of when they are taking place.

Right to speak at general meetings

The auditor has a right to be heard at general meetings which he attends, on any part of the business that concerns him as auditor.

Right in relation to written resolutions

The auditor has the right to receive a copy of any written resolution proposed. This means that he must receive a copy of any resolution which is proposed to terminate his engagement.

In practice, an auditor would not expect to have to invoke these rights very often, but the fact that they exist establishes his status in relation to the directors and makes it possible for him to get the co-operation that he needs in order to carry out his engagement.

14 Objective test answers: Presentation

1	A	Members do not inspect the accounting records – the auditors do this on their behalf.
2	A	Item (1) is now included as a current liability after the revision of IAS 1.
3	A	All of these items appear in the statement of changes in equity.
4	B	Item (2) is no longer required to be disclosed after the revision of IAS 1.
5	C	2 and 4 are distributions to/collections from shareholders, not income or expenses.
6	D	Authorised share capital is disclosed in the notes to the balance sheet, the other disclosures are made in the income statement or notes.
7	C	2 is a change of accounting estimate, 4 is specifically mentioned in IAS 8 as not constituting a change of accounting policy.
8	D	Material errors are treated in the same way as changes of accounting policy, by the application of retrospective restatement.
9	B	IAS 8 requires that a change in accounting policy is accounted for by retrospective application.
10	A	Changing the method of depreciation is a change of estimation technique not a change of accounting policy and therefore retrospective application is not required. However the current year figures must be changed to reflect the change in estimation technique and the change must be disclosed.

15 Section B answers: Presentation

(a) (i) **Materiality and aggregation**. Items which are material need to be shown separately in the financial accounts. Amounts which are not material, can be added together and the sub total can be shown.

(ii) **Offsetting**. Assets and liabilities should not be set off, unless it is permitted in a standard. This is because it hinders the users of financial statements in understanding what the transactions are.

(iii) **Consistency**. Transactions should be treated on a similar basis from year to year. Also, transactions of the same kind should be treated in the same way in each accounting period. This makes accounts **comparable** from one year to the next and between different companies.

(b) **Balance sheet as at 31 December 20X2** (in thousands of currency units)

	20X2	20X2	20X1	20X1
Assets				
Non-current assets				
Property, plant and equipment	X		X	
Goodwill	X		X	
Other intangible assets	X		X	
Investments in associates	X		X	
Available for sale investments	X̲		X̲	
		X		X
Current assets				
Inventories	X		X	
Trade and other receivables	X		X	
Other current assets	X		X	
Cash and cash equivalents	X		X	
		X̲		X̲
Total assets		X̲		X̲
Equity and liabilities				
Equity attributable to equity holders of the parent				
Issued capital	X		X	
Reserves	X		X	
Retained earnings	X̲		X̲	
		X		X
Minority interest		X		X
Non-current liabilities				
Long-term borrowings	X		X	
Deferred tax	X		X	
Long-term provisions	X̲		X̲	
		X		X
Current liabilities				
Trade and other payables	X		X	
Short term borrowings	X		X	
Current portions of long-term borrowings	X		X	
Short-term provisions	X̲		X̲	
		X̲		X̲
Total equity and liabilities		X̲		X̲

BPP PROFESSIONAL EDUCATION

Income statement

For the year ended 31 December 20X2 (in thousands of currency units)

	20X2	20X1
Revenue	X	X
Cost of sales	(X)	(X)
Gross profit	X	X
Other income	X	X
Distribution costs	(X)	(X)
Administrative expenses	(X)	(X)
Other expenses	(X)	(X)
Finance costs	(X)	(X)
Share of profit of associates	X	X
Profit before tax	X	X
Income tax expense	(X)	(X)
Profit for the period	X	X

(c) Companies might be expected to publish accounts using **standard formats** so as to ensure complete disclosure of material and important items and to ensure consistency between accounting periods and comparability between companies.

In addition, in certain European and other countries where standard formats have been in use for many years their use provides governments with consistent information for the preparation of national accounts and other economic statistics.

The detail shown in each of the standard income statements would enable users of accounts to calculate certain key ratios such as gross margins, net margins, ratio of administration costs to sales or profit and to identify the proportion of the net income arising from operations separately to that arising from financing transactions.

This information would be of use to shareholders and stockholders' analysts who will wish to assess the profitability of a company and compare it with possible alternative investments.

16 Leonardo

> **Pass marks**. This is a typical question on IAS and IFRS. In the first part you are required to discuss the standards and then to apply them in the second part.

(a) (i) **Discontinued operations**

An entity should disclose a single amount on the face of the income statement comprising the total of:

- The post tax profit or loss of discontinued operations

- The post-tax gain or loss recognised on the measurement to fair value less costs to sell or on the disposal of the assets constituting the discontinued operation.

This total should be analysed into the following components on the face of the income statement or in the notes.

- Revenue, expenses and pre-tax profit or loss

- Related income tax expense

- Gain or loss recognised on the measurement to fair value less costs to sell or on the disposal of the assets

- Related income tax expense

(ii) **Correction of prior periods errors**

Prior period errors are corrected retrospectively. This involves:

- either restating the comparative amounts for the prior periods in which the error occurred

- or, where the error occurred before the previous period, restating opening balances of assets, liabilities and equity for the period

(iii) **Changes in accounting policies**

Changes in accounting policies are rare and other than changes in IAS/IFRS are only required to enable more reliable/relevant information to be shown. The accounting treatment is to apply the change retrospectively to earlier accounting periods and adjust the opening balance of each component of equity with the cumulative total.

(b) **Leonardo**

Income statement for the year ended 30 September 20X8

	$'000
Revenue	6,840
Cost of sales (W1)	(3,988)
Gross profit	2,852
Distribution costs (W2)	(880)
Administrative expenses (W3)	(1,040)
Cost of fundamental reorganisation*	(560)
Profit on sale of property	1,200
Finance costs	(300)
Profit before tax	1,272
Income tax expense	(300)
Profit for the period	972

Note. Profit is stated after charging an exceptional bad debt of $400,000.

* These costs can be shown on the face of the income statement or in the notes.

Workings

1   *Cost of sales*

	$'000
Opening inventory	1,200
Purchases	3,670
Closing inventory (950 – 68)	(882)
	3,988

2   *Distribution costs*

As trial balance	880

3   *Administrative expenses*

As trial balance	590
Provision for doubtful debts (200 – 150)	50
Bad debt written off	400
	1,040

17 Objective test answers: Cash flow statements

1   A   It is important to know which way round the additions and subtractions go when preparing a cash flow statement.

2   D   Profit on disposal will be included in profit, so should be deducted.

3   C   These items do not affect cash flow.

4   D   The final figure in the cash flow statement is the increase or decrease in cash and cash equivalents.

5   B

	$'000
Retained earnings 31.12.X5	1,660
Retained earnings 31.12.X4	1,470
∴ Post tax profit for 20X5	190
Add back tax charge*	840
	1,030

* *Note.* This is the current liability at 31.12.X5, just as the 20X4 charge is the current liability at 31.12.X4.

6   A

Property, plant and equipment: cost

	$m		$m
Opening balance	40	Transfer disposal (balancing figure)	6
Cash – additions	16	Closing balance	50
	56		56

Property, plant and equipment: accumulated depreciation

	$m		$m
		Opening balance	10
Transfer disposal (balancing figure)	2	Income statement	6
Closing balance	14		
	16		16

Property, plant and equipment: disposal

	$m		$m
Transfer cost	6	Transfer depreciation	2
		Loss on sale	1
		Proceeds of sale (balancing figure)	3
	6		6

A   As above

B   As above but with loss of $1m on wrong side of disposal account

C   As above but with loss on sale omitted (written down value 6 – 2 taken)

7   B   Equity investments do not generally fulfil the description of cash equivalents

8   A   All of these items involve movements of cash

9   C   Depreciation and losses on disposal are added back.

10   A

	$'000
Cash from sales	
$3,600 + $600 – $700	3,500
Cash paid for purchases	
$2,400 + $300 – $450	(2,250)
Payments for expenses	(760)
	490

18 Cee Eff

> **Pass marks**. Assuming you know the format of cash flow statements, part (a) should have been quite straightforward, although the working for operating profit may have required some thought. In part (d) you should have been prepared to put forward your own ideas; you will be given credit for them as long as you can back them up.

(a)   **Calculation of operating profit**

Income statement

	$'000		$'000
Taxation*	19	Balance at 1.1.X4	55
Dividends	28	Profit for the year (bal fig)	69
Loan interest (80 × 15%)	12		
Balance at 31.12.X4	65		
	124		124

* Year end provision

(b)

	$'000	$'000
Profit for the year		69
Depreciation (90 – 56)		34
		103
Increase in inventory	(8)	
Increase in receivables	(7)	
Increase in payables	9	
		(6)
Cash generated from operations		97
Tax paid		(17)
Interest paid		(12)
Net cash flows from operating activities		68
Cash flows from investing activities		
Purchase of property, plant and equipment		(90)
Cash flows from financing activities		
Dividends paid	(26)	
Issue of shares	7	
Issue of loan stock	20	1
Net increase/decrease in cash and cash equivalents		(21)
Cash and cash equivalents at the beginning of the year		11
Cash and cash equivalents at the end of the year		(10)

(c)   *Cash and cash equivalents*

	31.12.20X4	31.12.20X3
	$'000	$'000
Cash in hand	–	11
Bank overdraft	(10)	–
	(10)	11

(d)   The cash flow statement shows a **decrease in cash of $21,000**. On the face of it, this is a **matter of concern** from the point of view of liquidity especially as the loans are all repayable in 20X8.

However, it is clear that the decrease in cash has **not** come about because of **unsuccessful operating activities**, which have in fact been cash generating. Additionally, the company is spending cash in order to **expand**: capital expenditure amounts to $90,000. This should lead to better operating results in future years when the assets purchased are brought into use, assuming that the investment in property, plant and equipment is now complete. A close eye must be kept on the cash situation, however, since many companies have gone under by trying to expand too quickly.

19 T cash flow

Pass marks. As with the preparation of the income statement and balance sheet, the key to this type of question is familiarity with the format of the statement and associated disclosures. The best way to achieve this is through practice.

(a) **T: Cash flow statement for the year ended 30 September 20X1**

Cash flows from operating activities

	$'000	$'000
Operating profit	3,600	
Adjustments for		
Depreciation	2,640	
Loss on disposal (2,600 – 900 – 730)	970	
Operating profit before working capital changes	7,210	
Increase in inventory (1,600 – 1,100)	(500)	
Increase in receivables (1,500 – 800)	(700)	
Decrease in payables (800 – 700)	(100)	
Cash generated from operations	5,910	
Interest paid	(24)	
Income taxes paid (W1)	(485)	
Net cash from operating activities		5,401
Cash flows from investing activities		
Purchase of property, plant and equipment	(8,000)	
Proceeds of sale of property, plant and equipment	730	
		(7,270)
Cash flows from financing activities		
Dividend paid (W2)	(1,000)	
Repayment of interest-bearing borrowings	(1,200)	
Proceeds from issue of shares (10,834 – 7,815)	3,019	
		819
Net decrease in cash and cash equivalents (1,200 – 150)		(1,050)
Cash and cash equivalents at 1 October 20X0		1,200
Cash and cash equivalents at 30 September 20X1		150

Workings

1 *Income taxes paid*

Income taxes

	$'000		$'000
Cash flow (bal fig)	485	Opening balance – current	685
Closing balance – current	1,040	Opening balance – deferred	400
Closing balance – deferred	600	Income statement	1,040
	2,125		2,125

2 *Dividend paid*

Dividend

	$'000		$'000
Cash paid (bal fig)	1,000	Opening balance	600
Closing balance	700	Income statement	1,100
	1,700		1,700

(b) At the end of **last year** T did have a **large cash balance**. The main elements of T's cash management this year have been to use that cash **to repay some of the outstanding interest-bearing borrowings**. However, due to a **huge investment in property, plant and equipment** the company has had to **raise funds** by a **share issue**. It could be argued that equity funds are more expensive than loan capital and therefore the loan should not have been repaid simply to be replaced by additional equity funds. However, if the loan was due for repayment during the year the company would have had **no choice**. T plc has also **chosen** to pay an **interim dividend** of $400,000 as well as the non-discretionary payments of income taxes and interest.

20 Objective test answers: Non-current assets, inventories and construction contracts

1 B 780 + 117 + 30 + 28 + 100 = 1,055

2 D They are all correct

3 B Capitalised development expenditure should be carried forward to be matched against future revenue.

4 D Neither internally generated goodwill not internally developed brands can be capitalised.

5 A Goodwill on acquisition is retained in the balance sheet and reviewed annually for impairment.

6 A Carriage outwards is charged to distribution, abnormal costs are not included in inventory.

7 D 1 Production overheads should be included in cost on the basis of a company's normal level of activity.

2 Trade discounts should be deducted but not settlement discounts.

3 The recent revision of IAS 2 does not allow the use of LIFO.

8 C

	$
Contract revenue recognised (900 × 60%)	540,000
Costs	(840,000)
Expected loss (900 – 1,200)	(300,000)
Costs incurred	720,000
Recognised loss	(300,000)
Progress billings	(400,000)
Due from customer	20,000

9 D None of these statements is correct.

Depreciation relating to a revaluation surplus can be transferred from the revaluation reserve to retained earnings, but there must still be a debit to the income statement.

10 C There must be 'readily ascertainable market value'. This implies that:

- the asset must be a member of a group of **homogenous assets** (ie they are all of the same kind), which are equivalent in all material respects

- There is an **active market** for that group of assets, evidenced by frequent transactions

Brands and publishing titles tend to be characterised as being 'unique' and hence most unlikely to have 'readily ascertainable market values'!

21 Section B answers: Non-current assets, inventories and construction contracts

(a) (i) IAS 38 does not allow the capitalisation of research costs.

IAS 38 lays down strict **criteria** to determine when carry forward of development costs is permissible.

– The expenditure attributable to the intangible asset during its development must be measurable.

– The technical feasibility of completing the product or process so that it will be available for sale or use can be demonstrated.

– The entity intends to complete the intangible asset and use or sell it.

– It must be able to use or sell the intangible asset.

– There must be a market for the output of the intangible asset or, if it is to be used internally rather than sold, its usefulness to the entity, can be demonstrated.

– Adequate technical, financial and other resources must exist, or their availability must be demonstrated, to complete the development and use or sell the intangible asset.

(ii) IAS 1 has three basic accounting assumptions: going concern, accruals and consistency.

Each of these concepts is relevant in considering the criteria discussed above for carrying forward development expenditure.

Going concern. The business must be in a position to continue its operations at least to the extent of generating resources sufficient to complete the development project and therefore to market the end product.

Accruals. The purpose of deferring development expenditure at all is to comply with the accruals concept by matching such expenditure with the income expected to arise from it.

Consistency. IAS 38 states that the criteria for deferral of expenditure should be consistently applied.

(b) **Income statement (extracts)**

	$'000
Depreciation charge	
North (($1.2m × 80%)/20 years)	48
Central (($4.8m × 140%)/40 years)	168
South ($2.25m/30 years)	75
	291
Loss on revaluation (20% × $1.2m)	240

Balance sheet (extracts)

	Cost/ revaluation $'000	Depreciation $'000	NBV $'000
North	960	48	912
Central	6,720	168	6,552
South	2,250	75	2,175
	9,930	291	9,639

At 1 January 20X0 the accumulated depreciation of the Central property is $1.2m, which represents 10 years' worth of depreciation, leaving 40 years remaining life. For the South and North properties, the

respective lives in these calculations are 30 and 20 years. If there is no previous revaluation surplus on the North property, then the loss in the current year is classed as an impairment, and must be taken to the income statement.

(c)   The general principle underlying IAS 2 is that inventories should be shown in financial statements at the **lower of cost and net realisable value**. This principle accords with both the matching concept, which requires costs to be matched with the relevant revenues, and the prudence concept, which requires that profits are not anticipated and any probable losses are provided for.

The **cost** of an item of manufactured inventory can include both external and internal costs and it is important that only correctly attributable costs are included. These are direct acquisition costs, direct inventory holding costs and production overheads based on a **normal** level of activity. General overheads are excluded.

Production overheads are usually incurred on a time basis and not in relation to the quantities of inventory produced. Most businesses, however, are assumed to continue to exist in the medium term and production overheads are part of the inevitable cost of providing production facilities in the medium term. Thus, so long as the scale of the overheads is not distorted by unusual levels of activity, it is reasonable to include them in the 'cost' of inventory produced in the period to which they relate. Identifying a 'normal' level of activity is more difficult where business is seasonal.

The establishment of NRV also poses a number of practical problems. For many intermediate products, and even for finished items, there may be a limited market and the inventory volumes may represent a significant proportion of the market especially if disposed of under distress conditions. Where a well-developed and liquid market does not exist, it is usually appropriate to base NRV on an orderly disposal after allowing for the reasonable additional costs of marketing and distribution.

22 Geneva

(a)   Treatment of construction contracts in the balance sheet

	$'000
Contract Lausanne	
Asset (1,000 + 240 – 1,080)	
Gross amount due from customers for contract work	160
Contract Bern	
Liability (1,100 – 200 – 950)	
Gross amount due to customers for contract work	50
Contract Zurich	
Liability (640 + 70 – 800)	
Gross amount due to customers for contract work	90

Treatment of construction contracts in the income statement

	Lausanne $'000	*Bern* $'000	*Zurich* $'000
Revenue	1,200	1,000	700
Cost of sales	960	1,200	630
Gross profit/(loss)	240	(200)	70

(b)   The accounting treatment of construction contracts reflects the **accruals** and **going concern concepts**.

The accruals concept means that the revenues generated in an accounting period should be matched with costs incurred to produce that revenue resulting in the profit for the period.

The going concern concept means that financial statements should be prepared on the basis that the business is expected to continue to operate in the future.

Due to the nature of construction contracts (extending beyond one accounting period) it is necessary to consider the application of both the accruals and going concern concepts. The amount of profit made on a construction contract can only be known with certainty after the completion of that contract, however this does not mean that the profit is not made until it is completed. It is generally considered that profit is earned proportionally as the contract progresses. Hence the recognition of profit only in the year that a contract is completed would hinder rather than assist in the year on year assessment of the profitability of companies, with each other and over time.

Hence, an assessment needs to be made at the end of each period of the amount to be recognised in the financial statements of the company. Generally, in the absence of any better information, **profit is assumed to accrue evenly over time**. The contract should be reasonably well advanced in order to assess the likely outcome and any losses foreseen should be accounted for immediately, in line with the concept of prudence.

23 Objective test answers: Distributable profits and capital transactions

1	C	The premium is transferred from share capital to share premium
2	C	$500,000 + $11,000
		Note that the forfeited shares each brought in a total of $2.60
3	D	Share capital $500,000 + $250,000 + $300,000 + $350,000
		Share premium $800,000 − $250,000 + $900,000 + $910,000
4	A	The called-up value will be debited to share capital and credited to a forfeited shares account.
5	D	All four are permitted.
6	A	$500,000 − $360,000 = $140,000
7	B	$100,000 purchase price minus $80,000 retained earnings
8	C	$80,000 retained earnings minus $50,000 premium on purchase (or $50,000 nominal value minus PCP $20,000)
9	D	If a shareholder fails to pay a call his shares are forfeited and the company is not obliged to return his money.
10	C	$120,000/1,500,000. For this purpose the bonus issue is treated as having taken place at the beginning of the year.

24 Objective test answers: Accounting standards I

| 1 | A | $^3/_{10} \times \$3,000$ |
| 2 | D | $^2/_6 \times$ $3,000 |

3   B   3   Obligations under finance leases due after twelve months will be shown under non-current liabilities.

           4   An asset held under an operating lease is not capitalised by the lessee.

4   D   Adjusting events are shown in the financial statements, not the notes.

5   C $1,800,000 – $116,000 – $20,000 = $1,664,000

6   B   Discovery of fraud, error or impairment, which will have existed at the balance sheet date.

7   D   These have all occurred after the balance sheet date.

8   C   1   Contingent liability that is possible, therefore disclose.
           2   Contingent liability but remote, therefore no disclosure.
           3   Non-adjusting post balance sheet event, material therefore disclose.

9   B   IAS 37 excludes retraining and relocation of continuing staff from restructuring provisions.

10   A   All three criteria must be present.

25 Objective test answers: Accounting standards II

1   C   Item 1 is not correct – if it is probable and the amount can be estimated reliably, then it must be provided for.

2   C   Customers, suppliers and providers of finance are not related parties.

3   C   In a finance lease, the risks and rewards of ownership are transferred.

4   A

	$
Deposit	30,000
Instalments (8 × $20,000)	160,000
	190,000
Fair value	154,000
Interest	36,000

$$\text{Sum of the digits} = \frac{8 \times 9}{2} = 36$$

6 months to				
June X1	$^8/_{36} \times \$36,000$			
Dec X1	$^7/_{36} \times \$36,000$			
June X2	$^6/_{36} \times \$36,000$			
Dec X2	$^5/_{36} \times \$36,000$			
June X3	$^4/_{36} \times \$36,000$	=	$4,000
Dec X3	$^3/_{36} \times \$36,000$	=	$3,000
			$7,000

5   A

Finance lease account

	$m		$m
20X1 1 Jan deposit	4,000	Non-current assets	15,400
31 Dec – instalment	4,000	Interest 15% × $11,400	1,710
Balance c/d	9,110		
	17,110		17,110
		Balance b/d	9,110
20X2 31 Dec – instalment	4,000	Interest 15% × 9,110	1,366

31 December 20X1

Current liabilities = 4,000 – 1,366
= $2,634

6   D   The fire is non-adjusting as it does not clarify the 31 December value of the building. It is therefore only disclosed if it threatens the company's going concern status.

Again the customer is assumed to be insolvent at 31 December. We simply did not know this and therefore it is an adjusting event and it should be accrued for.

The answer would be B if the customer had become insolvent after the year end.

7   C   The decision to close the division was taken after the year end and therefore does not affect the accounts for the year to 30 June 20X6 even though the division was loss-making. Option A confirms the final price of a transaction entered into before the year end and is therefore an adjusting event. Option B provides evidence of a diminution in value of an investment held at the year end and is therefore an adjusting event. Option D provides evidence that the previous estimate of accrued profit was inaccurate and therefore an adjustment should be made.

8   C   1   As the board decision had not been communicated to customers and employees there is assumed to be no legal or constructive obligation therefore no provision should be made.

2   As refunds have been made in the past to all customers there is a valid expectation from customers that the refunds will be made therefore the amount should be provided for.

3   There is no present obligation to carry out the refurbishment therefore no provision should be made under IAS 37.

9   C   The general requirements of IAS 24 for related party status are that two or more parties are related if:

- one party has control of the other
- the parties are subject to common control
- one party has influence over the financial and operating policies of another party
- the parties are subject to influence from the same source.

An 10% investment in another company does not fall into any of these categories.

10   B   Members of the close family of any key management of an entity are presumed to be related parties.

26 Section B answers: Accounting Standards

(a)   (i)   **Accounting treatment required**

This is the accounting treatment required under IAS 37:

- A provision should be accrued in the financial statements where it is probable that a future event will confirm a loss which can be estimated with reasonable accuracy at the date on which the financial statements are approved by the directors. Where the outcome is that a loss is only possible, the contingent loss should not be accrued.

- Contingent gains should not be accrued in the financial statements. When the realisation of the gain becomes reasonably certain then such a gain is not a contingency and an accrual would be appropriate.

Applying these principles to each of the four court cases we arrive at the following accounting treatment.

P: **'Possible' contingent gain: ignore**.
Q: **'Probable' contingent gain: disclose** in a note to the accounts but do not accrue any profit.
R: **'Possible' contingent loss: disclose** in a note to the accounts.
S: **'Probable' contingent loss = provision**: accrue $40,000.

  (ii)   The only journal entry necessary is in respect of the accrual required for case S.

DEBIT	Income statement		$40,000
CREDIT	Provision for legal case	$40,000	

(b)   **Adjusting events** are events that provide further evidence of conditions that existed at the balance sheet date.

Examples of adjusting events include:

(i)   The subsequent determination of the purchase price or of the proceeds of sale of non-current assets purchased or sold before the year end

(ii)   The renegotiation of amounts owing by customers or the insolvency of a customer

(iii)   Amounts received or receivable in respect of insurance claims which were in the course of negotiation at the balance sheet date

Non-adjusting events are indicative of conditions that arose subsequent to the balance sheet date.

Examples of non-adjusting events might be:

(i)   Losses of non-current assets or inventories as a result of a catastrophe such as fire or flood

(ii)   Closing a significant part of the trading activities if this was not begun before the year end

(iii)   The value of an investment falls between the balance sheet date and the date the accounts are authorised

(c)   IAS 17 is an example of economic substance triumphing over legal form. In legal terms, with a finance lease, the lessor may be the owner of the asset, but the lessee enjoys all the risks and rewards which ownership of the asset would convey. This is the key element to IAS 17. The lessee is deemed to have an asset as they must maintain and run the asset through its useful life.

The lessee enjoys the future economic benefits of the asset as a result of entering into the lease. There is a corresponding liability which is the obligation to pay the instalments on the lease until it expires. Assets and liabilities cannot be netted off. If finance leases were treated in a similar manner to the existing treatment of operating leases then no asset would be recognised and lease payments would be expensed through the income statement as they were incurred. This is 'off balance sheet finance'. The company has assets in use and liabilities to lessors which are not recorded in the financial statements. This would be misleading to the user of the accounts and make it appear as though the assets which were recorded were more efficient in producing returns than was actually the case.

27 Evans

> **Pass marks.** Start by preparing an interest and repayment schedule for the finance lease. The first instalment is paid prior to any interest accruing.

Income statement extract

	20X3
	$
Expenses (note 1)	X
Finance cost (note 2)	1,171

Balance sheet extract

	20X3
	$
Non-current assets	
Property, plant & equipment (note 3)	X
Finance leases liabilities	X
Non-current liabilities	
Loan notes	X
Obligations under finance leases (note 4)	52,054
	X
	$
Current liabilities	
Trade payables	X
Obligations under finance leases (note 4)	
Due within one year	7,687
Finance charges payable (W2)	1,171
	X

Notes

1 *Expenses*

	20X3
	$
Depreciation of owned assets	X
Depreciation of assets held under finance leases	6,157
Hire of plant and machinery – operating leases	10,000
Other expenses	X
	X

2 *Finance cost*

	$
Finance charges payable – finance leases (W2)	1,171

3 *Non current assets*

	$	$
Property, plant and equipment	*Owned*	*Leased*
Cost at 1 January 20X3	X	0
Additions	X	61,570
Cost at 31 December 20X3	X	61,570
Accumulated depreciation at 1 January 20X3	X	0
Charge for the year	X	6,157
Accumulated depreciation at 31 December 20X3	X	6,157
Net book value at 31 December 20X3	X	55,413
Net book value at 1 January 20X3	X	0

4   *Finance lease liabilities*

The minimum lease payments to which the company was committed at 31 December 20X3 are as follows.

	$
Under one year	12,000
Two to five years	48,000
Over five years	15,000
	75,000
Less: Interest allocated to future periods	15,259
	59,741
Due within one year (W3)	7,687
Due after more than one year (W3)	52,054
	59,741

Workings

1   *Depreciation charge for the year*

	$
Cost of asset	61,570
Useful life	10 years
Depreciation charge	$6,157

2   *Interest on finance lease*

	$
Cash price	61,570
Instalment 1 October 20X3	(3,000)
	58,570
Interest October – December 20X3 (2%)	1,171
Balance 31 December 20X3	59,741
Instalment 1 January 20X4	(3,000)
	56,741
Interest January – March 20X4 (2%)	1,135
Balance 31 March 20X4	57,876
Instalment 1 April 20X4	(3,000)
	54,876
Interest April – June 20X4 (2%)	1,098
Balance 30 June 20X4	55,974
Instalment 1 July 20X4	(3,000)
	52,974
Interest July – September 20X4 (2%)	1,059
Balance 30 September 20X4	54,033
Instalment 1 October 20X4	(3,000)
	51,033
Interest October – December 20X4	1,021
	52,054

	$
Total payments 26 × $3,000 =	78,000
Cash price	61,570
Total interest	16,430

3   *Obligations under finance leases*

	$
Balance at 31 December 20X3	59,741
Due within one year [12,000 – (1,135 + 1,098 + 1,059 + 1,021)]	7,687
Due after one year	52,054

28 Newcars

> **Pass marks.** This question required a knowledge of IAS 24 and the ability to apply it in deciding whether two companies are related parties.

(a)   One of the key elements in determining whether **parties are related** is the concept of **control or influence** and whether parties are under common control or influence. It would appear that **Arthur is a related party** of both Newcars plc and Oldcars plc. He has more than a **20% shareholding** in each company and as such a **significant influence** over the companies would normally be **presumed**. To reinforce this he is also a member of the board of directors of both companies. As such Arthur would be presumed to be a related party of both companies unless it can be demonstrated otherwise.

This means that Newcars and Oldcars are subject to **significant influence** from a common source (Arthur). Arthur is a member of the key management personnel of Newcars and also exerts significant influence over Oldcars. Per IAS 24 Newcars and Oldcars are thus related parties.

(b)   Assuming that Newcars and Oldcars are related parties, then IAS 24 requires disclosure of names and transaction details. The following **disclosures** will be required.

   (i)   Each company must state the other's **name** as a transacting related party.

   (ii)   There must be a **description of the relationship** between them which would need to include mention of Arthur and that both companies are subject to influence from him.

   (iii)   A **description of the transactions** must be given.

   (iv)   The **amount** of the transactions must be disclosed. This can be given in total.

   (v)   **Any other elements** of the transactions that are necessary for an understanding of the financial statements must be disclosed. For example, any unusual trade terms or the fact that the sales were not made at an arm's length price if this was the case.

   (vi)   **Any amounts due to or from the other company** at the balance sheet date must be disclosed.

(c)   When a user of financial statements reads the financial statements they will **assume** that the **transactions are all at arm's length** and that the organisation has always acted in its own best interests. If there are transactions with **related parties** then these **assumptions may not be valid** and therefore it is necessary to provide users with enough information about the related parties, the relationship and the transactions in order that users can make **informed decisions** from the financial statements.

For example if transactions had taken place between two related parties and these sales were not at a fair market value then the sales or cost of sales figures might be distorted. The details of disclosure that are required by IAS 24 mean that a user can assess the effect of these transactions and adjust the figures accordingly in order to gain a view as to the true profitability of the business.

Even if the transactions have been at arm's length it is still **useful information** for users to know of the existence of any related parties and particularly if the relationship is such that the business can be compelled to enter into transactions that are not necessarily in its own best interests.

29 L Manufacturing

L: Income statement for the year ended 30 June 20X1

	$m
Sales revenue	755
Cost of sales (W1)	262
Gross profit	493
Distribution costs (W1)	51
Administrative expenses (W1)	46
Net interest cost	5
Profit before tax	391
Income tax expense (30 – 10)	20
Profit for the period	371

L: Balance sheet as at 30 June 20X1

	$m	$m
Assets		
Non-current assets		
Property, plant and equipment (W3)		497
Current assets		
Inventories	16	
Trade receivables	57	
Bank	45	
		118
Total assets		615
Equity and liabilities		
Equity		
Called up share capital	100	
Share premium	60	
Retained earnings (W2)	221	
		381
Non-current liabilities		
Loans	76	
Provision for warranties	35	
		111
Current liabilities		
Trade payables	13	
Taxation	30	
Declared dividend	80	
		123
Total equity and liabilities		615

Workings

1   *Cost of sales, admin and distribution*

	Cost of sales	Administrative expenses	Distribution costs
	$m	$m	$m
Per trial balance	208	22	51
Warranties	8		
Research costs		8	
Depreciation			
Land and buildings			
534 × 2%		11	
Equipment			
(46 − 26) × 25%		5	
Plant and machinery			
(282 − 99) × 25%	46		
	262	46	51

2   *Retained earnings*

	$m
Balance b/f	38
Change of accounting policy (equipment depreciation)	(12)
Dividend paid	(96)
Profit for the period	371
Dividend declared	(80)
Balance at 30 June 20X1	221

3   *Property, plant and equipment*

	Property	Equipment	Plant	Total
	$m	$m	$m	$m
Cost	534	46	282	862
Depreciation b/f	(178)	(26)	(99)	(303)
Depreciation charge (W1)	(11)	(5)	(46)	(62)
	345	15	137	497

30 PW

Income statement for the year ending 31 December 20X5

	$'000
Revenue	18,000
Cost of sales (W1)	(9,062)
Gross profit	8,938
Distribution costs (696 + 360)	(1,056)
Administrative expenses (W4)	(4,078)
Finance costs	(100)
Profit before tax	3,704
Income tax expense (210 – 10)	(200)
Profit for the period	3,504

Balance sheet as at 31 December 20X5

	$'000	$'000
Assets		
Non-current assets		
Property, plant and equipment (W5)		5,680
Intangible asset: patent		540
		6,220
Current assets		
Inventory	3,900	
Receivables (W7)	3,192	
Bank	400	
		7,492
Total assets		13,712
Equity and liabilities		
Equity		
Share capital: ordinary		800
preferred		1,200
Revaluation reserve		700
Retained earnings		4,356
Total equity		7,056
Non-current liabilities		
Loan stock 5%	2,000	
Deferred tax (240 – 10)	230	
		2,230
Current liabilities		
Trade payables	3,500	
Interest payable	50	
Dividends payable	216	
Taxation payable	210	
Legal claim	450	
		4,426
Total equity and liabilities		13,712

Statement of changes in equity

	Share capital $'000	Other reserves $'000	Retained earnings $'000	Total $'000
Balance at 31 December 20X4	2,000	1,300	1,100	4,400
Loss on revaluation of property		(600)		(600)
Net profit for the period			3,504	3,504
Dividends			(248)	(248)
Balance at 31 December 20X5	2,000	700	4,356	7,056

Workings

1   *Cost of sales*

		$'000
Opening inventory		4,300
Purchases		8,662
Closing inventory		(3,900)
		9,062

2   *Depreciation*

		$'000
Property	((9,200 – 600) × 10%)	860
Plant and equipment	((3,000 – 1,200) × 20%)	360

3   *Provision for doubtful receivables*

	$'000
Adjusted provision (3,400 – 40 × 5%)	168
Provision b/f	(200)
Reduction in provision	(32)

4   *Administrative expenses*

	$'000
Per trial balance	2,300
Rent and rates	700
Legal claim less provision	150
Impairment loss on patent	60
Property depreciation	860
Bad and doubtful receivables (40 – 32)	8
	4,078

5   *Property plant and equipment*

	Property	Plant	Total
	$'000	$'000	$'000
Cost	9,200	3,000	12,200
Revaluation loss	(600)		(600)
Accumulated depreciation:			
(3,500 + 860) (W2)	(4,360)		(4,360)
(1,200 + 360) (W2)		(1,560)	(1,560)
Net book value	4,240	1,440	5,680

6   *Retained earnings*

	$'000
Per trial balance	1,100
Net profit for the year	3,504
Dividends	(248)
	4,356

7   *Receivables*

	$'000
Per trial balance	3,400
Bad debt written off	(40)
Provision for doubtful receivables (W3)	(168)
	3,192

31 Objective test answers: Short-term finance I

1   C   Since the compounding is to be done at six-monthly intervals, 5% (half of 10%) will be added to the value on each occasion. There will be six additions of interest during the three years, and the following expression can therefore be used:

$S = X(1 + r)^6$

where: S = Value of the investment at the end of the period
         X = Initial sum invested
         r = Interest rate

x^2

In this case: S = $10,000(1 + 0.05)^6$
               S = \$13,400

A is calculated using 5% compounded annually
B is calculated using 10% compounded annually
D is calculated using 10% compounded six monthly

2   D   A property mortgage is generally for a term longer than five years, and this is therefore a long-term source of finance.

3   A   Interest is only paid on the amount borrowed, not on the full facility.

4   D   This is also known as a documentary credit.

           A bill of exchange (A) is drawn by one party on another (not necessarily by a bank). An export guarantee (B) is insurance against defaults on exports. A banker's draft (C) is a cheque drawn by a bank on one of its own bank accounts.

5   D   The currency in which the loan is denominated will have little, if any, effect on the credit risk.

6   B   Although the level of return is a factor in the decision, it is more important to minimise the risk to the original capital invested.

7   C   Deciding what credit limits customers should be given.

8   A   Short-term cash surpluses will not normally be invested in equities owing to the risks associated with achieving a return over a short period.

9   B   The Miller-Orr model relates to cash management, not to interest rates.

10   A   The value can be found using the following expression:

Present value = \$100 × year 1–5 annuity factor
                   = 100 × 3.993
                   ≈ \$400

B would be the value if the first date of payment was today, and the annuity was paid for a further five years.

32 Objective test answers: Short-term finance II

1   B   Treasury bills are issued by the Bank of England on behalf of the government, to raise short-term cash (mostly for 90 days). They are traded 'second hand' on the discount market, and carry a low rate of interest because they are risk free.

          Other money market instruments carry slightly higher rates of interest. A sterling CD (A) is issued by a bank, acknowledging that a certain sum of money that has been deposited with it will become available on a given date to the certificate holder. CDs are also traded, on the CD market. Local authority deposits (D) and finance house deposits (C) are time deposits with local authorities and finance houses respectively. Local authorities raise money for short-term cash needs and finance houses raise money for re-lending.

2   D   R, effective rate $= \dfrac{6\%}{12}$

                                $= 0.5\%$

          $S = X(1 + r)^n = \$14,000 (1 + 0.005)^{24} = \$15,780.$

          If you chose one of the other answers, you did not use the monthly rate.

3   A   The company will be retaining the majority of its delivery vehicles, and it is safe to assume that reasonably priced contracted-out alternatives are available. This sale should not damage the long-term profitability of the company.

          B is not correct. It can be assumed that the blending of pigments to go into the china products is a core activity of the business. This plant should not be sold in these circumstances.

          C is not correct. Such a patent is likely to be a key to securing the long-term future profitability of the company. It should not be sold to meet short-term needs.

          D is not the most appropriate option. A 60% stake constitutes a controlling interest in a company. It could therefore be unsafe to sell this shareholding.

4   A   r = monthly rate = 0.5%

          R = 1 + r

          Using $S = A \left(\dfrac{R^n - 1}{R - 1} \right)$

          $10,000 = A \left(\dfrac{(1.005)^{36} - 1}{1.005 - 1} \right)$

          A = \$254

5   D   Convertible loan stock is a longer term investment, and transaction costs will be too high for a short-term investment.

          The minimum term for a local authority deposit (A) is normally overnight, and longer-term arrangements can also be made.

          If the company is large enough to lend directly on the money markets (B), it will be able to negotiate overnight, daily or weekly terms.

          Treasury bills (C) have a term of 91 days to maturity. No interest as such is paid, but the bills can be sold at any time.

6   B   Present value of a perpetuity of $\$1 = 1/_r = 1/_{0.12} = 8.333.$

          $8.333 \times \$3,000 = \$25,000.$

7　　C　　The interest yield is the **gross yield** divided by the **market value of the stock** expressed as a percentage, in this case $(11,000 \times 10\%) \div 10,000$.

You possibly arrived at A by multiplying the coupon rate by the market value and dividing by the nominal value. This is incorrect.

B is not correct. 10% is the coupon rate on this bond.

D is not correct. 12% is the average market rate of return which is irrelevant to the calculation of the yield of an individual bond.

8　　D　　Effective rate $= \dfrac{10\%}{\text{Quarter}} = 2.5\%$ compounded quarterly

$2,000 \times (1.025)^{16} = \$2,969$

9　　C　　Inflation does erode the capital value of amounts borrowed, but this favours borrowers and disfavours lenders. The value of the capital that borrowers have to repay is reduced.

A is true. The effect of inflation on the different costs and revenues of an enterprise cannot be known with certainty.

B is true. The fact that different elements of costs and earnings streams may have inflated at different rates makes comparison between business sectors and divisions of a business problematic.

D is true. There have, in fact, been negative interest rates in Japan at times. Effectively, people have had to pay their bank a percentage of the amount deposited to hold their money there.

10　　A　　With an inverted yield curve (short-term interest yields higher than long-term yields), bond prices will eventually fall as longer term interest yields are forced upwards. If bond yields rise and bond prices fall, shareholders will want higher yields too and so share prices will fall. Higher yields result in lower prices, for both bonds and shares.

33 Objective test answers: Short-term finance III

1　　B　　Present value $= \dfrac{10,000}{\text{Perpetuity factor}} - 10,000$ (Discount factor year 1)

$$= \dfrac{10,000}{0.1} - 10,000 \,(0.909)$$

$$= \$90,909$$

2　　B　　Inflation rate $= \left(\dfrac{(1 + \text{money rate})}{(1 + \text{real rate})} \right) - 1$

Year 1 $= \left(\dfrac{(1 + 0.09)}{(1 + 0.04)} \right) - 1$

$$= 4.81\%$$

Year 2 $= \left(\dfrac{(1 + 0.1)}{1 + 0.05)} \right) - 1$

$$= 4.76\%$$

Average $= \sqrt{(1.0481)(1.0476)} - 1$

$$= 4.78\%$$

3   D   This reflects the greater reward expected on long-term bonds.

4   B   Both statements are true.

5   A   Present value $= \dfrac{100}{(1+r)^n}$

$$= \dfrac{100}{(1+0.1)^{10}}$$

$$= \$39$$

6   D   Unsecured short-term loan notes issued by companies.

7   B   Terminal value $= X(1+r)^n$
$$= 100{,}000\,(1+0.08)^5$$
$$= \$146{,}933$$

8   A   It is a method of providing medium-term export finance.

9   C   Certificates of deposit are negotiable instruments.

10   B   Venture capital organisations may provide loan finance as well as equity finance to a company. They do not normally invest in established (stock market) companies.

34 Section B answers: Short-term Finance

Pass marks. You would get credit for explaining your rationale and drawing a conclusion. A time line diagram, showing what amounts were available in each period, would have helped ensure that you have covered all the possibilities.

(a)   **Short-term deposits**

Since interest rates are forecast to rise, the best solution is likely to be one in which only **short-term deposits** are made, thus allowing advantage to be taken of the rise in rates. Options structured in this way include the following.

	Amount $'000	Month invested	Period Months	Rate %	Income $
1	2,000	0	2	7.3	24,333
	6,000	2	2	8.0	80,000
	4,000	4	2	8.3	55,333
	Transaction costs				(300)
					159,366
2	2,000	0	4	7.4	49,333
	4,000	2	4	8.1	108,000
	Transaction costs				(200)
					157,133
3	2,000	0	4	7.4	49,333
	4,000	2	2	8.0	53,333
	4,000	4	2	8.3	55,333
	Transaction costs				(300)
					157,699

	Amount	Month invested	Period	Rate	Income
	$'000		Months	%	$
4	2,000	0	2	7.3	24,333
	2,000	2	2	8.0	26,667
	4,000	2	4	8.1	108,000
	Transaction costs				(300)
					158,700
5	2,000	0	6	7.5	75,000
	2,000	2	4	8.1	54,000
	2,000	2	2	8.0	26,667
	Transaction costs				(300)
					155,367
6	2,000	0	6	7.5	75,000
	4,000	2	2	8.0	53,333
	2,000	4	2	8.3	27,667
	Transaction costs				(300)
					155,700

It can be seen that Option 1 yields the best return.

(b) The spread will be calculated using the formula:

$$\text{Spread} = 3 \left(\frac{\frac{3}{4} \times \text{transaction cost} \times \text{variance of cash flows}}{\text{interest rate}} \right)^{1/3}$$

This gives: $3 \left(\dfrac{\frac{3}{4} \times 25 \times 9{,}000{,}000}{0.000236} \right)^{1/3} = 26{,}827$ 6.33 $\$C481$.

(variance of cashflows = standard deviation^2)

With a lower limit of $15,000 and a spread of $26,827, the upper limit of cash will be $41,827.

When the cash balance falls to $15,000 or reaches $41,827, cash will be transferred into or out of the account in order to bring the balance back to the **return point**. This is calculated as:

Lower limit + (spread × $^1/_3$)

This enables calculation of **how much** cash should be transferred. In this case the return point is:

15,000 + (26,827 × $^1/_3$) = $23,942

So, when the balance falls to $15,000, $8,942 will be transferred in to restore the balance to $23,942. When the balance reaches $41, 827. $17,885 will be transferred out to bring the balance back down to $23,942.

(c) **Features of an overdraft**

An **overdraft** is a negative balance on a current account at a bank. This constitutes borrowing and, because the balance will vary daily, the **interest** on the borrowing is normally computed on a **daily basis** at an **agreed rate**. A **maximum limit** to the overdraft is agreed with the bank and above this limit penalty **charges** will apply. In theory, the overdraft can be **cancelled immediately** if the bank is not happy with the company's **creditworthiness**. An overdraft can be **unsecured**, or **secured** on company assets or the personal assets of the proprietors.

The major advantage of an overdraft is that the company only pays interest when the overdraft is being used, in contrast to a bank loan.

Importance of overdraft

The overdraft is a key source of finance for working capital because of its **flexibility:** the finance varies automatically up to the agreed limit, enabling the company to handle peaks and troughs in cash flows without incurring excess interest charges. The potential disadvantage for an expanding company is that the **overdraft limit** may have to be **frequently renegotiated**. There is also a tendency for expanding companies to ignore the need to underpin their growth with longer term finance.

(d) **Alternatives to overdraft**

When considering alternatives to the bank overdraft, it is essential to consider the need for longer term funds (loans or equity funds) to **finance** the **permanent element** of working capital. Although such funds may be more expensive than short term finance, they provide a longer term stability for planning.

Short-term bank loans

A short-term bank loan (eg six months) can be arranged to **cover** a **forecast cash deficit**. The disadvantage compared with the overdraft is that the **interest is chargeable** on the **full amount** of the loan even if the finance is not required for part of the period.

Debt factoring

A **specialist organisation** will **collect the company's debts** and **advance cash**, effectively on the security of the company's receivables. The effective cost of the finance is sometimes difficult to compute but, for an expanding company, an advantage over overdrafts is that the source of finance effectively grows with the receivables ledger.

Discounting of invoices and bills of exchange

The company **presents invoices** or **bills of exchange** to the bank in return for immediate cash, slightly less than the face value (ie discounted). When the customers pay, the cash goes direct to the bank. The discount represents the **effective interest** on the funds advanced.

Supplier finance

Some suppliers will provide **extended credit periods** on inventory, or alternatively finance can be raised from finance houses on the security of inventory. Alternatively the company may exploit its relationships with suppliers by taking longer periods of credit. Unlike with an overdraft, the supplier may not charge any interest, but the company may lose **early payment discounts** and **supplier goodwill**.

Evaluation of different sources

The key to evaluating these different sources of finance is to **compute the true annual percentage interest rate** implicit in each arrangement and to quantify other **relevant cash flows**, such as administration costs, variations to selling prices and the likely effect on bad debts. Other issues which are less easy to quantify include the effect on customer, supplier and lender loyalty.

35 DF

(a) **Cost of discount**

The **percentage cost** of an **early settlement discount** to the company giving it can be estimated by the formula:

$$\left(\frac{100}{100 - d} \right)^{\frac{365}{t}} - 1$$

Where d is the size of discount (%)

t is the reduction in payment period in days necessary to achieve discount

d = 3%

t = 90 − 10 = 80

$$\% \text{ cost } = \left(\frac{100}{100 - 3} \right)^{\frac{365}{80}} - 1$$

$$= 14.9\%$$

The **annual equivalent rate of interest** in offering a 3% cash discount is therefore 14.9%.

Offer of discount

Other factors that DF should take into account before deciding on whether to offer a discount include:

(i) The **attractiveness** of the **discount** to FF, and the probability that it will be taken up

(ii) Whether the **discount** will encourage FF to **purchase larger volumes** than it would if the discount was not available

(iii) The interest **other customers** might show in taking a discount

(iv) The possibility of **withdrawing** from the discount arrangement without loss of FF's goodwill in the future

(b) To: Shareholders in DF
From: Management Accountant
Date: 11 December 20X1
Subject: Alternative methods of financing current assets

Introduction

The contract to supply FF means that DF will need to make a **significant additional permanent investment in current assets** (in the form of additional inventories and higher receivable balances). There will also be an additional temporary element which **fluctuates** with the level of sales. This will increase the amount of money needed by the company to finance these assets. There are a number of different sources of finance that could be considered.

Bank loan

A bank loan would normally be for a **fixed amount of money** for a fixed term and at a fixed rate of interest. The **size of this loan** and the **quality of security** available will be key factors in determining whether the bank is willing to make a further advance to cover the investment in current assets.

Advantages of bank loan

(i) **Bank finance** is **cheaper** than the cost of allowing a 3% **settlement discount**, and is also likely to be cheaper than using debt factoring or invoice discounting.

(ii) The **loan** can be **negotiated** for a **fixed term** and a **fixed amount**, and this is less risky than for example using an overdraft, which is repayable on demand.

Disadvantages of bank loan

(i) The company will have to **pay interest** on the **full amount of the loan** for the entire period. This could make it more expensive in absolute terms than using an alternative source of finance where interest is only payable on the amount outstanding.

(ii) The loan will **increase the level** of the company's **financial gearing**. This means that there could be greater volatility in the returns attributable to the ordinary shareholders.

(iii) The bank is likely to **require security**.

Overdraft

An overdraft is a form of lending that is **repayable on demand**. The bank grants the customer a **facility** up to a certain limit, and the customer can take advantage of this as necessary. Overdrafts are essentially short-term finance, but are renewable and may become a near-permanent source.

Advantages of overdraft

The attraction of using an overdraft to finance current assets is that **interest** is only **payable** on the **amount of the facility actually in use** at any one time. This means that the **effective cost of the overdraft** will be **lower** than that of the **bank loan**.

Disadvantages of overdraft

The main drawback to using an overdraft is that it will be **repayable on demand**, and therefore the company is in a more vulnerable position than it would be if a bank loan were used instead.

Loan stock

Loan stock finance is generally for the long-term and as such may be appropriate to finance the **non-current assets** and **permanent element of current assets** of DF.

Advantages of loan stock

(i) Loan stocks are a **cheaper form of finance** than shares because loan interest is tax-deductible.

(ii) Loan stocks should be **more attractive** to investors because they will be **secured** against the assets of the company.

(iii) **Issue costs** should be **lower** for loan stock than for shares.

(iv) There is **no immediate change** in the existing structure of control.

(v) There is **no immediate dilution** in earnings and dividends per share.

Disadvantages of loan stock

(i) **Interest** has to be paid on debt no matter what the company's profits in a year are. In particular DF may find itself locked into long-term debt at unfavourable rates of interest. The company is not legally obliged to pay dividends.

(ii) Money has to be made available for **redemption** or **repayment** of debt.

(iii) The Wong family may want a **higher dividend** from the company to compensate them for the **increased financial risk** of introducing debt.

Debt factoring

Factoring is an arrangement to have **debts collected** by a **factor company**, which advances a proportion of the money it is due to collect. Services offered by the factor would normally include administration of the receivables ledger and protection against bad debts.

Benefits of factoring

(i) **Growth** is **effectively financed through sales**, which provide the security to the factor. DF would not have to provide the additional security that might be required by the bank.

(ii) The **managers** of the business will **not** have to **spend time** on the problem of **slow paying customers**.

(iii) **Administration costs** will be **reduced** since the company will not have to run its own sales ledger department.

Disadvantages of factoring

(i) The **level of finance** is **geared** to the **level of sales**; in other words, finance lags sales. In practice, DF will need finance ahead of sales in order to build up sufficient inventories to meet demand.

(ii) Factoring may be **more expensive** than bank finance. Service charges are generally around 2% of total invoice value, in addition to finance charges at levels comparable to bank overdraft rates.

(iii) The fact that customers will be making payments direct to the factor may present a **negative picture** of the firm.

Invoice discounting

Invoice discounting is the **purchase of a selection of invoices**, at a discount. The discounter does **not take over** the **administration** of the client's sales ledger, and the arrangement is purely for the advance of cash.

Advantages of discounting

The arrangement is thus a **purely financial transaction** that can be used to release working capital, and therefore shares some of the benefits of factoring in that **further security** is **not required**. The discounter will make an assessment of the risk involved, and only good quality invoices will be purchased, but this should not be a problem to DF since FF is a large well established company.

Disadvantages of discounting

The main disadvantage is that **invoice discounting** is likely to be **more expensive** than any of the other alternatives. It is normally only used to cover a temporary cash shortage, and not for the routine provision of working capital.

Other options

(i) Finance can be obtained by **delaying payment to suppliers**. In theory this is potentially a **cheap source of finance.** The main disadvantage may be a **loss of supplier goodwill,** at a time when the company needs supplier co-operation to fulfil the new order.

(ii) Although we are told that **increased inventory levels** will be needed to **fulfil FF's requirements,** there may be scope for **reducing the inventory levels** necessary to fulfil other customers' requirements.

Conclusions

Of the options considered, factoring or some form of bank finance is likely to be the most appropriate. The final decision must take into account the full cost implications, and not just the relative rates of interest on the finance. DF must also consider the effect of the type of finance selected on the balance sheet, and the type of security that will be required. This could also impact on the ability of the company to raise further finance in the future.

36 Objective test answers: Working capital management I

1   A   Short-term finance is matched to fluctuating current assets. B is a conservative policy, while C and D are aggressive policies.

2   B   This is the ratio of current assets to current liabilities. C is wrong as the five year bank loan would not normally be included with current liabilities. A is the quick ratio (excludes inventories).

3   D   This is the ratio of current assets excluding inventories to current liabilities. C is wrong as the loan stock would normally be included with long-term liabilities. B is the current ratio.

4   D   Current assets: current liabilities $= 2{:}1$

Current liabilities $= 0.5 \times 100{,}000$
$$= 50{,}000$$

Working capital $= 100{,}000 - 50{,}000$
$$= 50{,}000$$

Working capital is 20% of capital employed

Capital employed $= \dfrac{50{,}000}{0.2}$

$$= 250{,}000$$

Sales: capital employed $= \dfrac{600{,}000}{250{,}000}$

$$= 2.4{:}1$$

5   A   The credit cycle begins with the receipt of the customer's order. Price negotiations take place prior to this point.

6   A $365 \times$ year end receivables $\div$ credit sales. B is calculated adding bad debts to total receivables. D is calculated using total sales, not credit sales. C makes both mistakes.

7   D   (Total sales $\times$ 2%) + $5,000. 'Without recourse' means that the factor carries the risk of the bad debts.

8   A   C ignores the effect of the changes on the level of inventories and payables. B and D are wrong because they assume that the financing cost will increase not decrease.

Current level of receivables $= \$2m \times {}^{90}/_{365} = \$493{,}151$
New level of receivables $= \$2m \times 80\% \times {}^{30}/_{365} = \$131{,}507$

Current financing requirement $= \$500{,}000 + \$493{,}150 - \$30{,}000 = \$963{,}150$
New financing requirement $= \$400{,}000 + \$131{,}507 - \$24{,}000 = \$507{,}507$

Reduction in financing requirement $= \$963{,}150 - \$507{,}507 = \$455{,}643$
Reduction in financing cost $= \$455{,}643 \times 10\% = \$45{,}564$ (round to $46,000)

9   C   Current ratio $= \dfrac{\text{Current assets}}{\text{Current liabilities}}$ and total current assets are unchanged.

10   B   Return on discount = $\left(\dfrac{100}{100-d}\right)^{\frac{12}{m}}$

where   d = % size of the discount
         m = reduction in payment period in months necessary to achieve discount

(see Formulae to learn in front pages)

Return on X's discount = $\left(\dfrac{100}{97}\right)^{4} - 1 = 12.96\%$

Return on Y's discount = $\left(\dfrac{100}{96}\right)^{3} - 1 = 13.02\%$

(Note that the formula here uses months rather than days. In this case, months is more accurate.)

37 Objective test answers: Working capital management II

1   C   The annual cost can be found using the following expression:

$$I = \left(\dfrac{100}{100-d}\right)^{\frac{365}{t}} - 1$$

where   i = implied annual cost in interest per annum
         d = the % size of the discount
         t = reduction in payment period in days which would be necessary to obtain the discount

In this case:

$$I = \left(\dfrac{100}{100-2.5}\right)^{\frac{365}{60-10}} - 1$$

$$= 20.3\%$$

2   D   Standing orders are used to make regular payments of a fixed amount. Payments to trade suppliers will vary in amount, and therefore a different method would be more appropriate.

3   B   The other main difference is that the payment can be for a variable amount each time, rather than for a fixed amount.

4   B

		$
Cash sales	February 220,000 × 1.1 × 25%	60,500
Credit sales	December 220,000 × $\dfrac{1}{1.1}$ × 75% × 48%	72,000
	January 220,000 × 75% × 50%	82,500
		215,000

If you chose A, you split sales incorrectly. If you chose C, you did not increase sales over time. If you chose D, you did not take the bad debts into account.

5 D The EOQ model can be used:

$$EOQ = \sqrt{\frac{(2C_oD)}{C_h}}$$

where EOQ = the reorder quantity
        C_o = cost of making one order
        C_h = holding cost per unit of inventory per year
        D = usage in units per year

In this case:

$$EOQ = \sqrt{\frac{(2 \times 25 \times 10,000)}{0.50}}$$

$$= 1,000$$

6 D $$EOQ = \sqrt{\frac{(2 \times 100 \times 40,000)}{2}}$$

$$= 2,000$$

Since 40,000 wheels are required each year, 20 orders will be placed.

7 A $$EOQ = \sqrt{\frac{(2 \times 400 \times 160,000)}{8}}$$

$$= 4,000$$

Since 160,000 wheels are required each year, 40 orders will be placed.

Orders will therefore be placed every 52 ÷ 40 = 1.3 weeks.

8 D Although the purchasing manager may sanction payments to suppliers, the payment will normally be raised by the finance department.

9 B A standing order is the simplest method to use for regular fixed payments. It is preferred to a direct debit because the person making the payment retains control over the amount paid.

10 D A banker's draft cannot be stopped or cancelled once it is issued, and is effectively a cheque drawn on the bank. It is accepted by most people as being as good as cash, but has none of the inconvenience that cash would involve in a payment of this size.

---

38 Objective test answers: Working capital management III

1 D Say Current assets are $75,000

Current liabilities are $50,000

30% decrease in both will be $15,000. Current assets will then be $60,000, current liabilities $35,000, and current ratio will be 60:35 = 1.71. This is an increase of less than 30%.

2 D No cash movements have taken place, and inventory levels are the same.

3 D Greater inventory levels lessen the risk of running out of inventory.

4 B Change in payables = Purchases – Cash paid

15,000 = 360,000 – Cash paid
Cash paid = $345, 000

5   B   The annual cash requirement is $120,000.

The interest cost of holding cash is 3% (5% − 2%)

Optimum amount to transfer $= \sqrt{\dfrac{2 \times 120,000 \times 50}{0.03}} = 20,000$

So $20,000 should be transferred in each transaction.

6   C   Cash cycle = Inventory turnover + Receivables turnover − Payables turnover

$$= \left(\left(\frac{6}{36 \times 0.8} \right) \times 365 \right) + \left(\left(\frac{8}{36} \right) \times 365 \right) - \left(\left(\frac{3}{36 \times 0.8} \right) \times 365 \right)$$

= 119 days

7   A $\text{EOQ} = \sqrt{\dfrac{2C_0 D}{C_h}}$

$$= \sqrt{\frac{2 \times 10 \times 36,000}{2}}$$

= 600 units

No of orders $= \dfrac{36,000}{600}$

= 60

8   C   Non-current assets are sold. The other answers may have limited or no effect on working capital.

9   B   BACS is mostly concerned with processing payrolls and transactions involving standing orders and direct debits. A is a definition of CHAPS.

10   D   Spread $= 3 \left[\dfrac{\frac{3}{4} \times \text{transaction cost} \times \text{variance of cash flows}}{\text{Interest rates}} \right]^{\frac{1}{3}}$

$$= 3 \times \left(\frac{\frac{3}{4} \times 20 \times 250,000}{0.00025} \right)^{\frac{1}{3}}$$

= $7,400

Maximum level = 7,400 + 1,000

= 8,400

39 Section B answers: Working Capital Management

(a)   **Length of operating cycle** $= 365 \left(\dfrac{\text{Average raw materials}}{\text{Purchases}} + \dfrac{\text{Average finished goods}}{\text{Cost of sales}} + \dfrac{\text{Average receivables}}{\text{Sales}} + \dfrac{\text{Average payables}}{\text{Purchases}} \right)$

$$= 365 \left(\frac{0.5(55 + 80)}{850} + \frac{185}{1,830} + \frac{0.5(114 + 200)}{1,996} - \frac{0.5(50 + 70)}{850} \right)$$

= 29.0 days + 36.9 days + 28.7 days −25.8 days

= 68.8 days

(b) The main factors to consider are:

(i) **Matching**

The traditional view is that **non-current assets** should be **financed** by **long-term sources** of **finance** and **current assets** by a **mixture of long-term and short-term sources**. Thus a company with a greater proportion of non-current assets and permanent current assets is also likely to have a higher proportion of long-term debt in its capital structure.

(ii) **Cost**

The company will seek to **minimise its cost of capital**. The cost of debt capital will be made up of the interest cost of the debt and the transaction costs incurred in arranging the finance. Short-term debt will need to be renegotiated more frequently and this will give rise to recurring transaction costs.

The **relative interest rates** carried by long-term and short-term debt will **vary over time** according to supply and demand and to market expectations of interest rate changes. Rates are generally higher on long-term loans than on short-term since the level of risk faced by the lender that interest rates may rise before repayment is due is higher.

(iii) **Security**

The company may find it easier to **raise short-term finance** with **low security** than long-term finance. However the cost of such loans is likely to be higher.

(iv) **Risk**

In opting for short-term debt, the company faces the risk that it may **not** be able to **renegotiate the loan** on such good terms, or even at all, when the repayment date is reached. Long-term loans are thus less risky. The fact that a firm is seeking a large amount of short-term debt, and is frequently going back to the market, may lead to a loss of confidence in the firm on the part of investors.

(v) **Flexibility**

Long-term debt may carry **early repayment penalties** if it is found that the loan is no longer needed or a more attractive form of finance becomes available. Short-term debt is **more flexible** since it allows the firm to react to interest rate changes and to avoid being locked into an expensive long-term fixed rate commitment at a time when rates are falling. Many firms use overdraft finance – a form of short-term credit whose amount varies from day to day according to the needs of the company. This avoids the company having to pay interest on funds which it does not actually need.

Pass marks. Note that sales are invoiced at the **end** of the month.

(c)

	October $'000	November $'000	December $'000	January $'000	Total $'000
Class A customers (W1)					
October sales			50	30	80
November sales				75	75
			50	105	155
Class B customers (W2)					
October sales		36	15	6	57
November sales			48	20	68
December sales				24	24
		36	63	50	149
Total cash received		36	113	155	304

Workings

1   *Class A customers*

October sales
50% received December $100,000 × 50% = $50,000
30% received January $100,000 × 30% = 30,000

November sales
50% received January $150,000 × 50% = $75,000

2   *Class B customers*

October sales
60% received November $60,000 × 60% = $36,000
25% received December $60,000 × 25% = $15,000
10% received January $60,000 × 10% = $6,000

November sales
60% received December $80,000 × 60% = $48,000
25% received January $80,000 × 25% = $20,000

December sales
60% received January $40,000 × 60% = $24,000

(d)   (i)   **Working capital management**

The **net working capital** of a business can be defined as its **current assets less** its **current liabilities**. The management of working capital is concerned with ensuring that **sufficient liquid resources** are **maintained** within the business. For the majority of businesses, particularly manufacturing businesses, trade payables will form the major part of the current liabilities figure.

Trade credit period

It follows that the **trade credit period** taken will be a major determinant of the working capital requirement of the company. This is calculated (in days) as the total value of **trade payables divided** by the level of **credit purchases** × 365.

Cash conversion cycle

A link can be made between working capital and liquidity by means of the **cash conversion cycle**. This measures the length of time that elapses between a firm **paying** for its **various purchases** and **receiving payment** for its **sales**. It can be calculated as the receivable days plus the inventory period less the trade credit period, and it measures the length of time for which net current assets must be financed.

(ii)   **Use of trade credit**

For many firms, trade payables provide a very **important source** of **short-term credit**. Since very few companies currently impose interest charges on overdue accounts, taking extended credit can appear to be a very cheap form of short-term finance. However, such a policy entails some risks and costs that are not immediately apparent, as follows.

(1)   If discounts are being forgone, the **effective cost** of this should be evaluated – it may be more beneficial to shorten the credit period and take the discounts.

(2)   If the company gains a reputation for slow payment this will **damage its credit standing** and it may find it difficult to obtain credit from new suppliers in the future.

(3)   Suppliers who are having to wait for their money may seek recompense in other ways, for example by raising prices or by placing a lower priority on new orders. Such actions could do **damage** to both the **efficiency and profitability** of the company.

(4) Suppliers may place the company **'on stop'** until the account is paid. This can jeopardise supplies of essential raw materials which in turn could cause production to stop: this will obviously provide the company with a high level of unwanted costs.

40 STK

Pass marks. (a) should be a standard economic order quantity calculation but make sure you use the right figure for ordering costs.

In (b) (i) you are required to incorporate a safety inventory into the calculations. You should therefore state clearly how you arrive at the average stock figure that you use, since there is more than one possible approach. The suggested solution to (b) (ii) is much fuller than is required. However, you should think widely about the implications of using a remote supplier, and take into account things you have learned from other sources.

(a) The economic order quantity (EOQ) is calculated as follows:

$$\text{Economic Order Quantity EOQ} = \sqrt{\frac{2C_oD}{C_h}}$$

Where C_o = cost of placing an order
D = annual demand
C_h = cost of holding one unit in inventory for one year

In the case of SSS:

C_o = \$200 per order (the delivery charge)

D = 10,000 units

C_h = \$4 + (\$400 × 3%) = \$16 per unit per year

$$\text{EOQ} = \sqrt{\frac{2 \times 200 \times 10,000}{16}}$$

= 500 units

The optimal order size for purchases from SSS is therefore 500 units.

(b) (i) To determine which supplier should be chosen, it is necessary to **compare the total annual purchasing costs** for each supplier.

Before this can be done we must first establish the purchasing costs if RRR Ltd is used.

The first step is to calculate the EOQ to determine whether this is above or below the minimum order size:

C_o = \$500

D = 10,000

C_h = \$4 + (\$398 × 3%) = \$15.94

$$\text{EOQ} = \sqrt{\frac{2 \times 500 \times 10,000}{15.94}}$$

= 792 units

This is below the minimum order size, and therefore it must be assumed that STK would order in batches of 1,000 units.

Average level of inventory if RRR is used = $\dfrac{\text{Order size}}{2}$ + Buffer inventory

$$= \dfrac{1{,}000}{2} + 600$$

$$= 1{,}100$$

If SSS Ltd is used, no buffer inventory will be necessary. The average level of inventory at any one time will therefore be just Order size/2, 500/2 = 250 units.

We can now compare the annual purchasing costs for the two suppliers:

		SSS		*RRR*
		$		$
Number of units purchased	10,000		10,000	
Unit price	$400		$398	
Total price paid		4,000,000		3,980,000
Number of orders placed				
(10,000/order quantity)	20		10	
Cost of placing one order	$200		$500	
Total ordering cost		4,000		5,000
Average inventory level	250		1,100	
Unit inventory holding cost	$16.00		$15.94	
Total inventory holding cost		4,000		17,534
Total annual cost		4,008,000		4,002,534

RRR should be the sole supplier because the annual purchasing costs are $5,466 lower than if SSS is used.

(b)   (ii)   **Factors that STK should take into account**

Potential costs of running out of inventory

In view of the fact that there is uncertainty about the lead times from RRR, these costs should be evaluated.

Safety inventory level

STK should consider whether this is sufficient in the light of possible variations in demand and lead time.

Dual sourcing

STK might consider trying to **order from both suppliers** for a while until it is confident that RRR can deliver reliably.

Quality of new supplier's products

STK should consider whether the quality is as good and **reliable** from RRR as it is from SSS.

Exchange risk

It is not clear whether RRR will be invoicing in sterling or in a different currency. If it is **not** invoicing in sterling then **STK** will face **exchange risks.** If RRR is invoicing in sterling, then it will carry the exchange risks. However, if there is a significant movement in the exchange rates this may affect RRR's ability to **continue to supply at the original price**.

Terms and conditions

STK should check whether the terms offered by the two suppliers are comparable, in particular the **payment terms** and the **period** for which the **prices quoted** are valid.

Local conditions

STK should investigate whether there are any local **political or economic conditions** in the country where RRR is based that could affect its ability to continue to supply reliably and at the price quoted.

Mock Exams

CIMA
Paper P7 (Managerial)
Financial Accounting and Tax Principles

Mock Exam 1

Question Paper	
Time allowed	**3 hours**
This paper is divided into three sections	
Section A	**Answer ALL sub-questions in this section**
Section B	**Answer ALL of the six short answer questions**
Section C	**Answer ONE question out of two**

DO NOT OPEN THIS PAPER UNTIL YOU ARE READY TO START UNDER EXAMINATION CONDITIONS

SECTION A – 50 marks

Answer ALL sub-questions in this section

Answer each of the sub-questions numbered from 1.1 to 1.25. Each is worth 2 marks

Question 1

1.1 A has a taxable profit of $100,000. The book depreciation was $10,000 and the tax allowable depreciation was $25,000. What was the accounting profit? 85K. ✗ 115

1.2 Company W makes an accounting profit of $300,000 during the year. This includes non-taxable income of $10,000 and depreciation of $35,000. In addition, $5,000 of the expenses are disallowable for tax purposes. If the tax allowable depreciation totals $30,000, what is the taxable profit?

- A $290,000
- B $295,000
- Ⓒ $300,000
- D $310,000

✓

1.3 Which of the following is a source of tax rules?

- A International accounting standards
- Ⓑ Supranational tax agreements
- C Local company legislation
- D Domestic accounting practice

✓

1.4 In no more than 15 words, complete the following sentence:

'An indirect tax is one that ....' 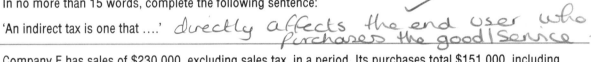 *directly affects the end user who purchases the good/service* ✓

1.5 Company E has sales of $230,000, excluding sales tax, in a period. Its purchases total $151,000, including sales tax. Purchases of $10,000 are zero rated. Sales tax is 17.5%. What is the sales tax payable for the period?

- A $7,830
- Ⓑ $9,580
- C $13,825
- D $19,250

✗ D

1.6 A company is resident in Country A. It has a branch in Country B. The branch has taxable profits of $100,000, on which tax of $15,000 is paid. The tax rate in Country A is 20% and there is a double taxation treaty between Countries A and B that allows tax relief on the credit basis. If the company has total taxable profits, including those of the branch of $150,000, how much tax will it pay in Country A?

- Ⓐ $10,000
- B $15,000
- C $20,000
- D $30,000

30k
20k. ✗

International financial Reporting Interepretations. Committee.

1.7 A committee of the International Accounting Standards Board (IASB) is known as the IFRIC.

What does the IFRIC stand for?

A International Financial Reporting Issues Committee
B International Financial Recommendations and Interpretations Committee
C International Financial Reporting Interpretations Committee
D International Financial Reporting Issues Council

XC

1.8 The IASB's Framework for the Preparation and Presentation of Financial Statements (Framework) lists the qualitative characteristics of financial statements.

Which THREE of the following are NOT included in the principle qualitative characteristics listed by the Framework?

(i)	Comparability	(v)	Understanding
(ii)	Relevance	(vi)	Matching
(iii)	Prudence ✗	(vii)	Consistency ✗
(iv)	Reliability		

A (i), (iii) and (vii)
B (i), (ii) and (v)
C (iii), (vi) and (vii)
D (iii), (iv) and (vi)

*Relevance ✓
Reliability ✓
Materiality
Comparability
Understandability*

1.9 Which of the following is NOT regarded as a related party of an enterprise by IAS 24 *Related party disclosures?*

A Directors of the enterprise
B A bank providing a loan to the enterprise
C The enterprise's employee pension fund
D A close relative of a director of the enterprise

1.10 IAS 10 *Events after the balance sheet date* distinguishes between adjusting and non-adjusting events.

Which of the following is an adjusting event?

A One month after the year end, a customer lodged a claim for $1,000,000 compensation. The customer claimed to have suffered permanent mental damage as a result of the fright she had when one of the enterprise's products malfunctioned and exploded. The outcome of the court case cannot be predicted at this stage.

B There was a dispute with the workers and all production ceased one week after the year end.

C A fire destroyed all of the enterprise's inventory in its furnished goods warehouse two weeks after the year end.

D Inventory valued at the year end at $20,000 was sold one month later for $15,000.

1.11 X signed a finance lease agreement on 1 October 20X2. The lease provided for five annual payments, in arrears, of $20,000. The fair value of the asset was agreed at $80,000.

Using the sum of digits method, how much should be charged to the income statement for the finance cost in the year to 30 September 20X3?

A $4,000
B $6,667
C $8,000
D $20,000

1.12 D purchased a non-current asset on 1 April 20X0 for $200,000. The asset attracted writing down tax allowances at 25% on the reducing balance. Depreciation was 10% on the straight-line basis. Assume income tax is at 30%.

The deferred tax balance for this asset at 31 March 20X3 is:

A $9,000
B $16,688
C $27,000
D $55,625

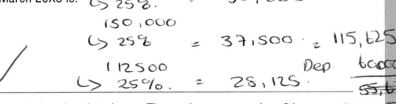

1.13 C started work on a contract to build a dam for a hydro-electric scheme. The work commenced on 24 October 20X1 and is scheduled to take four years to complete. C recognises profit on the basis of the certified percentage of work completed. The contract price is $10 million.

An analysis of C's records provided the following information:

Year to 30 September	20X2	20X3
Percentage of work completed and certified in year	30%	25%
	$'000	$'000
Total cost incurred during the year	2,900	1,700
Estimated cost of remaining work to complete contract	6,000	3,900
Total payments made for the cost incurred during the year	2,500	2,000

How much profit should C recognise in its income statement for the years ended:

	30 September 20X2	30 September 20X3
	$'000	$'000
A	100	375
B	330	375
C	330	495
D	500	825

1.14 F's year end is 30 June. F purchased a non-current asset for $50,000 on 1 July 20X0.

Depreciation was provided at the rate of 20% per annum on the straight-line basis. There was no forecast residual value.

On 1 July 20X2, the asset was revalued to $60,000 and then depreciated on a straight-line basis over its remaining useful life which was unchanged. On 1 July 20X3, the asset was sold for $35,000.

In addition to the entries in the non-current asset account and allowance for depreciation account, which TWO of the following statements correctly record the entries required on disposal of the non-current asset?

(i)   Debit income statement with a loss on disposal of $5,000.
(ii)   Credit income statement with a gain on disposal of $25,000.
(iii)   Transfer $60,000 from revaluation reserve to retained earnings as a movement on reserves.

(iv)   Transfer $30,000 from revaluation reserve to retained earnings as a movement on reserves.
(v)   Transfer $30,000 from revaluation reserve to income statement.
(vi)   Transfer $60,000 from revaluation reserve to income statement.

A   (i) and (iv)
B   (ii) and (iii)
C   (i) and (v)
D   (ii) and (vi)

1.15   S announced a rights issue of 1 for every 5 shares currently held, at a price of $2 each. S currently has 2,000,000 $1 ordinary shares with a quoted market price of $2.50 each. Directly attributable issue costs amounted to $25,000.

Assuming all rights are taken up and all money paid in full, how much will be credited to the share premium account for the rights issue?

A $200,000
B $308,333
C $375,000
D $400,000

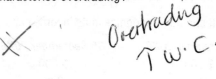

$$\frac{2,000,000}{5}$$

$$= 400000$$

$$= 400000 - 25,000$$

1.16   A company has a current ratio of 2.3 and a quick ratio (or acid test) of 0.8.

If it increases its overdraft in order to buy more inventory as a cash purchase, what will happen to the company's current ratio and quick ratio as a result of this transaction?

	Current ratio	Quick ratio
A	Increase	Increase
B	Increase	Decrease
C	Decrease	Increase
D	Decrease	Decrease

1.17   Which of the following is LEAST LIKELY to characterise overtrading?

A   Increased borrowing
B   Increased cash balances
C   Increased turnover
D   Reduced working capital

1.18   Which of the following is LEAST RELEVANT to the simple economic order quantity (EOQ) model for inventory?

A   Safety inventory
B   Annual demand
C   Holding costs
D   Order costs

1.19   Which of the following most appropriately describes *forfaiting*?

A   It is a method of providing medium-term export finance.

B   It provides short-term finance for purchasing non-current assets which are denominated in a foreign currency.

C   It provides long-term finance to importers.

D   It is the forced surrender of a share due to the failure to make a payment on a partly paid share.

1.20 Which of the following is likely to have the LOWEST expected rate of return?

    A   Unsecured bank loan.
    B   Preferred shares.
    C   Secured loan stock.
    D   Equity shares.

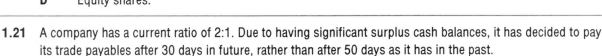

1.21 A company has a current ratio of 2:1. Due to having significant surplus cash balances, it has decided to pay its trade payables after 30 days in future, rather than after 50 days as it has in the past.

What will be the effect of this change on the company's current ratio and its cash operating cycle?

	Current ratio	Operating cycle
A	Increase	Increase
B	Increase	Decrease
C	Decrease	Increase
D	Decrease	Decrease

this will increase as payables have fallen.

$$\frac{50}{30} = 1.67:1.$$

$$\frac{\cancel{50}\;40}{20} = 2:1.$$

1.22 When receivables are sold to a debt factoring company, which of the following is LEAST likely?

    A   Cash will be received sooner than if debts were not sold.
    B   The receivables will be sold at a profit to the selling company.
    C   The debt factoring company will make a profit on the service provided.
    D   Working capital will decrease.

1.23 IAS 14 *Segment reporting* requires that segment revenue and result should be:

    A   Analysed by business segments and geographical segments
    B   Analysed by business segments
    C   Analysed by geographical segments
    D   Analysed by business segment and type of customer

1.24 The following balances were extracted from the books of A.

	31 March 20X3
	$'000
Sales	300
Cost of sales	200
Gross profit	100
Closing inventory	15
Trade receivables	36
Trade payables	28

Inventory turnover.

$$\frac{Inventory}{Cost\ of\ Sales} \times 365$$

$$\frac{15}{200} \times 365 = 27.375.$$

Receivables:

$$\frac{Rec}{Sales} \times 365 = \frac{36}{300} \times 365$$

$$\frac{15}{36} = 43.8.$$

A's average working capital cycle for the year ended 31 March 20X3 is

    A   11.0 days
    B   20.1 days
    C   34.7 days
    D   37.1 days

Payables.
Cost of Sales.

$$\frac{28}{200} \times 365 = 51.1\ days$$

1.25 R issued 500,000 new $1 equity shares on 1 April 20X2. The issue price of the share was $1.50 per share. Applicants paid $0.20 per share with their applications and a further $0.80 per share on allotment. All money was received on time.

A final call of $0.50 per share was made on 31 January 20X3. One holder of 5,000 shares failed to pay the call by the due date and the shares were forfeited. The forfeited shares were reissued for $1 per share on 31 March 20X3.

Which of the following is the correct set of accounting entries to record the reissue of the forfeited shares?

	Investment in own shares account	Bank account	Investment in own shares account	Share premium account
A	$5,000 credit	$5,000 debit	$2,500 debit	$2,500 credit
B	$5,000 credit	$5,000 debit	0	0
C	$5,000 credit	$5,000 debit	$2,500 credit	$2,500 debit
D	$5,000 debit	$5,000 credit	$2,500 credit	$2,500 debit

SECTION B – 30 marks

Answer ALL questions

Question 2

At the beginning of the accounting period, D had a credit balance of $40,000 on its current tax account, which was paid during the period. The opening balance on the deferred tax account was $250,000 credit.

The provision for tax for the current period is $50,000 and the balance on the deferred tax account is to be reduced to $225,000.

Required

Prepare extracts from the income statement, balance sheet and notes to the accounts. **(5 marks)**

Question 3 (Parts (a) and (b) refer to the same scenario)

(a)   A has an accounting profit of $100,000. This total is after charging depreciation of $25,000 and non-allowable expenses of $2,000. The figure also includes government grants received of $50,000.

The tax rate is 30%. Under A's tax regime, government grants are tax-free. If the tax allowable depreciation is $35,000, calculate the tax due for the current period.

(b)   A has paid a dividend during the accounting period of $8,500. The advanced tax rate is 15%. Calculate the following.

(i)   The advanced tax payable on the dividend.
(ii)   How much tax remains to be paid to the tax authorities at the end of the accounting period.

(5 marks)

Question 4

Discuss the usefulness of the audit report to a potential investor **(5 marks)**

Question 5

K Co has a minimum cash balance of $20,000. The variance of its daily cash flows is $2,250,000. It has a transaction cost of $100 for each purchase or sale of securities and the interest rate is 0.025 per cent per day.

Using the Miller-Orr model, calculate the upper limit for cash balances and the return point. **(5 marks)**

Question 6

What are the advantages of (a) centralised and (b) decentralised purchasing? **(5 marks)**

Question 7

IAS 8 *Accounting policies, changes in accounting estimates and errors* distinguishes between accounting policies and accounting estimates. Explain the distinction between accounting policies and accounting estimates, give an example of each and explain their treatment under IAS 8. **(5 marks)**

SECTION C – 20 marks

Answer ONE question out of two

Question 8

Hi, listed on its local stock exchange, is a retail organisation operating several retail outlets. A reorganisation of the entity was started in 20X2 because of a significant reduction in profits. This reorganisation was completed during the current financial year.

The trial balance for Hi at 30 September 20X3 was as follows:

	$'000	$'000
10% loan notes (redeemable 20Y0)		1,000
Retained earnings at 30 September 20X2		1,390
Administrative expenses	615	
Bank and cash	959	
Buildings	11,200	
Cash received on disposal of equipment		11
Cost of good sold	3,591	
Distribution costs	314	
Equipment and fixtures	2,625	
Interest paid on loan notes – half year to 31 March 20X3	50	
Interim dividend paid	800	
Inventory at 30 September 20X3	822	
Investment income received		37
Non-current asset investments at market value 30 September 20X2	492	
Ordinary shares of $1 each, fully paid		4,000
Provision for deferred tax		256
Provision for reorganisation expenses at 30 September 20X2		1,010
Allowances for depreciation at 30 September 20X2		
Buildings		1,404
Equipment and fixtures		1,741
Reorganisation expenses	900	
Revaluation reserve		172
Sales revenue		9,415
Share premium		2,388
Trade payables		396
Trade receivables	852	
	23,220	23,220

Additional information provided

(a)   The reorganisation expenses relate to a comprehensive restructuring and reorganisation of the entity that began in 20X2. Hi's financial statements for 20X2 included a provision for reorganisation expenses of $1,010,000. All costs had been incurred by the year end, but an invoice for $65,000, received on 2 October 20X3, remained unpaid and is not included in the trial balance figures. No further restructuring and reorganisation costs are expected to occur and the provision is no longer required.

(b)   Non-current asset investments are carried in the financial statements at market value. The market value of the non-current asset investments at 30 September 20X3 was $522,000. There were no movements in the investments held during the year.

(c)   On 1 November 20X3, Hi was informed that one of its customers, X, had ceased trading. The liquidators advised Hi that it was very unlikely to receive payment of any of the $45,000 due from X at 30 September 20X3.

(d) Another customer is suing for damages as a consequence of a faulty product. Legal advisers are currently advising that the probability of Hi being found liable is 75%. The amount payable is estimated to be the full amount claimed of $100,000.

(e) The income tax due for the year ended 30 September 20X3 is estimated at $1,180,000 and the deferred tax provision needs to be increased to $281,000.

(f) During the year, Hi disposed of old equipment for $11,000. The original cost of this equipment was $210,000 and accumulated depreciation at 30 September 20X2 was $205,000. Hi's accounting policy is to charge no depreciation in the year of the disposal.

(g) Depreciation is charged using the straight-line basis on non-current assets as follows.

Buildings	3%
Equipment and fixtures	20%

Depreciation is regarded as a cost of sales.

Required

Prepare the income statement for Hi for the year to 30 September 20X3 and a balance sheet at that date, in a form suitable for presentation to the shareholders, in accordance with the requirements of International Accounting Standards.

Notes to financial statements are NOT required, but all workings must be clearly shown. DO NOT prepare a statement of accounting policies or a statement of recognised income and expense.

(20 marks)

Question 9

The financial statements of YZ are given below:

BALANCE SHEET AT

	30 September 20X3		30 September 20X2	
	$'000	$'000	$'000	$'000
Property, plant and equipment		634		510
Current assets				
Inventory	420		460	
Trade receivables	390		320	
Interest receivable	4		9	
Investments	50		0	
Cash in bank	75		0	
Cash in hand	7		5	
		946		794
Total assets		1,580		1,304
Equity				
Ordinary shares $0.50 each	363		300	
Share premium account	89		92	
Revaluation reserve	50		0	
Retained earnings(loss)	93		(70)	
		595		322
Non-current liabilities				
10% loan notes	0		40	
5% loan notes	329		349	
		329		389
Current liabilities				
Bank overdraft	0		70	
Trade payables	550		400	
Income tax	100		90	
Accruals	6		33	
		656		593
Total equity and liabilities		1,580		1,304

INCOME STATEMENT FOR THE YEAR TO 30 SEPTEMBER 20X3

	$'000	$'000
Revenue		2,900
Cost of sales		(1,734)
Gross profit		1,166
Administrative expenses	(342)	
Distribution costs	(520)	
		(862)
		304
Income from investments	5	
Finance cost	(19)	
		(14)
Profit before tax		290
Income tax expense		(104)
Net profit for the period		186

Additional information

(a) On 1 October 20X2, YZ issued 60,000 $0.50 ordinary shares at a premium of 100%. The proceeds were used to finance the purchase and cancellation of all its 10% loan notes and some of its 5% loan notes, both at par. A bonus issue of one for ten shares held was made on 1 November 20X2; all shares in issue qualified for the bonus.

(b) The current asset investment was a 30 day government bond.

(c)   Property, plant and equipment include certain properties which were revalued in the year.

(d)   Property, plant and equipment disposed of in the year had a net book value of $75,000; cash received on disposal was $98,000.

(e)   Depreciation charged for the year was $87,000.

(f)   The accruals balance is interest payable of $33,000 at 30 September 20X2 and $6,000 at 30 September 2003.

(g)   Interim dividends paid during the year were $23,000.

Required

Prepare the following for YZ for the year ended 30 September 20X3, in accordance with IAS 7 *Cash flow statements*:

(a)   A cash flow statement, using the indirect method   **(18 marks)**

(b)   An analysis of cash and cash equivalents   **(2 marks)**

(Total = 20 marks)

Answers

A plan of attack

As you turned the page to start this exam any one of a number of things could have been going through your mind. Some of them may have been quite sensible, some of them may not.

The main thing to do is take a deep breath and do not panic. It's best to sort out a plan of attack before the actual exam so that when the invigilator tells you that you can begin and the adrenaline kicks in you are using every minute of the three hours wisely.

Your approach

This paper has three sections. The first section contains 20–25 multiple choice questions which are compulsory. The second has six short compulsory questions. The third has two questions and you must answer one of them.

OTs first again

However you find the paper, chances are you should **start with the objective test questions**. You should be able to do at least a few and answering them will give you a boost. **Don't even look at the other questions before doing Section A**. Remember how long to allocate to the OTs? That's right, 90 minutes. One and a half hours.

You then have a **choice**.

- Read through and answer Section B before moving on to Section C

- Go through Section C and select the question you will attempt. Then go back and answer the question in Section B first

- Select the question in Section C, answer it and then go back to Section B

Time spent at the start of each Section B and C question confirming the requirements and producing a plan for the answers is time well spent.

Question selection

When selecting the question from Section C make sure that you **read through all of the requirements**. It is painful to answer part (a) of a question and then realise that parts (b) and (c) are beyond you. By then it is too late to change your mind and do the other question.

When reviewing the requirements look at how many marks have been allocated to each part. This will give you an idea of how detailed your answer must be.

Doing the exam

Actually doing the exam is a personal experience. There is not a single *right way*. As long as you submit complete answers to the MCQs, question 1, the six Section B questions and one question from Section C, your approach obviously works.

One approach

Having done or guessed at the MCQs, I would work straight through Section B. There is no need to stop and make any choice until you get to Section C. The possible pitfall would be getting sucked too deeply into Section B and leaving insufficient time for Section C.

So lets look at the Section B questions in the pilot paper:

- Question 2 is a straightforward calculation of income tax liability. It would be a good idea to begin by putting the information into T accounts. Then the information just needs to be correctly presented. This can easily be done in 9 minutes.

- Question 3 is two small questions on tax and advanced tax. Easy as long as you know what to do.

- Question 4 is a trap. You can probably thing of lots of things to say about this and the worst thing you can do is to start writing them all down. You have 9 minutes for this, no more. Your plan(and you must have one) should be something like: 1. Limitations on its usefulness 2. Ways in which its usefulness is overestimated. Then think of the valid points you want to make in these two areas and make them briefly. Our answer does not use bullet points, but that would have been an equally valid approach.

- Question 5 is a gift. You are given the formula. Set your calculation out neatly and double-check your workings.

- Question 6 is crying out for bullet points and your answer will probably be similar to ours. The use of bullet points will save you from dangerous waffling.

- Question 7 is difficult and requires a good knowledge of IAS 8. If you had trouble with it, do revise this, as it could well come up.

Having hacked your way through Section B, taking no more than 9 minutes per question, you should now be left with 36 minutes to do your Section C question. The pilot paper gives a choice between a balance sheet/income statement and a cash flow. You probably know whether you feel more confident about balance sheet/income statement or cash flow. So check for any complicating factors in either of them, or any parts you feel unable to tackle, then make your choice and get on with it.

For the Section C Question you must proceed in a methodical way. Set out your format and then work through the question requirements, doing neat, readable calculations and fill out the figures. Even if you do not finish, you will get marks for what you have done, so do the easy bits first.

Time allocation

Be disciplined. Allocate your time according to the marks available but never go over the time allocation. The last few marks in a question are the hardest to earn.

Be sure to follow the requirements. If four advantages are required, give four. No extra credit will be given for five. Two advantages will only get you half marks.

Answer all of the question. Having a go at every part of all the Section B questions you are required to do will put you in a better position to pass than, say, only doing five questions. However difficult that sixth question seems at first there are marks to be earned.

If you have time left at the end of the exam ensure that you have attempted every part of every question. If you have, then scan through and ensure you complete any part of an answer you left earlier. Use the full three hours working towards a pass.

Marking the exam

When you mark your exam, be honest. Don't be too harsh though. Give yourself credit for the things you did well, but don't kid yourself with 'I would have done that in the real exam'. It may be worth your while making two lists; strengths and weaknesses.

Strengths will be areas of the syllabus you are confident with and also good exam technique. (Maybe you produced correct income statement and balance sheet formats.)

Weaknesses will be holes in your knowledge and poor exam technique (maybe you ran out of time and couldn't answer all the requirements of the last question).

Making this list will help you focus your last days of revision on the areas which require attention whilst reminding you of the areas you excel in.

SECTION A

Question 1

1.1

	$
Taxable profit	100,000
Less: depreciation	10,000
	90,000
Add: tax allowable depreciation	25,000
Accounting profit	115,000

1.2 The correct answer is C.

	$	$
Accounting profit		300,000
Add: depreciation	35,000	
disallowed expenses	5,000	
		40,000
		340,000
Less: non-taxable income	10,000	
tax allowable depreciation	30,000	40,000
Taxable profit		300,000

1.3 The correct answer is B. Supranational tax agreements (eg the EU rules on sales tax) are a source of tax rules. The other options are all sources of accounting rules.

1.4 An indirect tax is one that charges tax indirectly on the final consumer of the goods or services.

1.5 The correct answer is D.

	$
Output tax (230,000 x 17.5%)	40,250
Input tax ((151,000 − 10,000)/117.5 × 17.5)	21,000
Payable	19,250

1.6 The correct answer is B.

Total tax due is $30,000 ($150,000 x 20%) less double taxation relief of $15,000 (less than $100,000 x 20%), leaves $15,000 to pay.

1.7 C International Financial Reporting Interpretations Comittee

1.8 C Qualitative characteristics

- Relevance
- Reliability
- Understandability
- Comparability

1.9 B IAS 24 specifically excludes 'providers of finance in control of their business in that regard.'

1.10 D The subsequent sale provides evidence of the net realisable value of the inventory as at the year end.

1.11 B $(100,000 - 80,000) \times \dfrac{5}{5+4+3+2+1} = \$20,000 \times \dfrac{5}{15}$

$$= \$6,667$$

BPP
PROFESSIONAL EDUCATION

1.12 B *WDA*

		Capital allowance
	$	$
Cost 1.4 X0	200,000	
WDA 25%	50,000	50,000
WDV 31.3 X1	150,000	
WDA 25%	(37,500)	37,500
WDV 31.3 X2	112,500	
WDA 25%	(28,125)	28,125
WDV 31.3 X3	84,375	
Capital allowances claimed		115,625
Depreciation w/off		
3 yrs @ 10% straight line		60,000
Accelerated allowances		55,625
Tax rate		× 30%
		16,688

1.13 C

	20X2	*20X3*
	$'000	$'000
Costs to date	2,900	4,600
Costs to complete	6,000	3,900
Estimated total cost	8,900	8,500
Projected profit	1,100	1,500
Contract price	10,000	10,000
Completed	30%	55%
Cumulative profit	330	825
I/S credit	330	495

1.14 A

	Non-current asset	*Revaluation reserve*
	$	$
Cost 1.7.X0	50,000	
Depreciation to 1.7.X2		
20% × 2 yrs	20,000	
Book value 1.7.X2	30,000	
Revaluation increase	30,000	30,000
New carrying value 1.7.X3	60,000	
Depreciation: 1/3	20,000	
Value at 1.7.X3	40,000	
Disposal proceeds	35,000	
Loss on disposal	5,000	

1.15 C   Number of shares issued:

$$\frac{2,000,000}{5} = 400,000 \text{ shares}$$

	$
Issue price	2
Nominal value	1
Premium	1

	$
∴ Total premium	400,000
Less issue costs	25,000
Net to share premium	375,000

1.16 D   Say current assets are $230, current liabilities are $100 and inventory is $150 (hence current assets excluding inventory are $80).

Say overdraft is increased by $20 to pay for $20 inventory

New current ratio = 230 + 20: 100 + 20 = 2.08. Current ratio has decreased.

New quick ratio = 80: 100 + 20 = 0.67. Quick ratio has decreased.

1.17 B   Increased cash balances, Overtrading will generally result in a shortage of cash.

1.18 A   Safety inventory. B – D are all terms in the EOQ formula.

1.19 A   Forfaiting is a method of providing medium-term export finance.

1.20 C   Secured loan stock will have the lowest return, because it has the lowest risk due to the security.

1.21 A   Say current assets = 100, current liabilities = 50 giving a current ratio of 2:1.

Reducing current liabilities to 30 by paying trade payables sooner will reduce current assets to 80. The current ratio is 80:30, that is 2.67:1, and has therefore increased. The cash operating cycle will increase as payables have fallen.

1.22 B   The receivables will be sold at a profit to the selling company.

1.23 A   One of these will be its **primary** reporting format.

1.24 B   Inventory turnover $= \dfrac{\text{Inventory}}{\text{Cost of sales}} \times 365$ days

$$= \frac{15}{200} \times 365 = 27.4 \text{ days}$$

Receivables turnover $= \dfrac{\text{Receivables}}{\text{Sales}} \times 365$ days

$$= \frac{36}{300} \times 365 = 43.8 \text{ days}$$

Payables turnover $= \dfrac{\text{Payables}}{\text{Cost of sales}} \times 365$ days

$$= \frac{28}{200} \times 365 = 51.1 \text{ days}$$

Working capital cycle = inventory turnover + receivables turnover – payables turnover
= (27.4 + 43.8 – 51.1) days
= 20.1 days

BPP
PROFESSIONAL EDUCATION

1.25 A   Cash received on application and allotment

$1 × 5,000 = $5,000

Balance of share capital due = $2,500

Cash received on reissue of shares $1 × 5,000 = $5,000

Additional share premium:

INVESTMENT IN OWN SHARES ACCOUNT

	$		$
Call amount	2,500	Bank	5,000
Share premium	2,500		
	5,000		5,000

SECTION B

Question 2

	$
Income Statement (extract)	
Tax expense (Note 1)	25,000
Balance Sheet (extract)	
Current liabilities	
Tax payable	50,000
Non-current liabilities	
Deferred tax (Note 2)	225,000

Notes to the financial statements

1   *Tax expense*

	$
Provision for the current period	50,000
Decrease in deferred tax provision	(25,000)
	25,000

2   *Deferred tax*

	$
Balance brought forward	250,000
Decrease in provision	(25,000)
Balance carried forward	225,000

Question 3

(a)

	$'000	$'000
Accounting profit		100
Add: disallowable expenditure	2	
book depreciation	25	
		27
		127
Less: non-taxable income	50	
tax allowable depreciation	35	
		85
Taxable profit		42

The tax rate is 30%, so the tax due is $12,600 (30% × $42,000).

(b)   (i)   Advanced tax

As the advanced tax rate is 15%, the dividend paid is 85%.

$$\text{Advanced tax} = \frac{\$8,500}{85} \times 15$$

$$= \$1,500$$

(ii)   The tax due for the current period is unaffected by the advanced tax paid, it remains at $12,600.

However, the tax payable is reduced by the advanced tax paid.

Tax payable = $12,600 − $1,500

= $11,100

BPP
PROFESSIONAL EDUCATION

Question 4

Any potential investor will of course examine a company's latest set of audited accounts and will expect to see an unqualified audit report. If the report is qualified she/he will ask further questions. If it is a disclaimer or an adverse report, he will probably decide to invest elsewhere.

So, assuming that the report is unqualified, how useful will it be to him? The audit report is the expression of the auditor's **opinion**. The auditor has given his opinion that the accounts present fairly the financial position of the company and comply with the relevant legislation and accounting standards. The report will state that he has sought to obtain 'reasonable assurance' that the accounts are free from 'material misstatement'.

The reason he auditor feels able to give nothing more than 'reasonable assurance' is that he did not prepare the accounts and he will not have had time to examine all of the transactions. The auditor will begin by testing the internal control system. If the internal controls appear to be effective, he will reduce the time spent on substantive testing. If fraud or errors are well-hidden, and the auditor's suspicions have not been aroused, the chances of him stumbling across the discrepancy are not that high.

While the auditor will certainly give attention to any going concern issues, the audit report cannot be taken as any guarantee of the future viability of the entity. Nor does it assure the effectiveness or efficiency of management. These are probably the two factors which most interest an investor. The audit report is a useful addition to whatever other information the investor is able to obtain, but the above points mean that it cannot be used to frame an investment decision.

Question 5

Using the Miller-Orr model, the spread between the upper and lower cash limits will be:

$$3\left(\frac{\frac{3}{4}\times100\times2{,}250{,}000}{0.00025}\right)^{\frac{1}{3}} = \$26{,}314$$

As the minimum cash balance is $20,000, the maximum balance will be $46,314.

Return point = lower limit + $\frac{1}{3}$ × spread = $20,000 + $\left(\frac{26{,}314}{3}\right)$ = $28,771

Question 6

(a)   Centralised purchasing has the following advantages:

- The firm will be buying in larger quantities and so will be able to negotiate more substantial discounts.

- The organisation as a whole should be able to arrange more favourable credit terms than an individual branch

- Inventory handling functions will be mainly centralised, which should save costs.

- It should be possible to hold lower overall levels of inventory than if inventory was being held at each branch. This will reduce holding costs.

- Only one buying department will be needed, which will save staff costs.

(b)   Decentralised purchasing has the following advantages:

- Local branches will be more in control of their production and sales if they have local control of purchasing.

- The purchasing requirements of individual branches may vary. For instance, some lines of inventory may sell better in some areas than others.

- Local branches will be able to form their own relationships with suppliers. There may be a higher level of co-operation between a smaller organisation and its supplier.

- A local branch can be made more accountable for its own profitability and cash if it has control of its own purchasing function.

Question 7

Accounting policies are defined in IAS 8 as the 'specific principles, bases, conventions, rules and practices adopted by an entity in preparing and presenting financial statements'. In practice, accounting policies are formulated by reference to the appropriate IAS or IFRS. They should be applied consistently from one period to the next and for all similar transactions within a period.

An example of an accounting policy would be that non-current assets are held at historical cost and depreciated over their useful lives.

In applying an accounting policy, it is often necessary to make estimates. When a non-current asset is purchased, its expected life can only be estimated. An entity may have to estimate the expected level of bad debts, the possibility of some of its inventory becoming obsolescent, the fair value of assets and liabilities.

An example of an accounting estimate would be the method by which an asset was depreciated – this is the means by which the accounting policy of depreciation is applied. So a change from straight-line to reducing balance depreciation would be accounted for as a change of accounting estimate.

Changes of accounting policy are relatively rare and should be accounted for using **retrospective restatement**. The corresponding figures for previous periods are restated, so that the new policy is applied to transactions and events as if it had always been in use. Changes of accounting estimate are accounted for using **prospective restatement** – the change of estimate is applied to the current period and to future periods if they are affected.

SECTION C

Question 8

Pass marks. Notes to the accounts are not required, so you should not have wasted time preparing them. However workings need to be clear and almost a substitute for notes, for example non-current assets.

HI
INCOME STATEMENT FOR THE YEAR ENDED 30 SEPTEMBER 20X3

	$'000
Revenue	9,415
Cost of sales (W2)	4,410
Gross profit	5,005
Distribution costs	(314)
Administrative expenses (W3)	(760)
Reorganisation costs overprovision (W4)	45
Profit on disposal of asset (W1)	6
Interest cost (W5)	(100)
Investment income	37
Profit before tax	3,919
Income tax expense (W6)	(1,205)
Net profit for the period	2,714

HI
BALANCE SHEET AS AT 30 SEPTEMBER 20X3

	$'000	$'000
Assets		
Non current assets		
Property, plant and equipment (W1)		9,856
Investments (W7)		522
Current assets		
Inventory	822	
Receivables (852 – 45)	807	
Cash at bank and in hand	959	
		2,588
		12,966
Equity and liabilities		
Equity		
Ordinary shares of $1 each	4,000	
Share premium	2,388	
Revaluation reserve (W7)	202	
Retained earnings (1,390 + 2,714 – 800)	3,304	
		9,894
Non current liabilities		
Interest bearing borrowing	1,000	
Deferred tax	281	
Other provisions (W3)	100	
		1,381
Current liabilities		
Trade payables	396	
Taxation	1,180	
Accruals: restructuring (W4)	65	
loan note interest (W5)	50	
		1,691
		12,966

Workings

1   *Property, plant and equipment*

	Buildings $'000	Equipment and fixtures $'000	Total $'000
Cost			
Opening balance	11,200	2,625	13,825
Additions		-	-
Disposals		(210)	(210)
	11,200	2,415	13,615
Accumulated depreciation			
Opening balance	1,404	1,741	3,145
On disposals		(205)	(205)
Charge for year			
• $11,200 × 3%	336		
• $2,415 × 20%		483	819
Closing balance	1,740	2,019	3,759
Net book value	9,460	396	9,856

Profit on disposal:

	$'000	$'000
Sale proceeds		11
Net book value		
Cost	210	
Accumulated depreciation	205	
		5
Profit		6

2   *Cost of sales*

	$'000
Per trial balance	3,591
Depreciation (W1)	819
	4,410

3   *Administrative expenses*

	$'000
Per trial balance	615
Bad debt written off (Note 1)	45
Provision for legal claim re faulty product (Note 2)	100
	760

Notes

1   Although the customer went into liquidation after the year end, this provides additional evidence of conditions exiting at the balance sheet date. It is thus an adjusting event under IAS 10.

2   The obligation is probable, therefore a provision must be made.

4   *Reorganisation costs*

	$'000	$'000
Provision in 20X2 accounts		1,010
Reorganisation expenses	900	
Invoice received after y/e	65	
		965
Provision surplus		45

5   *Interest cost*

	$'000
Per trial balance: half year to 31 March 20X3	50
Accrual for six months to 30 September 20X3: 10% × $1m × 6/12	50
	100

6   *Taxation*

	$'000	$'000
Income tax payable		1,180
Deferred tax		
Provision b/fwd	256	
Provision required	281	
∴ Charge to income statement		25
		1,205

7   *Investments and revaluation reserve*

	Investments	Revaluation reserve
	$'000	$'000
Per trial balance	492	172
Revaluation of investments to market value	30	30
	522	202

Question 9

> **Pass marks**. This is fairly straightforward, although the bonus issue may have confused you.

(a)   YZ
CASH FLOW STATEMENT
FOR THE YEAR ENDED 30 SEPTEMBER 20X3

	$'000	$'000
Cash flows from operating activities		
Operating profit	304	
Adjustments for		
Depreciation	87	
Profit on disposal (W1)	(23)	
Operating profit before working capital changes	368	
Decrease in inventory	40	
Increase in receivables	(70)	
Increase in payables	150	
Cash generated from operations	488	
Interest paid (W2)	(46)	
Income taxes paid (W3)	(94)	
Net cash from operating activities		348
Cash flows from investing activities		
Purchase of property, plant and equipment (W1)	(236)	
Proceeds from sale of property, plant and equipment	98	
Interest received (W4)	10	
Net cash used in investing activities		(128)
Cash flows from financing activities		
Proceeds from issuance of share capital	60	
Repurchase of loan notes	(60)	
Dividends paid	(23)	
Net cash used in financing activities		(23)
Net increase in cash and cash equivalents		197
Cash and cash equivalents at beginning of period		
(Note (Part (b))		(65)
Cash and cash equivalents at end of period (Note (Part (b))		132

151

(b)   Analysis of cash and cash equivalents

	As at 30.9.X3 $'000	As at 30.8.X2 $'000	Change in year $'000
Cash in hand and balances at bank	82	5	77
Bank overdraft		(70)	70
Short-term investments	50	–	50
	132	(65)	197

Workings

1   *Property, plant and equipment*

PROPERTY, PLANT AND EQUIPMENT

	$'000		$'000
Bal b/fwd (NBV)	510	Disposals	75
Revaluation	50	Depreciation	87
Additions (bal fig)	236	Balance c/fwd (NBV)	634
	796		796

DISPOSALS

	$'000		$'000
Property, plant and equipment	75	Bank proceeds	98
Income statement (profit on sale)	23		
	98		98

2   *Interest paid*

INTEREST

	$'000		$'000
Paid (bal. fig)	46	Balance b/fwd	33
Balance c/fwd	6	Income statement	19
	52		52

3   *Income taxes paid*

TAXATION

	$'000		$'000
∴ Paid (bal.fig)	94	Balance b/fwd	90
Balance c/fwd	100	Income statement	104
	194		194

4   *Interest received*

INTEREST RECEIVABLE

	$'000		$'000
Balance b/fwd	9	Cash received	10
Income statement	5	Balance c/fwd	4
	14		14

CIMA
Paper P7 (Managerial)
Financial Accounting and Tax Principles

Mock Exam 2 (Pilot paper)

Question Paper		
Time allowed		**3 hours**
This paper is divided into three sections		
Section A	**Answer ALL sub-questions in this section**	
Section B	**Answer ALL six short-answer questions**	
Section C	**Answer ONE question out of two**	

DO NOT OPEN THIS PAPER UNTIL YOU ARE READY TO START UNDER EXAMINATION CONDITIONS

② Assets:

Contract Price	6m
Total Costs:	4,950
Expected total Profit	1,050

Attrib Profit $\frac{2m}{6m}$ = 1/3 of 1,050 = 350

Total Costs to date are:

	$'000
Cost of Sales:	2,200
Attrib Profit	350
	2,550
Prog. Payments Received	1,600
	950

Liabilities:

```
   1650
    550
  2,200
- 1,300
    900  - liability
```

⑤ optimal Sale / Transfer

$$= \sqrt{\frac{2 \times \text{Annual disbursements} \times \text{Cost Per Sale of securities}}{\text{Interest rates}}}$$

$$\sqrt{\frac{2 \times 240,000 \times 30}{0.05}} = 16,970$$

or 17,000 rounded up.

SECTION A – 50 marks

Answer ALL sub-questions in this section

Question 1

The rest balance each of them out.

1.1 Which ONE of the following transactions is most likely to affect the overall amount of working capital?

A Receipt of full amount of cash from a customer to settle their trade receivable account. *Cash↑ Rec↓ x*

B Payment of a trade payable account in full.

C Sale of a non-current asset on credit at its net book value. *– Non-current asset, rec↑ so working k goes up*

D Purchase of inventory on credit.

(2 marks)

1.2 B entered into a three-year contract to build a leisure centre for an entity. The contract value was $6 million. B recognises profit on the basis of certified work completed.

Construction Contracts.

At the end of the first year, the following figures were extracted from B's accounting records:

	$000
Certified value of work completed (progress payments billed)	2,000
Cost of work certified as complete	1,650
Cos of work-in-progress (not included in completed work)	550
Estimated cost of remaining work required to complete the contract	2,750
Progress payments received from entity	1,600
Cash paid to suppliers for work on the contract	1,300

What values should B record for this contract as 'gross amounts due from customers' and 'current liabilities – trade and other payables'?

	Gross amounts due from customers	Current liabilities – trade and other payables
A	$950,000	$350,000
B	$950,000	$900,000
C	$1,250,000	$600,000
D	$2,550,000	$900,000

(2 marks)

1.3 IAS 8 –*Accounting Policies, Changes in Accounting Estimates and Errors* specifies the definition and treatment of a number of different items. Which of the following is NOT specified by IAS 8?

✓ deals with

A The effect of a change in an accounting estimate. *– Only 2 reasons why you would Use IAS8*

B Prior period adjustments. *– Amend the AIC if found error or a change In a/c ing Policy. dealt with In IAS8*

C Provisions. *– IAS37 Covered.*

D Errors

(2 marks)

1.4 In no more than 15 words, complete the following sentence:

'A direct tax is one that...' *is levied directly on the person eg. excise duties / VAT.*

(2 marks)

I don't have to remember this formula.

1.5 A company uses the Baumol cash management model. Cash disbursements are constant at $20,000 each month. Money on deposit earns 5% a year, while money in the current account earns a zero return. Switching costs (that is, for each purchase or sale of securities) are $30 for each transaction.

What is the optimal amount (to the nearest $100) to be transferred in each transaction? **(2 marks)**

1.6 List (using no more than five words per item) the four main sources of tax rules in a country. **(4 marks)**

x Domestic legislation
x Legal decisions (court)
x Tax Authority Practice - Can make their own decisions
x International Treaties. & double tax treaties
x Supranational Bodies.

[Handwritten: Formula you have to learn: Cash discounts:]

1.7 WM's major supplier, INT, supplies electrical tools and is one of the largest companies in the industry, with international operations. Deliveries from INT are currently made monthly, and are constant throughout the year. Delivery and invoicing both occur in the last week of each month.

[Handwritten left margin:] $\left[\frac{100}{100-d}\right]^{\frac{365}{t}} - 1$

d - discount
T - time for cash discount, ie 30 days here.

[Handwritten right:] $\left(\frac{100}{100-2}\right)^{\frac{365}{30}} - 1$
$= 0.2786$
$\times 100 = 27.86\%$

Details of the credit terms offered by INT are as follows:

Normal credit period	Cash discount	Average monthly purchases
40 days	2% for settlement in 10 days	$100,000

WM always takes advantage of the cash discount from INT.

Calculate the annual rate of interest (to two decimal places) implied in the cash discount offered by INT. Assume a 365-day year. **(3 marks)**

1.8 A company has a current ratio of 2 :1. Due to having significant surplus cash balances, it has decided to pay its trade payable accounts after 30 days in future, rather than after 50 days, as it has in the past.

What will be the effect of this change on the company's current ratio and its cash operating cycle?

[Handwritten left margin: Current ratio will ↑ if you pay liabilities sooner.]

[Handwritten right: if you pay payables early, it will increase the cash op. cycle.]

	Current ratio	Cash operating cycle
A	Increase	Increase
B	Increase	Decrease
C	Decrease	Increase
D	Decrease	Decrease

(2 marks)

1.9 The following balances were extracted from the books of A:

[Handwritten: ③]
[Handwritten: Payables = 28, Cost of sales 200 × 365 = 51.1 days]

[Handwritten: ① $\frac{36}{300} \times 365 = 43.8$ days (Receivables). to get money back from cust.]

	Year ended 31 March 20X3 $000
Revenue	300
Cost of sales	200
Gross profit	100

[Handwritten: ② $\frac{Inv}{Cost\ of\ Sales} \times 365$. Inventory = $\frac{15}{200} \times 365 = 27.4$ days]

	At 31 March 20X3 $000
Closing inventory	15
Trade receivables	36
Trade payables	28

[Handwritten: 71.2 days altogether.]

[Handwritten left margin: Total WIC Cycle = 21.1 days with payables taken into A/C.]

Assume all revenue is credit sales and costs of sales equates to inventory purchases. What is A's average working capital cycle for the year ended 31 March 20X3? **(3 marks)**

1.10 Double tax relief is used to

A ensure that you do not pay tax twice on any of your income.
B mitigate taxing overseas income twice.
C avoid taxing dividends received from subsidiaries in the same country twice.
D provide relief where a company pays tax at double the normal rate. **(2 marks)**

1.11 A withholding tax is:

A tax withheld from payment to the tax authorities.
B tax paid less an amount withheld from payment.
C tax deducted at source before payment of interest or dividends.
D tax paid on increases in value of investment holdings. **(2 marks)**

1.12 Tax on an entity's trading profits could be referred to as:

(i)   Income tax
(ii)   Profits tax
(iii)   Indirect tax
(iv)   Direct tax
(v)   Earnings tax

Which TWO of the above would most accurately describe tax on an entity's trading profits:

A   (i) and (iii)
B   (i) and (iv)
C   (ii) and (iii)
D   (iv) and (v)   **(2 marks)**

1.13 An entity commenced business on 1 April 20X2. Revenue in April 20X2 was $20,000, but this is expected to increase at 2% a month. Credit sales amount to 60% of total sales. The credit period allowed is one month. Bad debts are expected to be 3% of credit sales, but other customers are expected to pay on time. Cash sales represent the other 40% of revenue.

How much cash is expected to be received in May 20X2?   **(3 marks)**

1.14 Which of the following types of taxes is regarded as an indirect tax?

A   Taxes on income.
B   Taxes on capital gains.
C   Taxes on inherited wealth.
D   Sales tax (Value added tax).   **(2 marks)**

1.15 E has an accounting profit before tax of $95,000. The tax rate on trading profits applicable to E for the year is 25%. The accounting profit included non-taxable income from government grants of $15,000 and non-tax allowable expenditure of $10,000 on entertaining expenses.

How much tax is E due to pay for the year?   **(2 marks)**

1.16 Which TWO of the following are underlying assumptions in the International Accounting Standards Board's Framework for the preparation and presentation of financial statements?

(i)   Accruals
(ii)   Relevance
(iii)   Comparability
(iv)   Going concern
(v)   Reliability

A   (i) and (v)
B   (ii) and (v)
C   (iii) and (iv)
D   (i) and (iv)   **(2 marks)**

1.17 The International Accounting Standards Board's Framework for the preparation and presentation of financial statements defines elements of financial statements. In no more than 30 words define an asset.   **(2 marks)**

The following data is to be used to answer questions 1.18 and 1.19 below

X acquired the business and assets from the owners of an unincorporated business: the purchase price was satisfied by the issue of 10,000 equity shares with a nominal market value of $10 each and $20,000 cash. The market value of X shares at the date of acquisition was $20 each.

The assets acquired were:

- Net tangible non-current assets with a book value of $20,000 and current value of $25,000.

- Patents for a specialised process valued by a specialist valuer at $15,000.

- Brand name, valued by a specialist brand valuer on the basis of a multiple of earnings at $50,000.

- Publishing rights of the first text from an author that the management of X expects to become a best seller. The publishing rights were a gift from the author to the previous owners at no cost. The management of X has estimated the future value of the potential best seller at $100,000. However, there is no reliable evidence available to support the estimate of the management.

| 1.18 | In no more than 30 words, explain the accounting treatment to be used for the publishing rights of the first text. | **(2 marks)** |

| 1.19 | Calculate the value of goodwill to be included in the accounts of X for this purchase. | **(4 marks)** |

| 1.20 | SK sells bathroom fittings throughout the country in which it operates. In order to obtain the best price, it has decided to purchase all its annual demand of 10,000 shower units from a single supplier. RR has offered to provide the required number of showers each year under an exclusive long-term contract. |

Demand for shower units is at a constant rate all year. The cost to SK of holding one shower unit in Inventory for one year is $4 plus 3% of the purchase price.

RR is located only a few miles from the SK main showroom. It has offered to supply each shower unit at $400 with a transport charge of $200 per delivery. It has guaranteed such a regular and prompt delivery service that SK believes it will not be necessary to hold any safety Inventory (that is buffer Inventory) if it uses RR as its supplier.

Using the economic order quantity model (EOQ model), calculate the optimal order size, assuming that RR is chosen as the sole supplier of shower units for SK. **(3 marks)**

| 1.21 | Which of the following would be LEAST LIKELY to arise from the introduction of a Just-in-Time inventory ordering system? |

    A   Lower inventory holding costs.
    B   Less risk of inventory shortages.
    C   More frequent deliveries.
    D   Increased dependence on suppliers.   **(2 marks)**

(Total marks = 50)

SECTION B – 30 marks

Answer ALL six short-answer questions

Question 2

– IAS16:

A new type of delivery vehicle, when purchased on 1 April 20X0 for $20,000, was expected to have a useful life of four years. It now appears that the original estimate of the useful life was too short, and the vehicle is now expected to have a useful life of six years, from the date of purchase. All delivery vehicles are depreciated using the straight-line method and are assumed to have zero residual value.

Required

~ See layout from memo _From Date:_ _To Subject_

As the trainee management accountant, draft a memo to the transport manager explaining whether it is possible to change the useful life of the new delivery vehicle. Using appropriate International Accounting Standards, explain how the accounting transactions relating to the delivery vehicle should be recorded in the income statement for the year ended 31 March 20X3 and the balance sheet at that date **(5 marks)**

Question 3

NDL drilled a new oil well, which started production on 1 March 20X3. The licence granting permission to drill the new oil well included a clause that requires NDL to "return the land to the state it was in before drilling commenced". _Decommissioning Costs this is known as._

NDL estimates that the oil well will have a 20-year production life. At the end of that time, the oil well will be de-commissioned and work carried out to reinstate the land. The cost of this de-commissioning work is estimated to be $20 million.

Required

As the trainee management accountant, draft a memo to the production manager explaining how NDL must treat the de-commissioning costs in its financial statements for the year to 31 March 20X3. Your memo should refer to appropriate International Accounting Standards. **(5 marks)**

Question 4

– Expected Values:

HRD owns a number of small hotels. The room occupancy rate varies significantly from month to month. There are also high fixed costs. As a result, the cash generated each month has been very difficult to estimate.

Christmas is normally a busy period and large cash surpluses are expected in December. There is, however, a possibility that a rival group of hotels will offer large discounts in December and this could damage December trade for HRD to a significant extent.

January is a poor period for the industry and therefore all the company's hotels will close for the month, resulting in a negative cash flow. The Finance Director has identified the following possible outcomes and their associated probabilities:

Weight Average these _Certain._

	$000	Probability
Expected cash balance at 30 November 20X3	+175	1.0 _–chance_
Net operating cash flow in December 20X3	+700	0.7 _–chance_
	–300	0.3 _– chance_
Net operating cash flow in January 20X4	–900	1.0 _– change._

Either/or: _1.0 = Certain_

Assume cash flows arise at month ends.

After January 20X4, trade is expected to improve, but there is still a high degree of uncertainty in relation to the cash surpluses or deficits that will be generated in each month.

Required

Calculate the expected cash balance or overdraft of HRD at 31 January 20X4.

Explain why your answer may not be useful for short-term cash planning and outline alternative approaches that could be used. **(5 marks)**

Question 5

On 1 January 20X3, SPJ had an opening debit balance of $5,000 on its tax account, which represented the balance on the account after settling its tax liability for the previous year. SPJ had a credit balance on its deferred tax account of $1·6 million at the same date.

SPJ has been advised that it should expect to pay $1 million tax on its trading profits for the year ended 31 December 20X3 and increase its deferred tax account balance by $150,000.

Required

Prepare extracts from the income statement for the year ended 31 December 20X3, balance sheet at that date and notes to the accounts showing the tax entries required. **(5 marks)**

Question 6

IAS 37 defines the meaning of a provision and sets out when a provision should be recognised.

Required

Using the IAS 37 definition of a provision, explain how a provision meets the International Accounting Standards Board's Framework for the preparation and presentation of financial statements definition of a liability. **(5 marks)**

Question 7 Contract lease:

A lessee leases a non-current asset on a non-cancellable lease contract of five years, the details of which are:

- The asset has a useful life of five years.
- The rental is $21,000 per annum payable at the end of each year.
- The lessee also has to pay all insurance and maintenance costs.
- The fair value of the asset was $88,300.

The lessee uses the sum of digits method to calculate finance charges on the lease.

Required

Prepare income statement and balance sheet extracts for years one and two of the lease. **(5 marks)**

SECTION C – 20 marks

Answer ONE question out of two

Question 8

AZ is a quoted manufacturing entity. Its finished products are stored in a nearby warehouse until ordered by customers. AZ has been re-organising the business to improve performance.

The trial balance for AZ at 31 March 20X3 was as follows:

	$000	$000
7% Loan Notes (redeemable 20X7)		18,250
Retained earnings at 31 March 20X2		14,677
Administrative expenses	16,020	
Bank and Cash	26,250	
Cost of goods manufactured in the year to 31 March 20X3 (excluding depreciation)	94,000	
Distribution costs	9,060	
Dividends paid	1,000	
Dividends received		1,200
Equity shares $1 each, fully paid		20,000
Interest paid	639	
Inventory as 30 March 20X2	4,852	
Plant and Equipment	30,315	
Allowance for depreciation at 31 March 20X2:		
Plant and Equipment		6,060
Vehicles		1,670
Allowance for doubtful trade receivables		600
Restructuring costs	121	
Sales revenue		124,900
Share issue expenses	70	
Share premium		500
Trade payables		8,120
Trade receivables	9,930	
Vehicles	3,720	
	195,977	195,977

Additional information provided

(i) Non-current assets are being depreciated as follows:

Plant & Equipment	20% per annum straight line
Vehicles	25% per annum reducing balance

Depreciation of plant and equipment is considered to be part of cost of sales, while depreciation of vehicles should be included under distribution costs.

(ii) Tax due for the year to 31 March 20X3 is estimated at $15,000.

(iii) The closing inventory at 31 March 20X3 was $5,180,000.

(iv) A dividend of 5 cents per ordinary share was paid in February 20X3.

(v) The 7% loan notes are 10-year loans due for repayment by 31 March 20X7. AZ incurred no other interest charges in the year to 31 March 20X3.

(vi)   The restructuring costs in the trial balance represent the cost of the final phase of a major fundamental restructuring of the entity to improve competitiveness and future profitability.

(vii)   At 31 March 20X3, AZ was engaged in defending a legal action against the entity. Legal advisers have indicated that it is reasonably certain that the outcome of the case will be against the entity. The amount of compensation is currently estimated at $25,000 and has not been included in the trial balance.

(viii) On 1 October 20X2, AZ issued 1,000,000 equity shares at $1·50 each. All money had been received and correctly accounted for by the year end.

Required

Prepare AZ's income statement for the year to 31 March 20X3, a balance sheet at that date, and a statement of changes in equity for the year. These should be in a form suitable for presentation to the shareholders, in accordance with the requirements of International Accounting Standards.

Notes to the financial statements are NOT required, but all workings must be clearly shown. DO NOT prepare a statement of accounting policies or a statement of recognised income and expenses.

(20 marks)

Question 9

The following information has been extracted from the draft financial statements of TEX, a manufacturing entity:

TEX – Income statement for the year ended 30 September 20X3

	$000
Revenue	15,000
Cost of sales	(9,000)
Gross profit	6,000
Other operating expenses	(2,300)
	3,700
Finance cost	(124)
Profit before tax	3,576
Income tax expense	(1,040)
Profit for the period	2,536

TEX – Balance sheets at 30 September

	20X3		20X2	
	$000	$000	$000	$000
Assets				
Non-current assets		18,160		14,500
Current assets:				
Inventories	1,600		1,100	
Trade receivables	1,500		800	
Bank	150		1,200	
		3,250		3,100
Total assets		21,410		17,600

	20X3		20X2	
	$000	$000	$000	$000
Equity and liabilities				
Equity:				
Issued capital		10,834		7,815
Retained earnings		5,836		4,400
		16,670		12,215
Non-current liabilities:				
Interest-bearing borrowings	1,700		2,900	
Deferred tax	600		400	
		2,300		3,300
Current liabilities:				
Trade payables	700		800	
Dividend payable	700		600	
Tax	1,040		685	
		2,440		2,085
		21,410		17,600

Non-current assets

	Property $000	Plant $000	Total $000
At 30 September 20X2			
Cost	8,400	10,800	19,200
Depreciation	1,300	3,400	4,700
Net book value	7,100	7,400	14,500
At 30 September 20X3			
Cost	11,200	13,400	24,600
Depreciation	1,540	4,900	6,440
Net book value	9,660	8,500	18,160

(i)   Plant disposed of during the year had an original cost of $2,600,000 and accumulated depreciation of $900,000; cash received on disposal was $730,000.

(ii) All additions to non-current assets were purchased for cash.

(iii) Dividends totalling $1,100,000 were declared before the balance sheet date.

Required

Prepare TEX's cash flow statement and associated notes for the year ended 30 September 20X3, in accordance with IAS 7 – *Cash flow statements*. **(20 marks)**

Cumulative present value of £1 per annum,

Receivable or Payable at the end of each year for n years $\frac{1-(1+r)^{-n}}{r}$

Periods (n)	Interest rates (r)									
	1%	2%	3%	4%	5%	6%	7%	8%	9%	10%
1	0.990	0.980	0.971	0.962	0.952	0.943	0.935	0.926	0.917	0.909
2	1.970	1.942	1.913	1.886	1.859	1.833	1.808	1.783	1.759	1.736
3	2.941	2.884	2.829	2.775	2.723	2.673	2.624	2.577	2.531	2.487
4	3.902	3.808	3.717	3.630	3.546	3.465	3.387	3.312	3.240	3.170
5	4.853	4.713	4.580	4.452	4.329	4.212	4.100	3.993	3.890	3.791
6	5.795	5.601	5.417	5.242	5.076	4.917	4.767	4.623	4.486	4.355
7	6.728	6.472	6.230	6.002	5.786	5.582	5.389	5.206	5.033	4.868
8	7.652	7.325	7.020	6.733	6.463	6.210	5.971	5.747	5.535	5.335
9	8.566	8.162	7.786	7.435	7.108	6.802	6.515	6.247	5.995	5.759
10	9.471	8.983	8.530	8.111	7.722	7.360	7.024	6.710	6.418	6.145
11	10.368	9.787	9.253	8.760	8.306	7.887	7.499	7.139	6.805	6.495
12	11.255	10.575	9.954	9.385	8.863	8.384	7.943	7.536	7.161	6.814
13	12.134	11.348	10.635	9.986	9.394	8.853	8.358	7.904	7.487	7.103
14	13.004	12.106	11.296	10.563	9.899	9.295	8.745	8.244	7.786	7.367
15	13.865	12.849	11.938	11.118	10.380	9.712	9.108	8.559	8.061	7.606
16	14.718	13.578	12.561	11.652	10.838	10.106	9.447	8.851	8.313	7.824
17	15.562	14.292	13.166	12.166	11.274	10.477	9.763	9.122	8.544	8.022
18	16.398	14.992	13.754	12.659	11.690	10.828	10.059	9.372	8.756	8.201
19	17.226	15.679	14.324	13.134	12.085	11.158	10.336	9.604	8.950	8.365
20	18.046	16.351	14.878	13.590	12.462	11.470	10.594	9.818	9.129	8.514

Periods (n)	Interest rates (r)									
	11%	12%	13%	14%	15%	16%	17%	18%	19%	20%
1	0.901	0.893	0.885	0.877	0.870	0.862	0.855	0.847	0.840	0.833
2	1.713	1.690	1.668	1.647	1.626	1.605	1.585	1.566	1.547	1.528
3	2.444	2.402	2.361	2.322	2.283	2.246	2.210	2.174	2.140	2.106
4	3.102	3.037	2.974	2.914	2.855	2.798	2.743	2.690	2.639	2.589
5	3.696	3.605	3.517	3.433	3.352	3.274	3.199	3.127	3.058	2.991
6	4.231	4.111	3.998	3.889	3.784	3.685	3.589	3.498	3.410	3.326
7	4.712	4.564	4.423	4.288	4.160	4.039	3.922	3.812	3.706	3.605
8	5.146	4.968	4.799	4.639	4.487	4.344	4.207	4.078	3.954	3.837
9	5.537	5.328	5.132	4.946	4.772	4.607	4.451	4.303	4.163	4.031
10	5.889	5.650	5.426	5.216	5.019	4.833	4.659	4.494	4.339	4.192
11	6.207	5.938	5.687	5.453	5.234	5.029	4.836	4.656	4.486	4.327
12	6.492	6.194	5.918	5.660	5.421	5.197	4.988	7.793	4.611	4.439
13	6.750	6.424	6.122	5.842	5.583	5.342	5.118	4.910	4.715	4.533
14	6.982	6.628	6.302	6.002	5.724	5.468	5.229	5.008	4.802	4.611
15	7.191	6.811	6.462	6.142	5.847	5.575	5.324	5.092	4.876	4.675
16	7.379	6.974	6.604	6.265	5.954	5.668	5.405	5.162	4.938	4.730
17	7.549	7.120	6.729	6.373	6.047	5.749	5.475	5.222	4.990	4.775
18	7.702	7.250	6.840	6.467	6.128	5.818	5.534	5.273	5.033	4.812
19	7.839	7.366	6.938	6.550	6.198	5.877	5.584	5.316	5.070	4.843
20	7.963	7.469	7.025	6.623	6.259	5.929	5.628	5.353	5.101	4.870

FORMULAE

Valuation models

(i) Future value of S, of a sum X, invested for n periods, compounded at $r\%$ interest: $\quad S = X[1 + r]^n$

(ii) Present value of £1 payable or receivable in n years, discounted at $r\%$ per annum:

$$PV = \frac{1}{[1 + r]^n}$$

(iii) Present value of an annuity of £1 per annum, receivable or payable for n years, commencing in one year, discounted at $r\%$ per annum:

$$PV = \frac{1}{r}\left[1 - \frac{1}{[1 + r]^n}\right]$$

(iv) Present value of £1 per annum, payable or receivable in perpetuity, commencing in one year, discounted at $r\%$ per annum:

$$PV = \frac{1}{r}$$

(v) Present value of £1 per annum, receivable or payable, commencing in one year, growing in perpetuity at a constant rate of $g\%$ per annum, discounted at $r\%$ per annum:

$$PV = \frac{1}{r - g}$$

Inventory management

(i) Economic Order Quantity

$$EOQ = \sqrt{\frac{2C_o D}{C_h}}$$

where: $\quad C_o \quad = \quad$ cost of placing an order

$\qquad C_h \quad = \quad$ cost of holding one unit in Inventory for one year

$\qquad D \quad = \quad$ annual demand

Cash management

(i) Optimal sale of securities, Baumol model:

$$\text{Optimal sale} = \sqrt{\frac{2 \times \text{Annual cash disbursements} \times \text{Cost per sale of securities}}{\text{interest rate}}}$$

(ii) Spread between upper and lower cash balance limits, Miller-Orr model:

$$\text{Spread} = 3\left[\frac{\frac{3}{4} \times \text{transaction cost} \times \text{variance of cash flows}}{\text{interest rate}}\right]^{\frac{1}{3}}$$

Answers

DO NOT TURN THIS PAGE UNTIL YOU HAVE
COMPLETED MOCK EXAM 2

A plan of attack

This is your second mock exam and you have seen the pilot paper before, so maybe you felt more comfortable tackling this paper. However, the adrenaline rush you get when you turn the paper over is not all bad. It does at least focus the mind. Then you can turn your attention to your plan of attack, and off you go.

Your approach

This paper has three sections. The first section contains 20-25 multiple choice questions which are compulsory. The second has six short compulsory questions. The third has two questions and you must answer one of them.

OTs first again

However you find the paper, chances are you should **start with the objective test questions**. You should be able to do at least a few and answering them will give you a boost. **Don't even look at the other questions before doing Section A**. Remember how long to allocate to the OTs? That's right, 90 minutes. One and a half hours.

You then have a **choice**.

- Read through and answer Section B before moving on to Section C

- Go through Section C and select the question you will attempt. Then go back and answer the question in Section B first

- Select the question in Section C, answer it and then go back to Section B

Time spent at the start of each Section B and C question confirming the requirements and producing a plan for the answers is time well spent.

Question selection

When selecting the question from Section C make sure that you **read through all of the requirements**. It is painful to answer part (a) of a question and then realise that parts (b) and (c) are beyond you. By then it is too late to change your mind and do the other question.

When reviewing the requirements look at how many marks have been allocated to each part. This will give you an idea of how detailed your answer must be.

Doing the exam

Actually doing the exam is a personal experience. There is not a single *right way.* As long as you submit complete answers to the MCQs, question 1, the six Section B questions and one question from Section C, your approach obviously works.

One approach

Having done or guessed at the MCQs, I would work straight through Section B. There is no need to stop and make any choice until you get to Section C. The possible pitfall would be getting sucked too deeply into Section B and leaving insufficient time for Section C.

So lets look at the Section B questions in the pilot paper:

- Question 2 is a straightforward question on IAS 16. As the question asks for a memo, give them a memo addressed to the transport manager. That will be one mark and you may as well have it. However remember that memos are short! Just give him the necessary information, nothing else.

- Question 3 is another memo, this time on IAS 37. Again, do the memo and say what you know. You may realise that there is something here that you do not know. Perhaps you knew a provision had to be made but did not know that the decommissioning costs could be capitalised. Don't waste time trying to remember it or figure it out. Just keep going.

- Question 4 is a cash flow forecast. You should be able to do this quite quickly. Make sure your workings are neat and legible. You should be able to score some marks on explaining the limitations of your answer, but don't spend more than a few minutes on it.

- Question 5 is a tax/deferred tax question. Put it into T accounts straight away and see what you are dealing with.

- Question 6 is yet another question on IAS 37, but also requires knowledge of the *Framework*. This is fairly simple, but don't let yourself waffle.

- Question 7 is no problem as long as you have mastered the treatment of leases, which of course you will have…

Having hacked your way through Section B, taking no more than 9 minutes per question, you should now be left with 36 minutes to do your Section C question. The pilot paper gives a choice between a balance sheet/income statement and a cash flow. You probably know whether you feel more confident about balance sheet/income statement or cash flow. So check for any complicating factors in either of them, or any parts you feel unable to tackle, then make your choice and get on with it.

For the Section C Question you must proceed in a methodical way. Set out your format and then work through the question requirements, doing neat, readable calculations and fill out the figures. Even if you do not finish, you will get marks for what you have done, so do the easy bits first.

Time allocation

Be disciplined. Allocate your time according to the marks available but never go over the time allocation. The last few marks in a question are the hardest to earn.

Be sure to follow the requirements. If four advantages are required, give four. No extra credit will be given for five. Two advantages will only get you half marks.

Answer all of the question. Having a go at every part of all the Section B questions you are required to do will put you in a better position to pass than, say, only doing five questions. However difficult that sixth question seems at first there are marks to be earned.

If you have time left at the end of the exam ensure that you have attempted every part of every question. If you have, then scan through and ensure you complete any part of an answer you left earlier. Use the full three hours working towards a pass.

Marking the exam

When you mark your exam, be honest. Don't be too harsh though. Give yourself credit for the things you did well, but don't kid yourself with 'I would have done that in the real exam'. It may be worth your while making two lists; strengths and weaknesses.

Strengths will be areas of the syllabus you are confident with and also good exam technique. (Maybe you produced correct income statement and balance sheet formats.)

Weaknesses will be holes in your knowledge and poor exam technique (maybe you ran out of time and couldn't answer all the requirements of the last question).

Making this list will help you focus your last days of revision on the areas which require attention whilst reminding you of the areas you excel in.

SECTION A

Question 1

1.1 **C** Non-current assets are not part of working capital.

1.2 **B** *Gross amounts due from customers*

	$'000
Certified value of work completed	2,000
Less cash received	(1,600)
	400
Add cost of work in progress	550
	950

Current liabilities – trade and other payables

	$'000
Cost of completed work	1,650
Cost of work in progress	550
	2,200
Less cash paid to suppliers	(1,300)
	900

1.3 **C** Provisions are covered by IAS 37.

1.4 A direct tax is one that is levied directly upon the individual who is expected to pay the tax.

1.5 Optimal transfer amount $= \sqrt{\dfrac{(2 \times 30 \times 240{,}000)}{0.05}}$

$= \$16{,}970$

$= \$17{,}000$ rounded

1.6
- Domestic legislation and legal decisions
- Tax authority practice
- International treaties
- Supranational bodies

1.7 Cost of discount $= (100/98)^{365/30} - 1$

$= 27.86\%$

1.8 **A** As the current ratio is 2:1 the reduction of cash and payables by the same amount will increase the ratio. Payable days reduce the cash operating cycle, so if these are reduced, the cycle increases.

1.9 Working capital cycle = 20.1 days

				Days
Receivables turnover days	=	$^{36}/_{300} \times 365$	=	43.8
Inventory turnover	=	$^{15}/_{200} \times 365$	=	27.4
				71.2
Payables payment period	=	$^{28}/_{200} \times 365$	=	(51.1)
				20.1

1.10 **B** Double taxable treaties deal with **overseas** income.

1.11 **C** Tax deducted at source before payment of interest or dividends.

1.12 **D** Direct tax and earnings tax.

1.13 Cash received in May

	$
May sales (20,000 × 1.02 × 40%)	8,160
April sales (20,000 × 60% × 97%)	11,640
	19,800

1.14 **D** Sales taxes such as VAT are indirect

1.15 Tax due = $22,500

	$
Accounting profit	95,000
Less non-taxable income	(15,000)
Add non- allowable expenditure	10,000
Taxable profit	90,000

Tax $= \$90,000 \times 25\%$
$= \$22,500$

1.16 **D** Accruals and going concern.

1.17 An asset is a resource controlled by an entity as a result of past transactions or events and from which future economic benefits are expected to flow to the entity.

1.18 The publishing rights cannot be recognised as they have no reliable monetary value as they were a gift and had no cost. The expected future value cannot be recognised as an asset as the event has not yet occurred.

1.19 Value of goodwill = $130,000

	$'000	$'000
Fair value of consideration – shares (10,000 × $20)		200,000
Cash		20,000
		220,000
Fair value of net assets acquired:		
Tangible non-current assets	25,000	
Patents	15,000	
Brand name	50,000	
		(90,000)
Goodwill		130,000

1.20 Optimal order size = 500 units

$$EOQ = \sqrt{\frac{2 \times \text{order costs} \times \text{demand}}{\text{holding cost}}}$$

$$EOQ = \sqrt{\frac{2 \times 200 \times 10,000}{\$4 + (3\% \times \$400)}}$$

EOQ = 500 units

1.21 **B** Inventory shortages are the most likely problem with JIT.

SECTION B

Question 2

MEMO

To: Transport manager
From: Trainee management accountant
Subject: Useful life

IAS 16 *Property, plant and equipment* requires that the useful lives of non-current assets should be regularly reviewed and changed if appropriate.

By 31 March 20X3 the delivery vehicle will have been depreciated for two years out of the original estimate of its useful life of four years:

	$
Cost	20,000
Depreciation ($20,000 $\times$ $^2/_4$)	(10,000)
Net book value at 31 March 20X2	10,000

The net book value at the start of the year ending 31 March 20X3 should now be written off over the remaining, revised useful life of four years giving an annual depreciation charge of $2,500 ($10,000/4).

In the income statement for the year ended 31 March 20X3 therefore the depreciation charge will be $2,500. In the balance sheet the delivery vehicle will appear at its net book value of $7,500 ($10,000 – 2,500).

Question 3

MEMO

To: Production manager
From: Trainee management accountant
Subject: De-commissioning costs

The accounting question regarding the de-commissioning costs is whether or not a provision should now be set up in the accounts for the eventual costs. According to IAS 37 any future obligations arising out of past events should be recognised immediately. The de-commissioning costs are a future obligation and the past event is the granting of the licence and the drilling of the site. — Although we can bring in and discount it back.

Therefore a provision should be recognised immediately in the accounts for the year ended 31 March 20X3. This will be $20million discounted to present value.

As this cost gives access to future economic benefits in terms of oil reserves for the next 20 years then the discounted present value of the de-commissioning costs can be capitalised and treated as part of the cost of the oil well in the balance sheet. However this total cost, including the discounted de-commissioning costs should be reviewed to ensure that the net book value does not exceed the recoverable amount. If there is no impairment then the total cost of the oil well and discounted de-commissioning costs should be depreciated for the next 20 years and a charge made to the income statement.

Question 4

Expected cash balance/overdraft

	$'000
Balance at 1 December	+ 175
December cash flow ((+700 × 0.7) + (-300 × 0.3))	+ 400
	+ 575
January	− 900
Expected overdraft	− 325

Using expected values and probabilities the expected value of the overdraft at the end of January is $325,000.

However this outcome will never actually occur. Given the two possibilities for the cash flow in December the reality is that there will be either an overdraft of $25,000 (+ 175 + 700 − 900) or an overdraft of $1,025 (+ 175 − 300 − 900).

The expected value of $325,000 is only of relevance for a situation that is happening time after time. For a one-off situation such as this there is therefore little point in basing any decision making on the expected value. Instead the short-term cash planning should be based upon both possible overdraft requirements rather than the expected value.

Question 5

INCOME STATEMENT (EXTRACT)

	$'000
Income tax expense (W1)	1,155

BALANCE SHEET (EXTRACT)

Non-current liabilities	
Deferred tax (W2)	1,750
Current liabilities	
Income tax	1,000

Workings

1 *Income statement*

	$
Income tax for year	1,000,000
Under-provision in previous year	5,000
Increase in deferred tax	150,000
Income tax expense	1,155,000

2 *Deferred tax*

	$
Opening balance	1,600,000
Increase in year	150,000
Closing balance	1,750,000

Question 6

IAS 37 defines a provision as a liability of uncertain timing or amount. It goes on further to state that a provision should only be recognised when:

(a)   There is a present obligation, either legal or constructive, arising as a result of a past event.

(b)   It is probable that an outflow of resources embodying economic benefits will be required in order to settle the obligation.

(c)   A reliable estimate of the amount of the obligation can be made.

This can be compared to the IASB's definition of a liability in its Framework for *Preparation and Presentation of Financial Statements:*

A liability is a present obligation of the entity arising from past events, the settlement of which is expected to result in an outflow of resources from the entity.

The key elements from the liability definition are all encompassed in the rules for recognising a provision.

(a)   **Obligation.** A liability is a present obligation and a provision is only recognised if there is an obligation. This obligation can either be a legal or a constructive obligation. A constructive obligation arises out of past practice or as a result of actions which have previously taken place which have created an expectation that the organisation will act in such a way.

(b)   **Past event.** A provision must arise out of a past event so the event must already have happened at the balance sheet date. If the event has not yet occurred then there is no provision as the entity may be able to avoid it.

(c)   **Outflow of resources.** A provision will only be recognised if it is probably that there will be an outflow of resources to settle the obligation which ties in with the IASBs definition of a liability.

Question 7

INCOME STATEMENT (EXTRACTS)

	Year 1	Year 2
	$'000	$'000
Finance charge (W1)	5,567	4,453
Depreciation charge (W3)	17,660	17,660

BALANCE SHEET (EXTRACTS)

	Year 1	Year 2
	$'000	$'000
Non- current assets		
Property, plant and equipment (W3)	70,640	52,980
Non-current liabilities		
Amounts due under leases (W2)	56,320	38,660
Current liabilities		
Amounts due under leases		
(72,867 – 56,320) (W2)	16,547	
(56,320 – 38,660) (W2)		17,660

Workings

1   *Finance charge*

		$'000
Total lease payments (5 × $21,000)		105,000
Fair value of asset		(88,300)
Total finance charge		16,700

Finance charge allocation

		$
Year 1	5/15 × 16,700	5,567
Year 2	4/15 × 16,700	4,453
Year 3	3/15 × 16,700	3,340
Year 4	2/15 × 16,700	2,227
Year 5	1/15 × 16,700	1,113
		16,700

2   *Lease liabilities*

		Finance charge	Repayment	
	$	$	$	$
Year 1	88,300	5,567	(21,000)	72,867
Year 2	72,867	4,453	(21,000)	56,320
Year 3	56,320	3,340	(21,000)	38,660
Year 4	38,660	2,227	(21,000)	19,887
Year 5	19,887	1,113	(21,000)	–

3   *Non-current assets*

Annual depreciation charge $= \dfrac{\$88,300}{5}$

$= \$17,660$

	$
Year 1	
Cost	88,300
Depreciation	(17,660)
Net book value	70,640
Year 2	
Depreciation	(17,660)
Net book value	52,980

SECTION C

Question 8

AZ
INCOME STATEMENT FOR THE YEAR ENDING 31 MARCH 20X3

	$'000	$'000
Revenue		124,900
Cost of sales (W1)		(99,735)
Gross profit		25,165
Distribution costs (9,060 + 513 (W2))	(9,573)	
Administration expenses (W3)	(16,045)	
Other operating expenses	(121)	
		(25,739)
		(574)
Income from other non current investments	1,200	
Finance cost (18,250 × 7%)	(1,278)	
		(78)
Loss before tax		(652)
Income tax expense		(15)
Net loss for the period		(667)

AZ
BALANCE SHEET AS AT 31 MARCH 20X3

	$'000	$'000
Non-current assets		
Property, plant and equipment (W4)		19,729
Current assets		
Inventory	5,180	
Trade receivables (9,930 – 600)	9,330	
Bank and cash	26,250	
		40,760
		60,489
Equity		
Called up share capital		20,000
Share premium (500 – 70)		430
Retained earnings (W5)		13,010
		33,440
Non-current liabilities		
7% loan notes	18,250	
Other provisions	25	
		18,275
Current liabilities		
Trade payables	8,120	
Tax payable	15	
Accruals (18,250 × 7% – 639)	639	
		8,774
		60,489

BPP
PROFESSIONAL EDUCATION

AZ

STATEMENT OF CHANGES IN EQUITY FOR THE YEAR ENDED 31 MARCH 20X3

	Share capital $'000	Share premium $'000	Retained earnings $'000	Total $'000
Balance at 31 March 20X2	19,000	–	14,677	33,677
Share issue	1,000	500		1,500
Share issue costs		(70)		(70)
Net loss for the period			(667)	(667)
Dividend			(1,000)	(1,000)
	20,000	430	13,010	33,440

Workings

1   Cost of sales

	$'000
Opening inventory	4,852
Manufacturing cost	94,000
Depreciation of plant and equipment (W2)	6,063
Less closing inventory	(5,180)
	99,735

2   Depreciation

	$'000
Plant and equipment (20% × 30,315)	6,063
Vehicles ((3,720 – 1,670) × 25%)	513

3   Administration expenses

	$'000
Per trial balance	16,020
Provision for legal claim	25
	16,045

4   Property, plant and equipment

	Plant and equipment $'000	Vehicles $'000	Total $'000
Cost	30,315	3,720	34,035
Accumulated depreciation			
(6,060 + 6,063) (W2)	(12,123)		
(1,670 + 513) (W2)		(2,183)	(14,306)
Net book value	18,192	1,537	19,729

5   Retained earnings

	$'000
Per trial balance	14,677
Net loss for the year	(667)
Dividend (20,000 × 0.05)	(1,000)
	13,010

Question 9

TEX

CASH FLOW STATEMENT FOR THE YEAR ENDED 30 SEPTEMBER 20X3

	$'000	$'000
Cash inflow from operating activities		
Cash receipts from customers (W1)		14,300
Cash paid to suppliers and employees (W4)		(8,290)
Cash generated from operations		6,010
Interest paid		(124)
Income taxes paid (W5)		(485)
Net cash from operating activities		5,401
Cash flows from investing activities		
Purchase of property, plant and equipment (W6)	(8,000)	
Proceeds from sale of equipment	730	
Net cash used in investing activities		(7,270)
Cash flows from financing activities		
Proceeds from issue of share capital (10,834 – 7,815)	3,019	
Repayment of borrowings (2,900 – 1,700)	(1,200)	
Dividends (W7)	(1,000)	
Net cash from financing activities		819
Net decrease in cash and cash equivalents		(1,050)
Cash and cash equivalents at 30 September 20X2		1,200
Cash and cash equivalents at 30 September 20X3		150

Notes

1 During the period property, plant and equipment was purchased for cash at a cost of $8 million.

2 Cash and cash equivalents included in the cash flow statement are made up of the following amounts:

	20X3	20X2
	$'000	$'000
Cash on hand and balances with banks	150	1,200

Workings

1 *Cash receipts from customers*

TRADE RECEIVABLES

	$'000		$'000
Opening balance	800	Cash received (bal fig)	14,300
Revenue	15,000	Closing balance	1,500
	15,800		15,800

2 *Purchases*

	$'000
Cost of sales	9,000
Less opening inventory	(1,100)
Add closing inventory	1,600
	9,500
Less depreciation (W3)	(2,640)
Less loss on disposal (2,600 – 900 – 730)	(970)
Purchases	5,890

3   *Depreciation*

DEPRECIATION PROVISION

	$'000		$'000
Disposal	900	Opening balance	4,700
Closing balance	6,440	Charge for year	2,640
	7,340		7,340

4   *Cash paid to suppliers and employees*

TRADE PAYABLES

	$'000		$'000
Cash paid (bal fig)	5,990	Opening balance	800
Closing balance	700	Purchases (W2)	5,890
	6,690		6,690

	$'000
Payments to suppliers	5,990
Other payments – operating expenses	2,300
	8,290

5   *Income taxes paid*

	$'000		$'000
Cash paid (bal fig)	485	Opening balance	
		Current	685
Closing balance		Deferred	400
Current	1,040		
Deferred	600	Income statement	1,040
	2,125		2,125

6   *Purchases of non-current assets*

	$'000		$'000
Opening balance	19,200	Disposal	2,600
Purchases (bal fig)	8,000	Closing balance	24,600
	27,200		27,200

7   *Dividends*

	$'000		$'000
Cash paid (bal fig)	1,000	Opening balance	600
Closing balance	700	Income statement	1,100
	1,700		1,700

Mathematical tables and exam formulae

PRESENT VALUE TABLE

Present value of £1 ie $(1+r)^{-n}$ where r = interest rate, n = number of periods until payment or receipt.

Periods					Interest rates (r)					
(n)	1%	2%	3%	4%	5%	6%	7%	8%	9%	10%
1	0.990	0.980	0.971	0.962	0.952	0.943	0.935	0.926	0.917	0.909
2	0.980	0.961	0.943	0.925	0.907	0.890	0.873	0.857	0.842	0.826
3	0.971	0.942	0.915	0.889	0.864	0.840	0.816	0.794	0.772	0.751
4	0.961	0.924	0.888	0.855	0.823	0.792	0.763	0.735	0.708	0.683
5	0.951	0.906	0.863	0.822	0.784	0.747	0.713	0.681	0.650	0.621
6	0.942	0.888	0.837	0.790	0.746	0.705	0.666	0.630	0.596	0.564
7	0.933	0.871	0.813	0.760	0.711	0.665	0.623	0.583	0.547	0.513
8	0.923	0.853	0.789	0.731	0.677	0.627	0.582	0.540	0.502	0.467
9	0.914	0.837	0.766	0.703	0.645	0.592	0.544	0.500	0.460	0.424
10	0.905	0.820	0.744	0.676	0.614	0.558	0.508	0.463	0.422	0.386
11	0.896	0.804	0.722	0.650	0.585	0.527	0.475	0.429	0.388	0.350
12	0.887	0.788	0.701	0.625	0.557	0.497	0.444	0.397	0.356	0.319
13	0.879	0.773	0.681	0.601	0.530	0.469	0.415	0.368	0.326	0.290
14	0.870	0.758	0.661	0.577	0.505	0.442	0.388	0.340	0.299	0.263
15	0.861	0.743	0.642	0.555	0.481	0.417	0.362	0.315	0.275	0.239
16	0.853	0.728	0.623	0.534	0.458	0.394	0.339	0.292	0.252	0.218
17	0.844	0.714	0.605	0.513	0.436	0.371	0.317	0.270	0.231	0.198
18	0.836	0.700	0.587	0.494	0.416	0.350	0.296	0.250	0.212	0.180
19	0.828	0.686	0.570	0.475	0.396	0.331	0.277	0.232	0.194	0.164
20	0.820	0.673	0.554	0.456	0.377	0.312	0.258	0.215	0.178	0.149

Periods					Interest rates (r)					
(n)	11%	12%	13%	14%	15%	16%	17%	18%	19%	20%
1	0.901	0.893	0.885	0.877	0.870	0.862	0.855	0.847	0.840	0.833
2	0.812	0.797	0.783	0.769	0.756	0.743	0.731	0.718	0.706	0.694
3	0.731	0.712	0.693	0.675	0.658	0.641	0.624	0.609	0.593	0.579
4	0.659	0.636	0.613	0.592	0.572	0.552	0.534	0.516	0.499	0.482
5	0.593	0.567	0.543	0.519	0.497	0.476	0.456	0.437	0.419	0.402
6	0.535	0.507	0.480	0.456	0.432	0.410	0.390	0.370	0.352	0.335
7	0.482	0.452	0.425	0.400	0.376	0.354	0.333	0.314	0.296	0.279
8	0.434	0.404	0.376	0.351	0.327	0.305	0.285	0.266	0.249	0.233
9	0.391	0.361	0.333	0.308	0.284	0.263	0.243	0.225	0.209	0.194
10	0.352	0.322	0.295	0.270	0.247	0.227	0.208	0.191	0.176	0.162
11	0.317	0.287	0.261	0.237	0.215	0.195	0.178	0.162	0.148	0.135
12	0.286	0.257	0.231	0.208	0.187	0.168	0.152	0.137	0.124	0.112
13	0.258	0.229	0.204	0.182	0.163	0.145	0.130	0.116	0.104	0.093
14	0.232	0.205	0.181	0.160	0.141	0.125	0.111	0.099	0.088	0.078
15	0.209	0.183	0.160	0.140	0.123	0.108	0.095	0.084	0.074	0.065
16	0.188	0.163	0.141	0.123	0.107	0.093	0.081	0.071	0.062	0.054
17	0.170	0.146	0.125	0.108	0.093	0.080	0.069	0.060	0.052	0.045
18	0.153	0.130	0.111	0.095	0.081	0.069	0.059	0.051	0.044	0.038
19	0.138	0.116	0.098	0.083	0.070	0.060	0.051	0.043	0.037	0.031
20	0.124	0.104	0.087	0.073	0.061	0.051	0.043	0.037	0.031	0.026

CUMULATIVE PRESENT VALUE TABLE

This table shows the present value of £1 per annum, receivable or payable at the end of each year for n years $\dfrac{1-(1+r)^{-n}}{r}$.

Periods (n)	Interest rates (r)									
	1%	2%	3%	4%	5%	6%	7%	8%	9%	10%
1	0.990	0.980	0.971	0.962	0.952	0.943	0.935	0.926	0.917	0.909
2	1.970	1.942	1.913	1.886	1.859	1.833	1.808	1.783	1.759	1.736
3	2.941	2.884	2.829	2.775	2.723	2.673	2.624	2.577	2.531	2.487
4	3.902	3.808	3.717	3.630	3.546	3.465	3.387	3.312	3.240	3.170
5	4.853	4.713	4.580	4.452	4.329	4.212	4.100	3.993	3.890	3.791
6	5.795	5.601	5.417	5.242	5.076	4.917	4.767	4.623	4.486	4.355
7	6.728	6.472	6.230	6.002	5.786	5.582	5.389	5.206	5.033	4.868
8	7.652	7.325	7.020	6.733	6.463	6.210	5.971	5.747	5.535	5.335
9	8.566	8.162	7.786	7.435	7.108	6.802	6.515	6.247	5.995	5.759
10	9.471	8.983	8.530	8.111	7.722	7.360	7.024	6.710	6.418	6.145
11	10.368	9.787	9.253	8.760	8.306	7.887	7.499	7.139	6.805	6.495
12	11.255	10.575	9.954	9.385	8.863	8.384	7.943	7.536	7.161	6.814
13	12.134	11.348	10.635	9.986	9.394	8.853	8.358	7.904	7.487	7.103
14	13.004	12.106	11.296	10.563	9.899	9.295	8.745	8.244	7.786	7.367
15	13.865	12.849	11.938	11.118	10.380	9.712	9.108	8.559	8.061	7.606
16	14.718	13.578	12.561	11.652	10.838	10.106	9.447	8.851	8.313	7.824
17	15.562	14.292	13.166	12.166	11.274	10.477	9.763	9.122	8.544	8.022
18	16.398	14.992	13.754	12.659	11.690	10.828	10.059	9.372	8.756	8.201
19	17.226	15.679	14.324	13.134	12.085	11.158	10.336	9.604	8.950	8.365
20	18.046	16.351	14.878	13.590	12.462	11.470	10.594	9.818	9.129	8.514

Periods (n)	Interest rates (r)									
	11%	12%	13%	14%	15%	16%	17%	18%	19%	20%
1	0.901	0.893	0.885	0.877	0.870	0.862	0.855	0.847	0.840	0.833
2	1.713	1.690	1.668	1.647	1.626	1.605	1.585	1.566	1.547	1.528
3	2.444	2.402	2.361	2.322	2.283	2.246	2.210	2.174	2.140	2.106
4	3.102	3.037	2.974	2.914	2.855	2.798	2.743	2.690	2.639	2.589
5	3.696	3.605	3.517	3.433	3.352	3.274	3.199	3.127	3.058	2.991
6	4.231	4.111	3.998	3.889	3.784	3.685	3.589	3.498	3.410	3.326
7	4.712	4.564	4.423	4.288	4.160	4.039	3.922	3.812	3.706	3.605
8	5.146	4.968	4.799	4.639	4.487	4.344	4.207	4.078	3.954	3.837
9	5.537	5.328	5.132	4.946	4.772	4.607	4.451	4.303	4.163	4.031
10	5.889	5.650	5.426	5.216	5.019	4.833	4.659	4.494	4.339	4.192
11	6.207	5.938	5.687	5.453	5.234	5.029	4.836	4.656	4.486	4.327
12	6.492	6.194	5.918	5.660	5.421	5.197	4.988	4.793	4.611	4.439
13	6.750	6.424	6.122	5.842	5.583	5.342	5.118	4.910	4.715	4.533
14	6.982	6.628	6.302	6.002	5.724	5.468	5.229	5.008	4.802	4.611
15	7.191	6.811	6.462	6.142	5.847	5.575	5.324	5.092	4.876	4.675
16	7.379	6.974	6.604	6.265	5.954	5.668	5.405	5.162	4.938	4.730
17	7.549	7.120	6.729	6.373	6.047	5.749	5.475	5.222	4.990	4.775
18	7.702	7.250	6.840	6.467	6.128	5.818	5.534	5.273	5.033	4.812
19	7.839	7.366	6.938	6.550	6.198	5.877	5.584	5.316	5.070	4.843
20	7.963	7.469	7.025	6.623	6.259	5.929	5.628	5.353	5.101	4.870

Exam formulae

Valuation models

(i) Future value of S, of a sum X, invested for n periods, discounted at r% interest per annum:

$S = X[1 + r]^n$

(ii) Present value of £1 payable or receivable in n years, discounted at r% per annum:

$PV = \dfrac{1}{[1+r]^n}$

(iii) Present value of an annuity of £1 per annum, receivable or payable for n years, commencing in one year, discounted at r% per annum:

$PV = \dfrac{1}{r}\left[1 - \dfrac{1}{[1+r]^n}\right]$

(iv) Present value of £1 per annum, payable or receivable in perpetuity, commencing in one year, discounted at r% per annum:

$PV = \dfrac{1}{r}$

(v) Present value of £1 per annum, receivable or payable, commencing in one year, growing in perpetuity at a constant rate of g% per annum, discounted at r% per annum:

$PV = \dfrac{1}{r - g}$

Inventory management

(i) Economic Order Quantity $EOQ = \sqrt{\dfrac{2C_oD}{C_h}}$

Where C_o = cost of placing an order   D = annual demand

C_h = cost of holding one unit in stock for one year

Cash management

(i) Optimal sale of securities, Baumol model:

$\text{Optimal sale} = \sqrt{\dfrac{2 \times \text{Annual cash disbursements} \times \text{Cost per sale of securities}}{\text{Interest rate}}}$

(ii) Spread between upper and lower cash balance limits, Miller-Orr model:

$\text{Spread} = 3\left[\dfrac{\frac{3}{4} \times \text{transaction cost} \times \text{variance of cash flows}}{\text{Interest rate}}\right]^{\frac{1}{3}}$

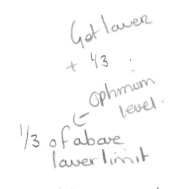

Review Form & Free Prize Draw – Paper 7 Financial Accounting and Tax Principles

All original review forms from the entire BPP range, completed with genuine comments, will be entered into one of two draws on 31 July 2005 and 31 January 2006. The names on the first four forms picked out on each occasion will be sent a cheque for £50.

Name: _____   Address: _____

_____

_____

How have you used this Kit?
(Tick one box only)

☐ Home study (book only)

☐ On a course: college _____

☐ With 'correspondence' package

☐ Other _____

Why did you decide to purchase this Kit?
(Tick one box only)

☐ Have used the complementary Study text

☐ Have used other BPP products in the past

☐ Recommendation by friend/colleague

☐ Recommendation by a lecturer at college

☐ Saw advertising

☐ Other _____

During the past six months do you recall seeing/receiving any of the following?
(Tick as many boxes as are relevant)

☐ Our advertisement in *CIMA Insider*

☐ Our advertisement in *Financial Management*

☐ Our advertisement in *Pass*

☐ Our advertisement in *PQ*

☐ Our brochure with a letter through the post

☐ Our website www.bpp.com

Which (if any) aspects of our advertising do you find useful?
(Tick as many boxes as are relevant)

☐ Prices and publication dates of new editions

☐ Information on product content

☐ Facility to order books off-the-page

☐ None of the above

Which BPP products have you used?

Text	☐	Kit	☑	i-Learn	☐	
Passcard	☐	CD	☐	i-Pass	☐	
Big Picture Poster	☐	Virtual Campus	☐			

Your ratings, comments and suggestions would be appreciated on the following areas.

	Very useful	Useful	Not useful
Effective revision and revision plan	☐	☐	☐
Exam guidance	☐	☐	☐
Questions	☐	☐	☐
'Pass marks' section in answers	☐	☐	☐
Content and structure in answers	☐	☐	☐
Mock exams	☐	☐	☐
'Plan of attack'	☐	☐	☐
Mock exam answers	☐	☐	☐

Overall opinion of this Kit	Excellent ☐	Good ☐	Adequate ☐	Poor ☐

Do you intend to continue using BPP products?   Yes ☐   No ☐

The BPP author of this edition can be e-mailed at: marymaclean@bpp.com

Please return this form to: Nick Weller, CIMA Range Manager, BPP Professional Education, FREEPOST, London, W12 8BR

Review Form & Free Prize Draw (continued)

TELL US WHAT YOU THINK

Please note any further comments and suggestions/errors below

Free Prize Draw Rules

1   Closing date for 31 July 2005 draw is 30 June 2005. Closing date for 31 January 2006 draw is 31 December 2005.

2   Restricted to entries with UK and Eire addresses only. BPP employees, their families and business associates are excluded.

3   No purchase necessary. Entry forms are available upon request from BPP Professional Education. No more than one entry per title, per person. Draw restricted to persons aged 16 and over.

4   Winners will be notified by post and receive their cheques not later than 6 weeks after the relevant draw date.

5   The decision of the promoter in all matters is final and binding. No correspondence will be entered into.

See overleaf for information on other
BPP products and how to order

CIMA Order

To BPP Professional Education, Aldine Place, London W12 8AW

Tel: 020 8740 2211 Fax: 020 8740 1184

email: publishing@bpp.com website: www.bpp.com

Order online www.bpp.com

Mr/Mrs/Ms (Full name)

Daytime delivery address

Postcode

Email

Date of exam (month/year)

Daytime Tel

Occasionally we may wish to email you relevant offers and information about courses and products. Please tick to opt into this service. ☐

	6/04 Texts £24.95	1/05 Kits £12.95	1/05 Passcards £9.95	Big Picture Posters £6.95	Success CDs £14.95	Virtual Campus	i-Pass £24.95	i-Learn
CERTIFICATE								
C1 Management Accounting Fundamentals	£24.95 ☐	£12.95 ☐	£9.95 ☐	£6.95 ☐	£14.95 ☐	£50 ☐	£24.95 ☐	
C2 Financial Accounting Fundamentals	£24.95 ☐	£12.95 ☐	£9.95 ☐	£6.95 ☐	£14.95 ☐	£50 ☐	£24.95 ☐	
C3 Business Mathematics	£24.95 ☐	£12.95 ☐	£9.95 ☐	£6.95 ☐	£14.95 ☐	£50 ☐	£24.95 ☐	
C4 Economics for Business	£24.95 ☐	£12.95 ☐	£9.95 ☐	£6.95 ☐	£14.95 ☐	£50 ☐	£24.95 ☐	
C5 Business Law	£24.95 ☐	£12.95 ☐	£9.95 ☐	£6.95 ☐	£14.95 ☐	£50 ☐	£24.95 ☐	
MANAGERIAL *7/04 Texts*								*i-Learn*
P1 Management Accounting - Performance Evaluation	£24.95 ☐	£12.95 ☐	£9.95 ☐	£6.95 ☐	£14.95 ☐	£90 ☐	£24.95 ☐	£34.95 ☐
P2 Management Accounting - Decision Management	£24.95 ☐	£12.95 ☐	£9.95 ☐	£6.95 ☐	£14.95 ☐	£90 ☐	£24.95 ☐	£34.95 ☐
P4 Organisational Management and Information Systems	£24.95 ☐	£12.95 ☐	£9.95 ☐	£6.95 ☐	£14.95 ☐	£90 ☐	£24.95 ☐	£34.95 ☐
P5 Integrated Management	£24.95 ☐	£12.95 ☐	£9.95 ☐	£6.95 ☐	£14.95 ☐	£90 ☐	£24.95 ☐	£34.95 ☐
P7 Financial Accounting and Tax Principles	£24.95 ☐	£12.95 ☐	£9.95 ☐	£6.95 ☐	£14.95 ☐	£90 ☐	£24.95 ☐	£34.95 ☐
P8 Financial Analysis	£24.95 ☐	£12.95 ☐	£9.95 ☐	£6.95 ☐	£14.95 ☐	£90 ☐	£24.95 ☐	£34.95 ☐
STRATEGIC *7/04 Texts*								
P3 Management Accounting - Risk and Control Strategy	£24.95 ☐	£12.95 ☐	£9.95 ☐	£6.95 ☐	£14.95 ☐	£90 ☐	£24.95 ☐	£34.95 ☐
P6 Management Accounting - Business Strategy	£24.95 ☐	£12.95 ☐	£9.95 ☐	£6.95 ☐	£14.95 ☐	£90 ☐	£24.95 ☐	£34.95 ☐
P9 Management Accounting - Financial Strategy	£24.95 ☐	£12.95 ☐	£9.95 ☐	£6.95 ☐	£14.95 ☐	£90 ☐	£24.95 ☐	£34.95 ☐
P10 Test of Professional Competence in Management Accounting (TOPCIMA)	£24.95 ☐	£24.95 ☐ (For 5/05: available 3/05)			£14.95 ☐			
Toolkit								
Learning to Learn Accountancy (7/02)	£9.95 ☐							

Total ☐

POSTAGE & PACKING

Study Texts and Kits

	First	Each extra	Online
UK	£5.00	£2.00	£2.00
Europe*	£6.00	£4.00	£4.00
Rest of world	£20.00	£10.00	£10.00

£ ☐
£ ☐
£ ☐

Passcards/Success CDs/Posters

	First	Each extra	Online
UK	£2.00	£1.00	£1.00
Europe*	£3.00	£2.00	£2.00
Rest of world	£8.00	£8.00	£8.00

£ ☐
£ ☐
£ ☐

Grand Total (incl. Postage) £ ☐

I enclose a cheque for (Cheques to *BPP Professional Education*)

Or charge to Visa/Mastercard/Switch

Card Number

Expiry date   Start Date

Issue Number (Switch Only)

Signature